NATIONAL GEOGRAPHIC

TRAVELER

Washington D.C.

NATIONAL GEOGRAPHIC

TRAVELER
Washington D.C.

John Thompson
Photography by Richard Nowitz

Contents

How to use this guide 6–7 About the author & photographer 8
The areas 49–230 Travelwise 231–262
Index 263–269 Credits 270–271

Page 1: Snapshot of the
Washington Monument
and the Reflecting Pool
Pages 2–3: The Jefferson
Memorial and cherry
blossoms draw crowds
on a spring evening.
Left: Colorful kayaks await
their turn on the water
beneath Key Bridge.

How to use this guide

See back flap for keys to text and map symbols.

The *National Geographic Traveler* brings you the best of Washington, D.C., in text, pictures, and maps. Divided into three main sections, the guide begins with an overview of history and culture.

Following are ten area chapters with featured sites selected by the author for their particular interest. Each chapter opens with its own contents list for easy reference. A map introduces the parameters covered in the chapter, highlighting the featured sites and locating other places of interest. Walks, plotted on their own maps, suggest routes for discovering the most about an area.

Features and sidebars offer intriguing detail on history, culture, or contemporary life.

The final section, Travelwise, lists essential information for the traveler—pre-trip planning, special events, getting around, practical advice, and emergency contacts—plus provides a selection of hotels and restaurants arranged by area, shops, activities, and entertainment possibilities.

To the best of our knowledge, all information is accurate as of Jan. 2002. However, it's always advisable to call ahead when possible, especially in light of security issues following the September 11, 2001, attacks.

Color coding

282

Each area of the city is color coded for easy reference. Find the area you want on the map on the front flap, and look for the color flash at the top of the pages of the relevant chapter. Information in **Travelwise** is also color coded to each region.

Corcoran Gallery of Art

www.corcoran.org

- Map p. 106
- 500 17th St., N.W., between E St. & New York Ave.
- 202-639-1700
- Closed Tues.
- $ Wed., Fri., Sat., Sun.; free Mon. (all day) & Thurs. after 5 p.m.
- Metro: Farragut West; Bus: 80

Visitor information

Practical information for most sites is given in the side column (see key to symbols on back flap). The map reference gives the page number of the map and grid reference. Other details are address, telephone number, days closed, entrance charge in a range from $ (under $5) to $$$$$ (over $25), and nearest Metro station and most important bus routes for sites in Washington. Other sites have information in italics and parentheses in the text.

TRAVELWISE

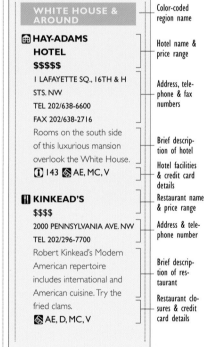

Hotel & restaurant prices

An explanation of the price bands used in entries is given in the Hotels & Restaurants section (beginning on p. 238).

AREA MAPS

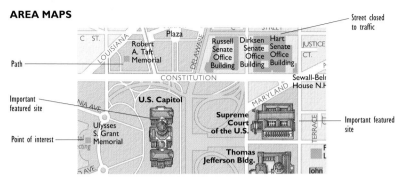

Path

Important featured site

Point of interest

Street closed to traffic

Important featured site

- A locator map accompanies each area map and shows the location of that area in the city.

WALKING TOURS

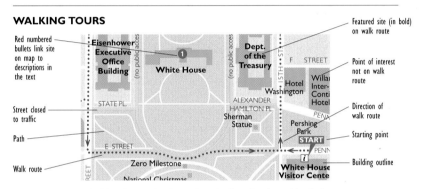

Red numbered bullets link site on map to descriptions in the text

Street closed to traffic

Path

Walk route

Featured site (in bold) on walk route

Point of interest not on walk route

Direction of walk route

Starting point

Building outline

- An information box gives the starting and ending points, time and length of walk, and places not to be missed along the route.

REGIONAL/EXCURSION MAPS

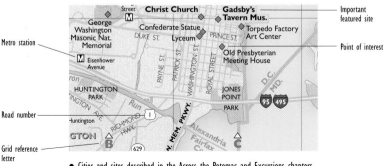

Metro station

Road number

Grid reference letter

Important featured site

Point of interest

- Cities and sites described in the Across the Potomac and Excursions chapters (p. 203 & pp. 216–217) are bolded and highlighted in yellow on the map. Other suggested places to visit are also bolded and are shown with a red diamond symbol.

NATIONAL GEOGRAPHIC
TRAVELER
Washington D.C.

About the author & photographer

John Thompson has authored or contributed to more than a dozen National Geographic books. His forthcoming Society publications include a book on the National Historic Trails and the Central Appalachians volume for the America's Outdoors series. A former resident of Washington, D.C., he now lives in Charlottesville, Virginia.

Richard Nowitz's work as a contract photographer with National Geographic WORLD magazine over the past ten years has taken him around the globe. Nowitz has also been the principal photographer of more than 15 large format photo and travel guides. In 1996 he was honored by the Society of American Travel Writers as Travel Photographer of the Year. He lives in Maryland with his wife and three children.

With contributions by:
David Montgomery, a reporter with the *Washington Post* Style section, wrote "Washington today" on pp. 10–17.
Thomas Head, *Washingtonian* magazine's Executive Wine and Food Editor, wrote the Travelwise section.
Sean Groom, "City on the river" feature on pp. 32–33
Mark Rogers, "Politics at work" feature on pp. 58–59
James Yenckel, "Famous denizens of Georgetown" feature on pp. 158–159

History
& culture

**The gold-leaf eagle has
landed—atop Union Station.**

Washington today

A NEW SELF-CONFIDENCE IS DAWNING IN WASHINGTON, D.C., AS THE CITY demonstrates it is a city, not some unclassifiable zone dubbed the District of Columbia— a phrase that appears in speeches but never in conversation.

To natives and long-time transplants, home is just Dee-Cee, thank you, or Wahr-shington in soft Southern-accented tones slightly edged by the oddly Elizabethan flint of dialects around the Chesapeake Bay. Washington never forgets that the government is the reason this once marshy lowland was reclaimed and the federal city was planted at a twinkling bend in the Potomac River. Yet the city is transcending its role as a bland backdrop to the grandeur of the monuments, museums, and great American history hereabouts. Those things are why many people come—but not why they stay.

The map looks as if something took a ragged bite out of the once perfect 100-square-mile diamond-shaped District. That happened in 1846, when Virginia reclaimed its share of the land donated to create the capital. The remaining 68 square miles, originally part of Maryland, make an intimate city of 572,000 people.

The other physical dimension of the intimate city is up, and in Washington ambition soars higher than architecture. No building stands taller than the Capitol dome; in the densest part of town—the K Street canyon populated by lawyers and lobbyists—offices top out at the 12th floor. This architectural homage to the Capitol means the typical Washington street has one of the biggest skies in urban America. It makes walking a pleasure in a city designed with walkers in mind, with wide avenues and breathtaking sight-lines anchored by Pierre Charles L'Enfant's ceremonial circles. Turn a corner and you might see the upper quarter of the Washington Monument peeking above the modest roofline of a modern office building —a juxtaposition of the monumental capital and the working city that is quintessentially Washington.

The dual nature of the city's soul is reflected in myriad ways as power Washington and workaday Washington mingle serendipitously. Spend time shopping on Connecticut Avenue, lunching on Wisconsin, or talking politics on Pennsylvania, and you'll be startled to see motorcycle police appear out of nowhere and block traffic. Next you'll hear the sirens and see the speeding motorcade: The President on his way to some engagement. Look through the limo's tinted glass and you might catch a wave in return. Then the police vanish—maestros of that Washington ballet, the rolling blockade.

Washingtonians always know when someone important has moved down the block. Suddenly fit-looking men and women in plain clothes wearing earpieces linger about. Not long ago, Capitol Hill residents reported that Attorney General John Ashcroft was an excellent piano player. They could hear his baby-grand renditions of show tunes and classical melodies floating out the windows of his row house. And the latest parlor game in Glover Park is trying to guess which neighbor's house conceals the entrance to the secret FBI tunnel under the old Soviet Embassy.

Not that the privilege of being the nation's capital isn't sometimes a burden. When that happens, Washington, ever the gracious Southern hostess, can also play the irreverent Northern wag. The lack of a vote in Congress is a sore point. Washingtonians pay 2.5 billion dollars a year in federal income taxes—more per capita than 49 of the states—yet have no say in how the money is spent. The Constitution dictates the District cannot be a state, but Congress could grant it a vote in the federal legislature. In 2000, the city's 200th anniversary as the capital, a resident came up with a new license plate motto, meant to be a cheeky civics lesson that might surprise visitors: "Taxation Without Representation."

As Washington strides into the future, its aspirations rise in glass and limestone amid the marble totems of its past. Construction cranes hover like a new kind of Washington monu-

A rosy dawn catches a mirror image of the U.S. Capitol and an equestrian statue of Ulysses S. Grant in the waters of the Capitol Reflecting Pool.

ment over downtown's east end—the newly buzzing Seventh Street corridor. Nineteenth-century government landmarks like the Tariff Building are being fitted for new uses, such as a luxury hotel, while the equally august National Portrait Gallery, the National Archives, and other museums undergo extensive renovations.

Preservation guidelines are intended to ensure that development travesties don't mar the best of the old, but there's always a fear that shiny new facades and high rents will doom quirky neighborhood joints. A buttoned-down town like Washington needs as many of these places as it can get. People take infinite comfort that Ben's Chili Bowl on U Street continues to purvey the best chili dogs in the free world. All around Ben's, the street once known as the "Black Broadway," where Duke Ellington used to perform, is undergoing a resurgence beneath the soulful gaze of

Ellington himself—painted larger than life on the blank side of a building.

Postcard Washington is a vision of famous buildings, but the people make the city. Contrary to reputation, this is not a population of transients, a capital of people from someplace else getting ready to leave. When a presidential administration changes, or a new Congress is seated, only a few thousand people arrive to replace the few thousand on their way out.

Marilyn Monroe is a regular on the busy corner of Calvert Street and Connecticut Avenue, popular for its ethnic restaurants.

Most Washingtonians don't work for the government. Many settled here because of opportunities in technology, education, public policy, international affairs. There is also a large core of native Washingtonians, particularly African American families, who moved

here from the South generations ago, when jobs in the federal government afforded one of the few avenues of advancement for blacks. Now about 60 percent of the population is black, 31 percent white. The growing Hispanic community is about 8 percent.

In the late 1990s Washingtonians began hearing real estate agents use an unaccustomed term for the city: "Hot!" Suburban traffic congestion, falling crime, and an improving economy merged to make city living fashionable again. Decades of population loss subsided, replaced by slight annual gains. The newcomers are busy restoring row houses in once-neglected neighborhoods and discarding at least one of their two cars for sensible shoes and the clean comfort of the Metro.

Even longtime Washingtonians can afford to be choosy about how they savor monumental Washington. They stand at the top of the

Capitol steps and try again to absorb the perfect landscape geometry lesson that is the Mall. They visit their favorite Smithsonian exhibits religiously. They wait to see the Washington Monument at sundown, when the marble turns rose and gold. The Franklin Delano Roosevelt Memorial is popular for late-evening romantic interludes amid the mood-lit waterfalls.

But Washingtonians would just as soon leave the Mall and zip up to the National

Downtown sidewalks such as this one on 17th Street fill with folks on lunchtime errands or simply taking a break from work.

Arboretum in Northeast to study the exquisite bonsai tree exhibition. Or take the kids on an excursion to the remains of the Civil War forts that once ringed the city. Or disappear into the wilds of Rock Creek Park, where you can forget your are in a city. It is places like this—beyond

the Mall—where the heart of the living city beats in four quadrants. The perfect coda to seeing the Lincoln Memorial is a visit to the Frederick Douglass house in Anacostia. During the Potomac springtime, when the perfume of Southern blooms intoxicates even the most hopeless workaholic, by all means see the cherry blossoms suspended like pink breath around the Tidal Basin—but also don't miss the less crowded and still spectacular blossom display at Dumbarton Oaks in Georgetown.

Spanish will get you as far as English in Adams Morgan, where club music blares until 2 a.m. and the cuisine runs from El Salvador to Afghanistan to Ethiopia to Lebanon and back again. Hop a Metro to the southwest waterfront and find the latest Pulitzer Prize-winning play being presented at Arena Stage or the freshest catch from the Chesapeake being sold on the Maine Avenue docks.

In the neighborhoods Washington comes most clearly into perspective. Climb the hill in Anacostia that John Wilkes Booth crossed during his escape from the city after assassinating Abraham Lincoln, and take in the view from the parking lot of Our Lady of Perpetual Help Church. Or find a perch on the Brookland heights occupied by the Basilica of the National Shrine of the Immaculate Conception. The bitten-off diamond city

Weekly jam sessions add a beat to beautifully landscaped Meridian Park.

spreads before you—the low downtown skyline slipping into expanding rings of row house neighborhoods stretched along the long lines of L'Enfant's broad boulevards.

And there, too, are the white dome and the obelisk—still grand at this distance, but not so dominating, and part of a larger picture. ∎

History of Washington

GEORGE WASHINGTON, PIERRE CHARLES L'ENFANT, AND THE MANY OTHERS involved knew they were engaged in something momentous when they set out to design the capital of the United States. In an age when preplanned cities of this scale were unheard of, here was a chance to lay out a worldwide center of culture, commerce, and learning. Somewhat like the Constitution, the resulting city design was the product of a lively give-and-take among some of 18th-century America's greatest minds. Awkward and unattractive at first, the city has matured into a metropolis of unfinished grace and beauty—a reflection of the imperfect and ever evolving democracy it governs.

DOING IT ON PURPOSE

Seven years had passed since the Revolutionary War when, in July 1790, Congress agreed on the location of a new capital. Until that time, citizens of the new nation had identified primarily with their home state, thinking of themselves as Virginians or New Yorkers rather than Americans. Local ties would continue to command the loyalties of many, but it was clear that establishing the seat of a central government was essential to holding the loosely joined republic together.

One key was to avoid the mistakes of the European empires that had failed the very people who were here now. This was to be a government of the people, so the placement and design of the capital would set the tone for a federal government that aspired to be strong but not domineering. The capital, by extension, must be grand yet welcoming.

The first step in that tall order was to pick an appropriate place. With the 13 Colonies strewn the length of the eastern seaboard, it was logical to locate the capital about halfway down. In a classic display of democratic compromise, Secretary of the Treasury Alexander Hamilton agreed to urge northern states to vote for a southern capital if Virginia Representative James Madison would support federal assumption of state war debts (he did). So despite occupying the approximate midpoint of the coast, Washington was deemed a "Southern" town from the outset. This characterization had much to do with the fact that Washington lay (and lies) 60 miles south of the Mason-Dixon Line—the Maryland-Pennsylvania border that also divides the North from the South.

As for the precise size and site of the city, Congress left President Washington somewhat in the dark. The representatives decreed only that the capital was not to exceed 10 miles square, and that it must be positioned on the Potomac River somewhere between the mouth of the Eastern Branch (now the Anacostia River) and Conococheague Creek, some 70 miles upriver. The rest was up to Washington.

In January of 1791, Washington selected a swatch of land at the highest navigable point on the Potomac River, where it was joined by the Eastern Branch. The site was partly a marriage of convenience: The preexisting riverport towns of Alexandria, Virginia, and Georgetown, Maryland, could easily receive shipments of the lumber and foodstuffs the city would need to sustain construction.

Laid out in a square carved from Maryland (mostly) and Virginia, the capital was named "City of Washington" to honor America's first President. Surveyor Andrew Ellicott and Benjamin Banneker—his self-taught, freeborn black assistant—delimited a square 10 miles on a side, with the corners pointing in the cardinal directions.

Though President Washington had trained as a surveyor, like any good leader he was quick to recognize those moments when he needed expert advice. For his chief engineer he chose a well-connected young Frenchman who had fought against the British during the Revolutionary War and had gone on to design a temporary headquarters for the federal government in New York. The idea of creating an important city out of nothing appealed mightily to the brilliant Pierre Charles L'Enfant—and apparently daunted him not at all.

Charles Willson Peale's "George Washington" (1772) portrays the future president as a young colonel in a Virginia regiment.

Angling for the job, he wrote these words to President Washington in 1789: "No nation, perhaps, had ever before the opportunity offered them of deliberately deciding on the spot where their Capital City should be fixed."

L'Enfant got the job.

Throughout 1791, he could be seen standing high atop Jenkins Hill (now Capitol Hill) or striding the woods of Tiber Creek (modern-day Constitution Avenue), his surveying instruments in hand, measuring distances and elevations. By contrast, L'Enfant's motivation —a vision of a grand city of broad avenues, monumental government edifices, and stirring vistas—remained invisible to all but himself. "I see the capital city as something more than a place to live and work," he wrote. "I see it as a symbol.... [W]e should plan now with the realization that a great nation is going to rise on this continent.... Right now, we have a chance which no nation has ever given itself.... How can America plan for less than greatness?"

L'ENFANT TERRIBLE

L'Enfant's extraordinary prescience and pride were voiced at a time when the country's most populous city, Philadelphia, claimed only 28,522 residents. Yet here was L'Enfant, imagining a capital of 800,000 citizens— larger than many of the European cities such as Paris that had served as his models.

As it turned out, L'Enfant was dead on: At its population peak in 1950, Washington was home to 802,000 people. (That number has since subsided to 572,000.)

Standing a mile apart but joined by Pennsylvania Avenue, the Capitol building and the President's House formed a barbell at the core of L'Enfant's design. (The presidential residence would not be officially named the White House until 1901.) Several broad streets would radiate from these two powerhouses, signifying their openness and accessibility. The avenues would unspool at length before ending at circular intersections atop existing hills, thus creating views of "magnificent distances."

Two years into the War of 1812, British soldiers gut the White House with fire in this painting by Leslie Saalburg.

The Capitol would divide the city into quadrants, while a grid of numbered and lettered streets would be superimposed on the radiating avenues. The Mall, extending about 1 mile west from the Capitol to the Potomac River, would be a grand esplanade similar to the one L'Enfant had beheld in Marly, near Versailles. The Frenchman foresaw fine baroque houses lining it on either side.

Within a year, L'Enfant had been fired by President Washington for insubordination and refusal to compromise. Even so, his plan was largely enacted: Trees and buildings may veil several of those hoped-for views of "magnificent distances," yet Dupont and Scott Circles, among others, still clearly display the beauty of the original design.

Despite its ambitious origin, the city hardly

sprang up overnight. Congressmen arriving for the Inaugural session in 1800 looked out upon a dismal scene. The streets were muddy. Mosquitoes and snakes bred in abundance. Hogs and cattle roamed at will, while the unfinished Capitol and President's House had spawned attendant clusters of huts and shacks resembling refugee villages. One newly minted statesman dubbed this hardship post "a mudhole equal to the great Serbonian bog."

With no property tax on government buildings, the city relied on real estate speculation for funding. Yet buyers were scarce: By 1800, less than 10 percent of city lots had been sold. Washington grew from 8,208 people by 1810 to 18,826 by 1830, a rate far below the national average. Gazing upon these wide, uncluttered avenues going nowhere, Charles Dickens would dub Washington "the City of Magnificent Intentions."

WAR COMES TO WASHINGTON

The War of 1812 proved to be a turning point in the city's fortunes, which mirrored those of the country at large. In August 1814, with the British victory sealed, redcoats landed in Maryland and marched on Washington, where they torched the Capitol, the President's House, and all federal buildings except the old Blodgett's Hotel, which housed both the Post Office and the Patent Office at the time.

Afterward, Congress came close to voting that the capital be relocated. But with local bankers promising to help rebuild the city—and galvanized by the strong sense of community that often follows a disaster—Washington

"The Peacemakers" (1868) by George P. A. Healy depicts William Sherman, Ulysses S. Grant, President Lincoln, and David Porter dicussing peace terms just before the Civil War's end.

dug in and bounced back. President Madison repaired to the Octagon (see p. 122), Congress moved to the Patent Office (and from there to a temporary building on the site of the present-day Supreme Court), and life went on.

The third of the District lying west and south of the river was ceded back to Virginia in 1846. Not only did the federal government have no need for the land on that side of the Potomac River, but Alexandria—having lost political advantages by its inclusion in the District—had petitioned the state to re-embrace it. This reduced Washington City to a parcel of land covering just 68 square miles.

A SECOND CITY

History's most bitter irony may be that this bastion of freedom was built on slave labor. Beginning in the 1790s, plantation owners in Maryland and Virginia were paid for the use of their slaves to supplement the meager supply of skilled workers constructing the capital.

In a parallel development, this city of so-lons became a magnet for the disenfranchised. Situated at the northern extreme of the upper South, Washington was a natural gateway for runaway slaves. Though slavery would not be outlawed in the city until 1862, by 1830 Washington contained more free blacks than slaves. A "second city"—one composed largely of African Americans—sprang to life within the federal city.

Lacking an entrenched society but rich with a transient mix of foreigners and congressmen, Washington was generally more tolerant of blacks than were other Southern cities. From 1807 to 1861, more than 15 private black schools flourished in the district.

Occasionally, however, race riots erupted. On the heels of the Nat Turner rebellion in 1831, the Snow Riot of 1835 was ignited by two unrelated events: A slave allegedly tried to murder the widow of the U.S. Capitol designer, William Thornton, and a white physician was arrested for possession of abolitionist tracts, whose publication or distribution was forbidden in D.C.

Rebuffed from lynching the doctor, a white mob turned its fury on Mr. Beverly Snow, the free black owner of a local restaurant. Though Snow escaped, roving bands attacked black churches, schools, restaurants, and tenements for the next week. Before long the city had tightened its black codes—discriminatory

Federal troops parade from the Capitol to the President's House to commemorate the end of the Civil War in April 1865.

laws governing the behavior of free blacks.

In the 1830s and '40s, Congress heard numerous petitions to banish slavery in Washington—the only place over which it exercised total control. Each time, shamefully, Georgetown's Southern-leaning aristocracy joined with the proslavery segment of Congress to keep the issue from being seriously debated.

In April 1848, 77 Washington slaves boarded the schooner *Pearl* at a city wharf and tried to escape to freedom down the Potomac River. Captured within a day, the slaves—many of them privileged house servants with only a few years' bondage remaining—were sold off to agents in Louisiana and Georgia. The deep passions stirred by the affair led the House of Representatives to pass a resolution that year calling for an end to the slave trade in Washington.

The resolution was nothing but paper. Slavery itself continued. Free blacks were only marginally better off. Black or white, poor neighborhoods were plagued by violent crime. The seedier areas of town included Swampoodle (now the area north of Massachusetts and New Jersey Avenues) and Murder Bay (today's Federal Triangle). The latter—located between President's Park (the Ellipse) and the fetid Washington City Canal (since covered by Constitution Avenue)—was especially notorious. "Crime, filth, and poverty seem to vie with each other in a career of degradation and death," a police superintendent characterized Murder Bay in 1866. "Whole families…are crowded into mere apologies for shanties."

BROTHER AGAINST BROTHER

Monumental Washington started to take shape in the years leading up to the Civil War. Work began on the Washington Monument in 1848, but within six years funds had dried up, the monument was mired in political controversy, and construction was suspended with the building just 152 feet tall. By the time work resumed in 1880, white marble from the original quarry was no longer available; the white marble furnished by the second quarry has weathered differently from the base, yielding the two-tone tower in evidence today.

In 1855 the distinctive red-sandstone Smithsonian Castle rose beside the Mall, paving the way for several national museums. A forerunner to the National Theatre was in place on Pennsylvania Avenue by 1835. The

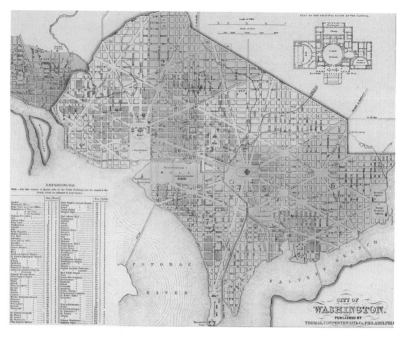

Willard and other fine hotels popped up in the neighborhood by the 1850s. Amid the statuary and posh town houses of Lafayette Square, the White House had settled into a state of manorial dignity, complete with greenhouses, flower gardens, and fruit trees.

Destined to tower above it all, the Capitol's cast-iron dome (replacing its wood dome of 1822) was under way by the Civil War's outbreak in April 1861. Despite an absence of building funds during that conflict, Lincoln ordered the Capitol's construction to go forward as a sign that the Union would endure.

Considered a remote and somewhat sleepy town before the war, Washington now entered the national consciousness as the staging ground for Union forces and the embattled capital of a divided nation. With the Confederate capital of Richmond just 100 miles distant, the war's major battles—Fredericksburg, Antietam, Gettysburg—formed an arc within easy striking distance of Washington. The first and second battles of Bull Run, for example, took place just 30 miles west of city limits.

To keep the Rebels at bay should they outflank the Union Army, a ring of 68 forts was hastily thrown up around Washington. These

installations proved their worth in July 1864, when a large Confederate force led by Gen. Jubal Early dashed through Maryland and reached the city's northern portal of Fort Stevens. Early's assault was repulsed within a day, but it gave the President a vivid taste of combat: Observing the skirmish from the fort's parapet, the 6-foot-4-inch top-hatted Lincoln made such a tempting target for enemy sharpshooters that a Union officer reprimanded him, "Get down, you damn fool, before you get shot!" The words were out of his mouth before the speaker—Lt. Col. (and future Supreme Court justice) Oliver Wendell Holmes, Jr.—realized he was upbraiding the President.

Washington was eventually overwhelmed—by its own troops. Bone-weary soldiers arrived by ship and rail, thronging the streets, falling asleep on vacant lots and sidewalks.

A time-lapse photograph of Dupont Circle on a winter's night (below) shows that L'Enfant's vision of central circles and radiating streets (opposite) is alive and well.

Horse-drawn guns and caissons rutted the muddy streets; livestock grazed on the Mall; a bakery and barracks opened in the Capitol.

With more than 4,000 prostitutes in residence, a newspaper reported, the "majority of the women on the streets were openly disreputable." Troops under Gen. Joseph Hooker were such constant patrons of the red-light district southeast of the Treasury Department that the area was dubbed "Hooker's Division."

As battle casualties poured into Washington, the city scrambled to treat as many as 50,000 sick or injured soldiers at once. Practically every church, public building, and large private home in the city was pressed into service as military housing.

HAPPY DAYS AGAIN

The population explosion unleashed by the war—during which the city grew from 60,000 to 140,000 inhabitants, including 40,000 former slaves—continued to boom in peacetime. Freedmen's Village in Arlington and Barry Farm in Anacostia received federal aid to

Politics as unusual

If it is true that all politics is local, Washington seems more than happy to oblige. Native Washingtonians, fueled by the injustice of being deprived of full congressional representation, often focus on the local political scene to the point of obsession.

Except for a brief flowering of self-governance from 1812 to 1871, Congress and the President have always controlled the city government and appointed its officials. In 1970, Washington was finally allowed to send a delegate to the House of Representatives, yet that deputy (in common with emissaries from Puerto Rico and other U.S. territories) could not vote, except in committees.

In 1973 Civil Rights and home rule activists won Washington the right to elect its own mayor and city council. Unwilling to cede power completely, Congress retained the right to interfere in local government whenever it deemed necessary.

That's exactly what happened in April 1995: With district finances in a shambles, Congress created a presidentially appointed D.C. financial control board to manage city spending. Two years later, Congress stripped Mayor Marion Barry of most of his authority—a move Barry lambasted as a "rape" of democracy—and the control board took over the city reins.

Under new mayor (and formerly chief financial officer of the city) Anthony Williams, elected in 1998, the city's overall health has improved dramatically. With the city having produced four consecutive balanced budgets, the control board went dormant on September 30, 2001. ■

Washington had elected its own mayors and aldermen since 1820. With the city in debt and apprehensive over the power of the newly granted black vote, Congress scrapped that system in 1871 and replaced it with a territorial government headed by a presidentially appointed governor. Other parts of the new city government included boards of public works and health; a nonvoting delegate to Congress; an elected house of delegates; and a president-appointed council, with Frederick Douglass one of three blacks among its 11 members.

President Ulysses S. Grant wanted to hand the governorship of this newborn political entity to his crony Alexander R. "Boss" Shepherd. He backed down when the city's conservative old guard protested his choice, but Shepherd wormed his way into power nonetheless: He was named vice president of public works, a post that allowed him to run the entire city.

"How is our new governor like a sheep?" went a riddle of the time.

"He is led by A. Shepherd" was the answer.

By hook but mostly by crook, Boss Shepherd led the way for the next three years. During his reign the city added miles of sewers, water lines, gas lines, sidewalks, and roads, as well as 60,000 trees and more than 1,000 houses and buildings. Most important, Shepherd saw to it that miles upon miles of streets were leveled and paved. Working people adored him for the jobs and civic improvements; blue bloods despised him for raising their taxes.

As it turned out, citizens were amply justified in feeling fleeced. Authorized to spend four million dollars on the city, Shepherd approved the expenditure of 20 million instead. This put the city in hock but landed Shepherd in a mansion on Farragut Square, two blocks from the White House.

Armed with Grant's tacit approval, Shepherd bullied the city into submission. When the Baltimore & Ohio Railroad delayed removing its tracks from the Capitol grounds, Shepherd loyalists materialized at midnight to rip up the offending ties and rails. He invited critics of such tactics to "git up and git."

Shepherd's undoing was the financial panic of 1873. The next year, Congress dissolved the territorial government and installed three presidentially appointed commissioners. The Organic Act of 1878 abolished home rule for

house northward-migrating blacks.

With the help of radical Republicans bent on Reconstruction, black Washington enjoyed a sudden (if short-lived) heyday in the late 1860s and early 1870s. Howard University and the nation's first black high school—both staffed by top-notch instructors turning out well-educated graduates—were founded during this period. At the same time, blacks moved into jobs as officials and clerks, launched newspapers and other businesses, and mingled in white society.

Servicemen and friends form a conga line in front of the Red Cross Building on 17th Street to celebrate the end of World War II.

good, giving the three commissioners "near-absolute power." It also set up the system, still in place today, whereby the district receives an annual operating subsidy from the federal government, compensating the district for the costs that the federal presence places on the city. (In 1997, however, that federal payment was suspended; in return, D.C. got tax breaks and a guarantee that the federal government would cover the district's substantial pension shortfall.)

INTO THE 20TH CENTURY

In Washington as in many other American cities, the final quarter of the 19th century was a fin-de-siècle free-for-all. Hotels, public buildings, and arriviste villas mushroomed along the city's main avenues. Though industry was confined to a handful of gristmills and breweries in Georgetown and Foggy Bottom, Washington's main employer—the federal government—provided thousands of jobs. In addition to the clerks needed to run the many newly born government agencies, construction workers were in demand to complete the long-delayed Washington Monument (1884), to construct the Library of Congress (1897),

and to erect many other buildings that are city landmarks today. The National Zoological Park (1889) and Rock Creek Park (1890) were also created around this time, putting the pleasures of nature within easy reach of downtown museums and monuments.

Even as official Washington flourished, the city was nurturing seeds of discontent. Thousands of poor people had gravitated to the capital, lured by the simple notion that the President's adoptive home town would welcome them as well. Rarely was that the case. Washington's alleys, home to more than 17,000 residents, were notorious incubators of filth, crime, and disease. Most of these alleys would ultimately be torn down or gentrified, driving the poor underclass from one neighborhood to another.

To help the growing city fully realize the beauty envisioned by L'Enfant, in 1901 Senator James McMillan proposed a commission that would upgrade the Mall, expand the White House and the park system, and place judicial and congressional office buildings facing the Capitol. McMillan recruited four brilliant designers—architects Charles McKim and Daniel Burnham, landscape architect

Frederick Law Olmsted, and sculptor Augustus Saint-Gaudens—whose plans, drawn up free of charge, would be transformed into reality by the U.S. Army Corps of Engineers.

With Burnham leading the way, the city beautiful began to take shape. Railroad tracks crisscrossing the Mall were torn out. The Mall was extended to stretch all the way from the Capitol to the site of a planned memorial to Abraham Lincoln at its far west end. Gardens, fountains, and a reflecting pool were slated for the Mall as well. An opulent Union Station, designed by Burnham himself, rose north of the Capitol.

Not every aspect of the plan was enacted, yet it furnished a blueprint for future growth of the city core. It's fair to say that the McMillan Plan made possible the Mall's current status as a national showpiece.

STRUGGLES FOR FREEDOM

During the 1910s, the city's population swelled again as workers flooded in to support America's role in World War I. By decade's end, nearly 450,000 people called Washington home—a 32 percent increase since 1910. The Mall, which had begun to feel like a park, became a vast parking lot for hundreds of new automobiles that suddenly appeared in Washington.

With the proliferation of relief agencies during the Great Depression and President Franklin D. Roosevelt's New Deal, the number of workers on Washington's federal payroll rose from 70,261 in June 1933 to 108,673 in June 1935. Construction added many new facades to the cityscape: the Supreme Court building, the Federal Triangle buildings, the Library of Congress Annex (now called the John Adams Building), the Longworth House Office Building, and nearly 5,000 houses, apartment buildings, and office buildings.

As the city focused on winning World War II, the early 1940s brought yet another influx of new Washingtonians. Thousands of female office workers and servicemen descended on the city, and many of them stayed on after the war. By 1950, the district's population would peak at just over 800,000.

Once again, the Mall became a warehouse for the nation's needs. A beehive of "tempos"—temporary government office buildings made of cement and asbestos board—were

built along both sides of the Mall, adding to those thrown up during World War I.

By war's end in 1945, Washington found itself the capital of the most powerful nation on Earth. It had evolved from a provincial Southern town to a world leader in little more than half a century. The city seemed to be flexing its new muscles, spearheading a Cold War against communism worldwide.

On a local level, however, the story of Washington was increasingly a tale of two cities. More and more, white and black Washingtonians led separate lives in separate parts of town. Throughout the 1940s, D.C.'s schools,

parks, playgrounds, restaurants, theaters, and water fountains remained as segregated as those in any Southern town.

Then, in 1954, came the U.S. Supreme Court ruling, in *Brown v. Board of Education,* that "separate but equal education facilities are inherently unequal." The ensuing rapid integration of D.C. public schools served as a model for the nation.

In the late 1950s, blacks outnumbered whites for the first time in Washington's history. The far reaches of the city's Northeast and Southeast quadrants had drawn a raft of new residents ever since World War II, most of

Dr. Martin Luther King, Jr., salutes a crowd of Civil Rights activists during the August 23, 1968, March on Washington.

them from rural backgrounds. Now, with whites leaving the severely overcrowded city for new housing in the suburbs, middle-class blacks moved en masse into such upper Northeast neighborhoods as Fort Totten and Brookland. From 1950 to 1975, the city's black population rose from 35 percent to more than 70.

With the appointment of Walter Washington as mayor-commissioner in 1967, black Washington gained a degree of control over its affairs for the first time since the dissolution of the territorial government nearly 100 years earlier. Congress, however, retained final say over city governance—and it continues to wield that power today. This has created a troubling and inequitable political quirk: Washingtonians are the only modern Americans who suffer "taxation without representation," as some city vehicle licenses protest. D.C. voters can elect only nonvoting delegates (as opposed to representatives) to Congress, yet that body holds veto power over Washington's laws and budgets—a bone of lingering local contention and resentment.

THE PEOPLE'S PARADE GROUND

The Mall—the country's unofficial forum—has long been a rallying point for social causes. The women's suffrage movement, for example, demonstrated here in the 1910s; two decades later, thousands of Bonus Marchers descended on the Capitol to demand veterans' benefits, only to be run off by Gen. Douglas MacArthur's cavalry.

On August 28, 1963, more than 200,000 people marched on Washington to demand jobs and freedom for blacks. The event culminated in the rousing "I Have a Dream" speech delivered by Dr. Martin Luther King, Jr., on the steps of the Lincoln Memorial. Television cameras caught the historic moment on film, projecting it into living rooms and minds across the nation.

This encouraging progress was brought to a tragic end in April of 1968, when Dr. King fell to an assassin's bullet on a motel balcony in Memphis, Tennessee. Around the country, grief erupted in spasms of violence. In Washington, rioting, burning, and looting broke out near the intersection of 14th and U Streets and spread outward from there. Eventually the conflagration gutted 57 blocks in the heart of the city, crippling the once-thriving retail district downtown. Twelve people died and several hundred were injured amid the chaos.

It took 4,000 U.S. Army and National Guard troops three days to restore the peace, and the scars lingered for years. Not until the late 1990s did some areas recover. The U Street corridor, for instance—once the epicenter of Washington nightlife—has been spruced up and now draws visitors from all backgrounds.

A FRESH START

The seeds of the city's rejuvenation had been planted several years before the 1968 riots. In 1961, President John F. Kennedy and his wife, Jackie, initiated improvements to the city core. They applied a mix of historic preservation and urban renewal to Lafayette Square and to the part of Pennsylvania Avenue from the White House to the Capitol. A few years later, the urban landscape received another official facelift from Lady Bird Johnson and her "Beautify America" campaign, which added tulips, daffodils, and flowering trees and shrubs to the banks of Rock Creek and the Potomac River.

1971 was pivotal in the city's growing emphasis on aesthetics. The Mall's tempos (see p. 28) were finally removed to make way for Constitution Gardens—a 50-acre park north of the Reflecting Pool—and the John F. Kennedy Center for the Performing Arts opened on the Potomac River just above the Theodore Roosevelt Memorial Bridge. Inscribed on a wall of the Kennedy Center are the words of arts patron JFK: "This country cannot afford to be materially rich and spiritually poor."

As of 2000, the first of Kennedy's conditions remained elusive: Per capita income for the District of Columbia's 572,000 residents was nearly $40,000, but close to 17 percent were below the poverty line. That number contrasts starkly with statistics for the larger metropolitan area, which reveal that the world's richest country is led by the nation's richest megalopolis.

Poking fun at Washington politics has become a national pastime, yet the city possesses a beauty and grandeur that can win over the most hardened cynic. After Lincoln's assassination in 1865, Congressman James Garfield reportedly assured a mob in New York City: "Fellow citizens! God reigns, and the Government at Washington still lives!" Sixteen years later, Garfield, by then President himself, would be assassinated. But Washington's business went on, as it still does—through wars, deaths, financial crises, and administrations good and bad. As long as we have a United States, we will have a Washington, D.C. ■

A candlelit vigil at the Lincoln Memorial honors the victims of the September 11, 2001, attack on the World Trade Center and the Pentagon.

Washingtonians soak up sunrays at Georgetown's Washington Harbour against a background of Watergate, the Kennedy Center, and Memorial Bridge.

City on the river

Most people don't think of Washington as a riverside city, yet the Potomac is the wildest watercourse running through any major metropolis. To experience this contradiction yourself, explore Washington by water. In the process you'll leave a world of traffic, concrete, and crowds for a realm where turtles bask on logs, an osprey wings low over the water with a fish flashing in its talons, and your only neighbor glides by in a scull.

The Potomac River has been the heart of Washington since Georgetown was founded as a shipping center in 1751. By the 1790s the harbor was exporting more tobacco than any other port in the country. Later, the Chesapeake & Ohio Canal (whose towpath you can still amble) connected Georgetown to villages inland, fueling both their growth and that of the capital city.

With affluence came effluence: The Potomac was declared unfit for bathing as early as 1894, and even touching the bacteria-laden water was deemed unwise as late as 1971. The 1970s brought a concerted, community-wide effort to clean up the river, with the result that today it has been reborn. The fish are back, the birds have returned, and the water bobs with all manner of recreational craft: canoes,

kayaks, rowing shells, sailboats, and—alas—jet skis.

Washington's iconic landmarks appear grander and more intimate from the water. You can get especially close-up views of the Lincoln Memorial, Kennedy Center, and Jefferson Memorial. As you glide beneath one of the nine graceful arches of Memorial Bridge, Robert E. Lee's home, Arlington House, looms above Arlington Cemetery on the Virginia shore. Opposite Washington Harbour, heavily wooded, 88-acre Theodore Roosevelt Island makes a delightfully natural destination teeming with geese, snapping turtles, and beaver.

Many people take to the river aboard a narrated cruise—there are brunch, lunch, dinner, and moonlight options. Capitol River Cruises (301-460-7447) and Shore Shot Cruises (202-554-6500) offer 50-minute excursions from Washington Harbour (31st & K Sts., N.W.). A 90-minute tour by Potomac Riverboat Company (703-548-9000) leaves from Old Town Alexandria or Georgetown. A quirky choice is the tour offered by D.C. Ducks (202-832-9800); after rolling past the Mall's monuments, your amphibious vehicle plunges into the river for a waterborne view of town. The Alexandria Seaport Foundation (703-549-7078) conducts a

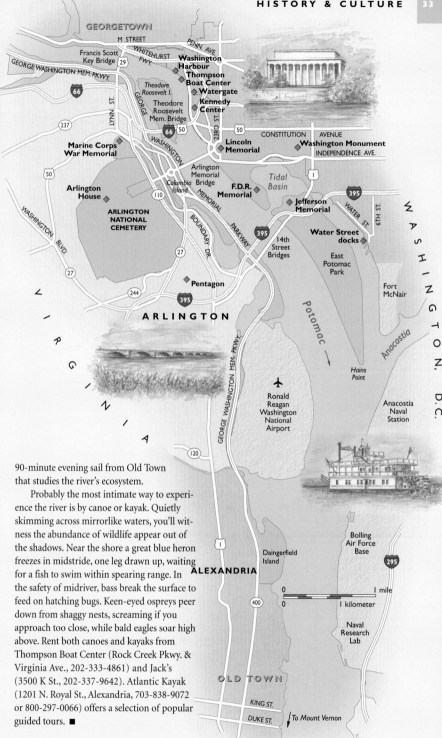

90-minute evening sail from Old Town that studies the river's ecosystem.

Probably the most intimate way to experience the river is by canoe or kayak. Quietly skimming across mirrorlike waters, you'll witness the abundance of wildlife appear out of the shadows. Near the shore a great blue heron freezes in midstride, one leg drawn up, waiting for a fish to swim within spearing range. In the safety of midriver, bass break the surface to feed on hatching bugs. Keen-eyed ospreys peer down from shaggy nests, screaming if you approach too close, while bald eagles soar high above. Rent both canoes and kayaks from Thompson Boat Center (Rock Creek Pkwy. & Virginia Ave., 202-333-4861) and Jack's (3500 K St., 202-337-9642). Atlantic Kayak (1201 N. Royal St., Alexandria, 703-838-9072 or 800-297-0066) offers a selection of popular guided tours. ■

The arts

WASHINGTON IS A RECENT ARRIVAL ON THE BIG-LEAGUE ART SCENE. DESPITE the city's status as the birthplace of many gifted musicians and actors—among them John Philip Sousa, Duke Ellington, Helen Hayes, and Pearl Bailey—an artistic community of note did not really coalesce here until 1971, when the John F. Kennedy Center for the Performing Arts welcomed the first music and theater patrons to its riverside venue. Since then, Washington has distinguished itself in just about every field of artistic endeavor, making it a leading center of the arts worldwide.

CLASSICAL MUSIC

One of the nation's finest orchestral companies, the National Symphony Orchestra was officially incorporated in 1931. At the opening of the Kennedy Center 40 years later, the NSO premiered Leonard Bernstein's "Mass," a work commissioned for the occasion. The orchestra now has a busy 52-week season that includes local performances in the Kennedy Center Concert Hall, tours in this country and abroad, televised Independence Day and Memorial Day concerts on the West Lawn of the U.S. Capitol, and programs for visiting heads of state—about 175 concerts a year in all.

Its fifth music director, Leonard Slatkin, has guided the NSO since 1996. "The status of contemporary music is probably in better shape now than it's been in the last 25 years," says Slatkin. "What I think is coming in new compositions is a real infusion of the Americans from other cultures who are here—the Latino Americans, the Asian Americans."

From a regional company struggling to make its name in 1956, the Washington Opera has evolved into a world-class organization playing to sellout audiences in the Opera House at the Kennedy Center. In the early 1980s, the company scheduled 16 performances of four operas every year; it now stages 70 performances of eight operas a year. The Washington Opera has been under the artistic direction of Placido Domingo since 1996.

A commitment to staging new American operas, bringing out lesser known important works, and nurturing young talent keeps this company in the mainstream of the opera world. A 1984 innovation—projecting surtitles above the stage—helped attract a wider audience. The 1980s were also important growth years because of the enthusiastic support of local philanthropist David Lloyd

Kreeger and the inventive direction of Martin Feinstein. Among the outstanding talents that have worked on Washington Opera productions are Gian Carlo Menotti, Franco Zeffirelli, Bruce Beresford, and Werner Herzog. Conductors have included Daniel Barenboim, Rafael Fruhbeck de Burgos, Mstislav Rostropovich, and Max Rudolf.

Washington music lovers can find a concert any night of the week, whether performed by a D.C.-based or visiting group. The Kennedy Center has hosted renowned companies from around the world, including the Berlin Philharmonic Orchestra, the Metropolitan Opera, and La Scala, while the Millennium Stage program brings free daily performances of all sorts of musical genres to the Kennedy Center's Grand Foyer.

Nor is the Kennedy Center the only game in town. Nearby Lisner Auditorium at George Washington University is a comfortable 1,490-seat hall, and other area universities feature classical music by local and guest artists. Downtown churches and museums often schedule musical events: Concerts at the National Gallery of Art, the Corcoran Gallery of Art, the Phillips Collection, and Dumbarton Oaks can be wonderfully intimate occasions. The 670-seat auditorium at the National Academy of Sciences, with its excellent acoustics, occasionally offers free concerts, often of new music. Another small venue, the Folger Shakespeare Library, presents medieval, Renaissance, and baroque music in an Elizabethan setting.

Many music aficionados consider the District of Columbia to be the nation's capital of

A ballerina performs the Washington Ballet's *Carmen* at the Kennedy Center, which presents touring companies and solo artists.

D.C. native and jazz maestro Duke Elling-ton gazes from a painting on sale at Eastern Market.

choral music. Prominent groups include the Master Chorale of Washington (formerly the Paul Hill Chorale) and the Choral Arts Society of Washington. Both frequently perform in concert with the National Symphony Orchestra and touring orchestras.

In the summer, the place to go with a picnic and a group of friends is Wolf Trap Farm Park, off the Dulles Toll Road or Va. 7. You can sit on the lawn or in the Filene Center—the open-air auditorium of this delightful park—and enjoy al fresco programs of the National Symphony Orchestra, touring opera companies, jazz, rock, or blues.

POPULAR MUSIC

Washington has historically excelled at military band music. The U.S. Marine Band received a great boost in 1868 when a local 13-year-old boy signed up as an apprentice. His name was John Philip Sousa, and within 12 years he would assume leadership of the

band. Dismayed by the band's outdated and poorly arranged music, Sousa sent off to Europe for scores by Wagner, Berlioz, and other modern composers of the day. He also began writing music of his own. Demanding excellence from others as well as from himself, Sousa drilled the band into shape. Many members quit within a year, but those who stayed became a well-honed and disciplined unit. In 1892 Sousa formed his own band and toured the United States and abroad. His tuneful lifetime outpouring ultimately included 140 original military marches, among them "The Washington Post" march (1889) and "The Stars and Stripes Forever" (1896).

Heart-poundingly patriotic performances of the illustrious U.S. Marine Band and other military combos are staged free of charge on summer evenings at the Sylvan Theater (on the grounds of the Washington Monument) and on the East Terrace of the Capitol. Alternatively, you might enjoy an evening tattoo at the Marine Barracks on Capitol Hill.

Another local musician who made good was jazz legend Edward Kennedy "Duke" Ellington. Born at 1217 22nd Street, N.W., in

1899 and raised in the Shaw neighborhood, Ellington studied classical music with a neighbor who taught music at Dunbar High School. At 24 he headed off to New York City—and thence into the Big Band and Jazz Hall of Fame. Washington jazz has enjoyed a devoted following ever since. When the Howard Theatre opened at 7th and T Streets in 1910, it marqueed such standouts as W. C. Handy, Fletcher Henderson, Bessie Smith, and Count Basie. Duke Ellington and Pearl Bailey were among the local talents who debuted at the Howard. Another star-studded black showcase, the 1922 Lincoln Theater on U Street, N.W., closed for a short while but reopened as a movie theater in the 1970s; renovated in 1994, the 1,250-seat theater today features a mixture of concerts, dance recitals, plays, and movies.

Blues Alley in Georgetown has long worn the crown as the best—sometimes the only—place in town to catch big-name jazz acts. This comfortable den has low ceilings, high cover charges, and a serious and sophisticated clientele. Other reliable spots for hearing live jazz most nights of the week include Georgetown's One Step Down, which promotes local artists, and City Blues Café on Connecticut Avenue.

Various venues host the occasional jazz concert. The most popular acts take the stage at DAR Constitution Hall, the Kennedy Center's Concert Hall, and Wolf Trap; others show up in smaller locales such as the Terrace Theater in the Kennedy Center or Baird Auditorium in the National Museum of Natural History.

If you get a chance to catch local piano virtuoso John Eaton in concert, don't pass it up. One of the country's leading exponents of classic jazz, Eaton played the piano bar circuit for years before graduating to his current trademark lecture-concerts. They are high-order entertainment.

An endless number of options exist for rock and other popular music. These range from headliner concerts at the 20,000-seat MCI Center downtown to eclectic local acts (and some up-and-coming national ones) at popular hangouts such as the 9:30 Club on V Street and the Black Cat on 14th Street. On the east side of Rock Creek Park, Carter Barron Amphitheatre is a fun summer weekend place for watching pop, rock, blues, and jazz.

Acoustic folk and bluegrass have also carved out solid niches in the Washington area; the Birchmere in Alexandria, which nurtured Grammy-winner Mary Chapin Carpenter and bluegrass pioneers The Seldom Scene, is the top choice.

THEATER

Home to more than 78 active theaters as of early 2002, the Washington metro area can boast more playhouses than any city besides New York. Whether the show is a classic drama, a local original, off-Broadway, pre-Broadway, or post-Broadway, the best of standard and contemporary theater captivates Washington audiences on a nightly basis.

Most prominent is the Kennedy Center, with two large theaters: The 1,100-seat Eisenhower Theater is a plush venue for touring productions of dramas and comedies, while the adjacent 2,200-seat Opera House presents elaborate musicals and performances of the Washington Ballet and other dance troupes.

Washington theater does not begin and end at the Kennedy Center, however. A theater has operated continuously on the Pennsylva-

nia Avenue site of the National Theatre, rebuilt in the early 1920s, since 1835. In 1845 fire destroyed the building during a performance of *Beauty and the Beast*—the first of five such conflagrations in the theater's history.

Until 1873, blacks were confined to the balcony; after that, they were not admitted at all. Finally, in 1948, local Civil Rights activists campaigned to desegregate the National. They picketed the facility, and the actors playing at the time in a touring production of *Oklahoma!* voted to honor the picket lines; for the next four years, as a result, the theater staged only movies (it reopened as a live theater in 1952).

John Wilkes Booth, Jenny Lind, Helen Hayes, John Barrymore, Sarah Bernhardt, Vivien Leigh, and Katharine Hepburn have all trod the boards of the National, which has premiered such groundbreaking productions as *West Side Story, M. Butterfly,* and many other shows. The National also continues its tradition of offering big glittery Broadway and pre-Broadway productions.

Half a block away on 13th Street, the Warner Theatre opened in 1924 as a silent-

Putting on arias: Opera—in this case, a performance of "Figaro"—is just one of the musical offerings on tap at Wolf Trap Farm Park for the Performing Arts in Vienna, Virginia.

movie palace and vaudeville stage. From 1945 to the late 1960s, it presented movies only. It then deteriorated, as did much of downtown Washington, but stayed alive with a menu of porn films and rock concerts. After closing for three years, the Warner reopened in 1992 with its rococo finery intact. It now offers a mix of musicals, dramas, and concerts.

About three blocks east of the Warner, Ford's Theatre on 10th Street had been in business for only four years when, in 1865, it became notorious as the scene of Lincoln's assassination. Restored to its 1860s appearance, it reopened in 1968 with a staging of *John Brown's Body*. Ford's Theatre now offers contemporary plays and musicals.

Probably the city's best program of serious and innovative drama is offered at the Arena Stage, on the waterfront in Southwest Washington. Since its 1950 founding by Zelda and Thomas C. Fichandler and Edward Mangum, the Arena has pioneered the resident theater movement; part of the fun is seeing your favorite local actors perform a wide variety of roles. Arena Stage also owns the distinction of being the first playhouse outside New York City to win a Tony award (the 1976 Regional Theatre Tony Award). James Earl Jones, Ned Beatty, Jane Alexander, and other notable actors cut their teeth here. Three theaters in one, the Arena holds the Fichandler Stage, a theater in the round with 827 seats sloping down to the stage; the 514-seat Kreeger Theater; and the cozy 200-seat Old Vat Room, which often presents new and local works.

After 20 praiseworthy years in its original home at the Folger Shakespeare Library, the Shakespeare Theatre moved in 1992 to a larger, 451-seat theater in the Lansburgh on Seventh Street, N.W. Richard Thomas and Kelly McGillis are among the luminaries who have played in this acclaimed local company. The September through June season includes works by Shakespeare and other dramatists; the group also stages the "Shakespeare Free For All," a summer Shakespeare play put on free of charge for two weeks at Carter Barron Amphitheatre.

Two theaters in the Logan Circle area have garnered outstanding reputations. The Source Theatre on 14th Street presents the work of new or local playwrights, as well as a more orthodox slate of classic plays by the likes of Anton Chekhov and Arthur Miller.

Known for its offbeat contemporary plays, the Studio Theatre on P Street has claimed many Helen Hayes awards. These homegrown awards for theatrical excellence recognize the formative contributions to local drama of Hayes, a Washington native who first appeared on a D.C. stage at the age of six and later won an Academy Award for her portrayal of the title character in 1932's *The Sin of Madelon Claudet.*

Perhaps seeking deliverance from the real-life hams on Capitol Hill, Washingtonians are flocking to comedy clubs. Two well-established companies spin out partially improvised political satire on a regular basis. The Capitol Steps, consisting of current and former congressional staffers, offer witty, well-polished songs and skits every Friday and Saturday night at the Ronald Reagan Building on Pennsylvania Avenue. Inside the Naval Heritage Theater farther east on Pennsylvania, the no-holds-barred Gross National Product presents a wilder, almost guerrilla-style lampoonery, whether skewering Democrats in "All the President's Women" or Republicans in "Son of a Bush." The Connecticut Avenue comedy club known as Improv features headliners as well as promising locals doing traditional stand-up.

FINE ARTS

In a city of monumental buildings and larger-than-life statuary created by some of the nation's finest architects and sculptors, D.C. art has tended to be powerful and realistic, depicting powerful people and real events. With a preponderance of these pieces being commissioned—and with many of them requiring committee approval—it's a wonder the city holds so many truly fine works of art.

The U.S. Capitol, for example, is a trove of officially sanctioned art. Its chief muralist, Italian artist Constantino Brumidi (1805–1880), was known as the Michelangelo of the Capitol; his 1865 "Apotheosis of George Washington" graces the ceiling of the Rotunda. Acclaimed artist John Trumbull (1756–1843) painted the eight large historical scenes hanging in the Rotunda.

Much of the city's great painting and sculpture is housed in established museums:

the National Gallery of Art, the Corcoran Gallery of Art, the Phillips Collection. Significant works of art created on site in Washington have tended to be in portraiture and open-air sculpture (see pp. 44–45).

Early painting in Washington was documentary as well as aesthetic: Public figures, it was agreed, should have their portraits painted for posterity. Thus locals such as George Washington, James Madison, and the wife of Capitol designer William Thornton sat for eminent portrait painter Gilbert Stuart (1755–1828), who lived in Philadelphia and Boston.

Another leading portrait painter, Charles Willson Peale (1741–1827), completed seven life paintings of George Washington, as well as portraits of Benjamin Franklin, Thomas Jefferson, and John Adams. His son Rembrandt Peale (1778–1860) parlayed his family connections into a precocious start in painting: At age 17 he produced a life portrait of George Washington. The younger Peale studied under his father, whose sharply modeled neoclassic style exerted a strong influence; Rembrandt Peale's 1805 portrait of Jefferson, now owned by the New-York Historical Society, is considered his masterpiece—and our best likeness of the third President.

The White House, too, has a Rembrandt Peale oil of Jefferson, as well as other important portraits. The Reception Rooms of the Department of State hold several portraits by the Peales, Stuart, and Thomas Sully (1783–1872). Other places to look for early Washington faces include the National Portrait Gallery and the National Gallery of Art.

What did the city look like in its infancy? Thanks to the efforts of several minor artists, we have a fairly good idea. Sketches by surveyors and architects show the lay of the land around the Capitol, the White House, and other government buildings as they were going up. Views of Washington by painter George Jacob Beck depict the Georgetown waterfront in the 1790s as a Constable-style landscape, where a country lane stands sprinkled with little houses.

City views by August Kollner in the 1830s show a Potomac busy with sailboats and the new steamboats. The latter owed their existence to engineer and painter Robert Fulton (1765–1815), who in 1807 invented the first

commercially successful steamboat; in the early 1800s Fulton had stayed with friends who owned a country estate that would become the Kalorama neighborhood, and he painted its pastoral scenes.

An 1832 lithograph of the west front of the Capitol by Hudson River artist Thomas Doughty (1793–1856) is a decidedly bucolic setting; the wooded hills and cultivated fields around Jenkins Hill (now Capitol Hill) make the government structure seem almost comically out of place. Washington's rural aspect would continue to be emphasized as late as the 1880s in the sketches and drawings of isolated cabins by DeLancey W. Gill (1859–1940), an illustrator for the Smithsonian Institution's

Bureau of American Ethnology. Perhaps these were in wistful lament for a town changing into a city?

An artists' salon blossomed in Washington at the turn of the 20th century. It met at the studio-home of painter and playwright Alice Pike Barney (1857–1931), at 2306 Massachusetts Avenue, next to the current Turkish Embassy. Overlooking Sheridan Circle, Barney's Studio House became the venue for poetry readings, plays, art shows, and other creative undertakings of the sort now associated with a multitude of Dupont addresses. Barney helped establish the Sylvan Theatre on the Mall. Both George Bernard Shaw and Alice Roosevelt Longworth sat for portraits by her hand.

Nowadays the homes of the rich and au courant are graced by abstract art turned out by Washington Color School artists, who rose to prominence in the 1960s. Gene Davis (1920–1985), known for his boldly striped canvases, worked as a White House correspondent during the Truman years before settling down to abstract art. Sam Gilliam (1933–) stepped into the limelight with his "drape paintings" in the late 1960s—stained, unframed canvases thrown over sawhorses and furniture, hung from ceiling beams, or draped

Mary Cassatt's "Little Girl in a Blue Armchair" (1878) gazes in eternal ennui from a wall of the National Gallery of Art.

on walls. The *Washington Post* described a 1999 show of his glass-enclosed collages of acrylic on birch plywood as "cubist African kimono sculptures." Gilliam's work has been commissioned for the Washington Convention Center and Ronald Reagan National Airport. He has also been honored with solo exhibitions at the Corcoran Gallery of Art and other showcases.

novels often aspire to capitalize on their settings by tackling the city's major industry: politics. The first classic "Washington novel"—an insider's look at the political machinations of the federal government—was probably *The Gilded Age*, an 1873 satire of political and financial shenanigans coauthored by Mark Twain and newspaper editor Charles Dudley Warner. It was followed in 1880 by *Democracy,*

At Kramer Books & afterwords café, a literary landmark just north of Dupont Circle, browsers converge to flip pages, sip coffee, and, on weekends, listen to live music.

LITERATURE

In more than two centuries as the nation's capital, Washington has embraced a succession of bards—writers who have succeeded in capturing this elusive power spot in prose or verse. The district's standout chroniclers have included Henry Adams, Allen Drury, and Gore Vidal.

Unlike literature set elsewhere, Washington

an American Novel, a mysterious and anonymously authored exposé that became wildly popular for blowing the lid off corruption in the Grant Administration. Despite widespread public and private conjecture about the identity of the crusading novelist, not until the author's death in 1918 would it be revealed that *Democracy* had been written by Henry Adams.

Published more than 40 years ago but still

relevant today, Allen Drury's *Advise and Consent* (1959) broke new ground for its startling portrayal of backroom politics. Focusing mainly on the U.S. Senate and a controversial nominee for secretary of state, the book won the former newspaper reporter a Pulitzer Prize in 1960; the 1962 movie version, starring Henry Fonda and Charles Laughton under the direction of Otto Preminger, remains one of Hollywood's more intelligent treatments of Washington.

Many consider Gore Vidal to be Washington's modern laureate, though the erudite author of *Washington, D.C.: a Novel* (1967) and more than 25 other books seems determined to flee that distinction; Vidal has lived in Ravello, Italy, since the early 1970s. Born in West Point, New York, in 1925, Vidal spent much of his childhood inhaling politics at the Rock Creek Park home of his grandfather, Thomas P. Gore, a populist senator from Oklahoma. Vidal himself ran for Congress (unsuccessfully) in 1960 and for the Senate (with identical results) in 1982. He was already a novelist by his first campaign, but his most popular work was still decades away: *Lincoln* (1984) painted a balanced and human portrait of a President who had been only canonized until then. Vidal's novel *1876* puts recent political history into perspective: In that year Republican Rutherford B. Hayes stole the election from Democrat Samuel J. Tilden, who had won the popular vote; one of the states whose election returns were contested was Florida.

In a city of often secret doings, those who bring them to light can achieve near-mythic acclaim. Bob Woodward and Carl Bernstein, who broke the scandalous story of the Watergate break-in and burglary in the early 1970s, are but two of the many Washington reporters who have used journalism as a springboard to literary fame. Their post-Watergate work includes the jointly authored *All the President's Men* and *The Final Days*, as well as individual efforts by Woodward such as *Veil: The Secret Wars of the CIA, 1981-1987* and *The Brethren*.

Another scribe-turned-literary lion, Ward Just, reported for the *Washington Post* until the late 1960s. While covering Richard Nixon's 1968 presidential campaign, Just concluded that fiction was the only medium capable of conveying the true nature of politics. His work ranges from *The Congressman Who Loved Flaubert*, a 1973 collection of political short stories, to *Echo House*, a 1997 portrait of D.C. government that spans eight decades and three generations.

Novelist Gore Vidal frequently based his fiction on events in Washington history.

Newsweek columnist Joe Klein hit the jackpot with his first book, the 1996 best-seller *Primary Colors*. In common with Henry Adams's *Democracy* of a century earlier, Klein's book—a thinly veiled fictionalization of Bill Clinton's 1992 campaign—was first published anonymously.

Carrying a book by any of four other leading local lights—satirical novelist Christopher Buckley, hard-boiled detective writer George P. Pelecanos, espionage master Charles McCarry, or journalist Stanley Karnow—should mark you instantly as a Washingtonian in the know.

Poets, too, have been pivotal in the city's literary life. Walt Whitman, who helped care for wounded soldiers in Washington during the Civil War, wrote one of his greatest poems here: the moving elegy to Lincoln, "When Lilacs Last in the Dooryard Bloom'd." Its lines let the reader see the slain President's funeral cortege clatter by: "With the tolling tolling bells' perpetual clang, / Here, coffin that slowly passes, / I give you my sprig of lilac." Ironically, 1865 was the same year that Whitman was

Stories
in stone

Filled with monumental architecture and heroic statuary, Washington is a city that can be read even by the illiterate. The pediment of the Supreme Court's west facade, for example, shows an enthroned Liberty holding the scales of justice. The busy scene depicted on the pediment of the National Archives uses winged horses, rams, and papyrus flowers as classical symbols of aspiration, parchment, and paper.

The more somber the structure, the less evident the signage. Nowhere on the outside of the Supreme Court is the building's function identified. Nor will you find the words "Abraham Lincoln" until you walk inside the Lincoln Memorial.

Yet building exteriors cannot narrate the welter of stories that Washington has to tell. As you walk around the district, you'll encounter more equestrian statues than in any other North American city. These sculptures—most of them depicting military men astride horses in various stances—came into vogue in the late 19th century, when the nation's compulsion to honor its Civil War heroes dovetailed with the rapid growth of its capital city. It's an urban myth, by the way, that a horse with one hoof raised denotes its rider was wounded in battle; nor is it true that both hooves in the air denote the rider died in battle.

Befitting its wartime role as the Federal capital, Washington bristles with Union generals in bronze. Only one Confederate officer is so honored: Even then, the statue of Brig. Gen. Albert Pike—at Third and D Sts., N.W.—recognizes his service not as a soldier but as a Mason. Otherwise you'll have to cross the river to Alexandria, Virginia, to find the nearest Confederate statue—the Rebel soldier who stands at Prince and South Washington Streets in Old Town, head downcast, arms crossed, back turned resolutely on the North.

Washington's late 19th-century renaissance in statuary also coincided with America's emergence as an environment favorable to artists. A nation of growing affluence and power demanded artists to document its glory. As a result, many world-renowned sculptors have work on display in Washington. One of them was Augustus Saint-Gaudens (1848–1907), a Dublin-born artist who grew up in New York City. His 1890 Adams Memorial (see p. 190), commissioned by author Henry Adams to honor his wife, Clover, is one of the most beautiful, moving, and remote pieces of sculpture in the city: It is tucked away in a grove of Japanese yews in Rock Creek Cemetery.

The most famous sculpture in Washington, if not the entire country, is Daniel Chester French's 1922 marble figure of Lincoln, who sits in brooding majesty 19 feet high inside the rectangular marble Lincoln Memorial at the

east end of Memorial Bridge. Lincoln clenches his left hand to show strength and resolve; his right lies open to signal compassion (it's another urban myth that he is signing "A.L.").

Thanks to the lobbying efforts of certain groups and the personal fortunes of certain individuals, tributes to elusive or lost causes dot the cityscape as well. The Temperance Fountain (ca 1880) at Pennsylvania Avenue and Seventh Street, for example, is a mini-temple surmounted by a long-legged crane; a San Francisco dentist donated the drinking fountain to advocate the salutary effects of water over spirits. Though the fountain no longer functions, a bar across the street stays busy.

So what does it take to get yourself memo-

The 19-foot-high marble statue of Abraham Lincoln dominates the open-air Lincoln Memorial, built from 1914 to 1922 in the likeness of a Doric temple.

rialized in the nation's capital? First, you must form a citizens' group to petition Congress. A vote must then be taken, a sculptor commissioned, an approval granted by the Commission of Fine Arts, and funds raised. Only a fraction of proposals make the long journey from paper to stone.

For a guide to more than 400 of the city's open-air sculptures, take a look at James M. Goode's *Outdoor Sculpture of Washington, D.C.* (Smithsonian Institution Press, 1974). ■

fired from his job as a clerk in the Indian Bureau. The charge: writing offensive poetry.

Another world-class poet served a Washington sojourn, but not by choice. Indicted for treason in 1945 for having broadcast Fascist propaganda during World War II, Ezra Pound was remanded to the care of St. Elizabeth's Hospital (formerly St. Elizabeth's Lunatic Asylum). Upon his release in 1958, Pound proclaimed: "All of America is an insane asylum."

wise created a capital context for her capital crimes, strewing corpses around tourist sites from the Kennedy Center to the Smithsonian.

ARCHITECTURE

Conceived as a grand capital, Washington has attained a unifying look about its core. One of the main proponents of a neoclassic-style capital was architect-philosopher-statesman Thomas Jefferson. The great buildings and

The restrained symmetry of the Georgian Carlyle House (left) in Old Town Alexandria sets off the 1800 federal-style Octagon (right), a house museum and national historic landmark.

Nicer surroundings were in store for the many writers who have stayed at the Willard Hotel on Pennsylvania Avenue, among them Mark Twain, Emily Dickinson, and Charles Dickens. Julia Ward Howe wrote the "Battle Hymn of the Republic" during an 1861 stay. Martin Luther King, Jr., penned parts of his "I Have a Dream" speech here in August 1963.

In the capital's quirkiest epistolary pattern, presidential progeny have authored a host of murder mysteries with a Washington locale. FDR's son Elliott Roosevelt set a number of his books in the White House, where characters meet untimely ends in the West Wing, the East Room, the Executive Mansion, the Oval Office, the Blue Room, and the Rose Garden. Margaret Truman, daughter of Harry S., like-

monuments, harking back to ancient Greek and Roman models, were designed to impress with their massiveness and their references to earlier democracies. Weighty columns of marble and pediments embellished with allegorical scenes are the general rule for these early (and many later) federal buildings.

Precious few 18th-century edifices remain. The White House and the Capitol were started in the early 1790s, but both were burned in 1814—and both have undergone all sorts of alterations and renovations since their rebuilding to look the way they do. The Capitol recalls the Pantheon in Rome, begun in 27 B.C. as a temple for worshiping the gods. A less grandiose style was chosen for the executive mansion: Its Georgian format was popular in many manor houses of the day, among them Mount Vernon, Woodlawn, and Gunston Hall, all in Virginia. All three abodes feature porticoes, cornices, steep roofs pierced by several chimneys, and near-perfect symmetry.

The federal style flourished in tandem with Washington's growth in the 19th century. Alexandria and Georgetown, already well established, built scores of elegant brick town houses and row houses for prosperous local

breathtakingly cavernous interior. It was nearly razed in the 1960s.

The Old Executive Office Building—the world's largest office building at the time of its 1888 construction—was ridiculed and likewise threatened with demolition. Harry S. Truman, for one, called it the "greatest monstrosity in America." Apparently the 33rd President's appreciation of architecture did not match his statecraft; the Gilded Age building,

In Georgetown, the 1868 Italianate villa (left) of Cooke's Row on Q Street is a private residence; Victorian eclecticism reigns along a P Street block (right).

merchants. Residences from the early 1800s tend to be unadorned, while those built after the Civil War betray unmistakable Victoriana: They sport rosettes, urns, swags, and decorative ironwork. The finest examples of the federal style in Washington are the 1800 Octagon at 1799 New York Avenue, N.W. and the 1816 Tudor Place at 1644 31st Street, N.W. The latter, despite its name, blends neoclassic and federal elements. Conceived as private homes by Capitol designer, William Thornton, both are now national historic landmarks.

Other building styles began to appear later in the 1800s, but architects risked opprobrium if they strayed too far from the city's neoclassicism. Completed in 1887, the redbrick Pension Building (National Building Museum) has a

with its mansard roofs and hundreds of window pediments and columns, is now recognized as an outstanding American example of French Second Empire-style architecture.

Daring and exuberant, the Old Post Office (1899) was likewise slated for obliteration until it was saved in the late 1970s and converted into a retail-office complex. Though it hunkers uneasily among its sedate neighbors on Pennsylvania Avenue, the castlelike building has become a beloved landmark.

Popular in the first half of the 20th century, the beaux arts style, with its use of columns and other classical elements, meshed well in Washington. Union Station (1908) by Daniel Burnham and John Russell Pope's National Archives (1935) and National Gallery of Art

(1941) are grand without ostentation.

Though many downtown buildings were razed in the mid-20th century and replaced with concrete cubes, a few noteworthy buildings did go up. Edward Durell Stone's National Geographic Society 17th Street building (1964) and Kennedy Center (1971) may be boxy, but their interplay of columnar elements and white stone is well suited to Washington.

Other styles have made their way into the cityscape, yet they send symbolic nods to their

Since its 1988 restoration, Union Station has been a hub of shopping, dining, & trainsportation.

forerunners. Architect I. M. Pei's radically modernist East Building (1978) of the National Gallery, for instance, is faced with the same pink marble as the traditional West Building (1941). In general, no city building is allowed to rise more than 20 feet higher than the width of the street on which it stands. ■

Grand marble halls of law, justice, and knowledge top Washington's most prominent hill. But here, too, you'll discover a more prosaic world of lively markets, soothing parks, and flower-filled gardens.

Capitol Hill

The Capitol Rotunda
from below

Capitol Hill

"A PEDESTAL WAITING FOR A MONUMENT" CITY PLANNER PIERRE CHARLES L'Enfant called the swell of land then known as Jenkins Hill, on the city's southeastern side. Today beautiful monuments grace this hill, including the Capitol and the Supreme Court. Humanizing the grandeur of marble buildings and plazas are tree-lined residential streets. The heart of Washington, Capitol Hill is a good place to begin your tour.

For nearly one hundred years, the Capitol was the only building created for the use of the nation's legislature. To the east spread an orderly neighborhood of brick row houses. But by the end of the 19th century, the Library of Congress's Jefferson Building had risen across from the Capitol, followed shortly by architect Daniel H. Burnham's imposing Union Station and adjacent City Post Office. The early 1900s saw construction of the Cannon Building (1908) and Russell Building (1909), the first House and Senate office buildings. In the 1930s, the Supreme Court, the Folger Shakespeare Library, and the Adams Building of the Library of Congress added more density to Capitol Hill.

By the mid-20th century, much of the residential area was in decline as middle-class families abandoned the city for the suburbs. Then in the 1970s, urban pioneers, lured by low real estate values and the convenient location, began moving in and revitalizing the area. With the Eastern Market *(7th & C Sts., S.E.)* as an anchor, Capitol Hill became a vibrant neighborhood once again. Spruced up historic houses, shops, and restaurants from the Capitol to Lincoln Park make this a pleasant and lovely place to live in and visit.

You will need a full day to see all the sights here, two days to see them in detail. Union Station and Capitol South Metro stops are about equidistant from the Capitol. If you start from one, you can work your way to the other or do a leisurely loop back to your starting point. Either way, plan on getting some exercise—the area was designed on a grand scale. Walking gives you a chance to savor the magnificent architecture from various points.

As you walk, bear in mind that these buildings are both historical museums and working halls of democracy. Touring them gives you a sense of the great enterprise upon which the Founding Fathers embarked. If the free world has a geographical center, it is Capitol Hill. ∎

Row houses cluster in the desirable Capitol Hill neighborhood.

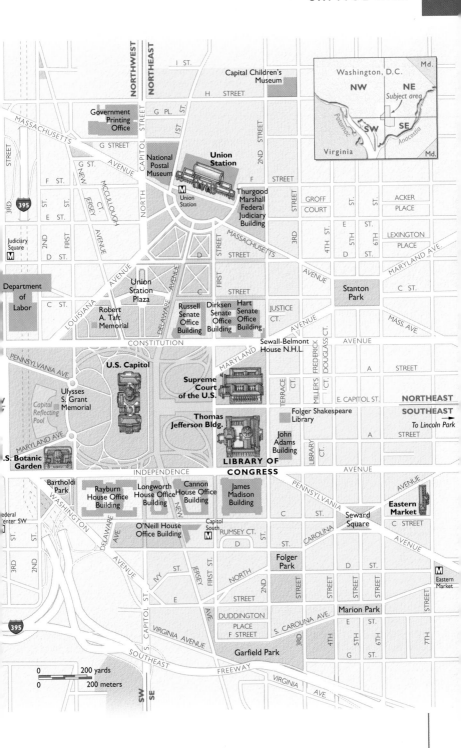

NORTHWEST
NORTHEST

I ST.

Capital Children's Museum

H   STREET

Washington, D.C.

NW   NE
Subject area

Potomac

SW   SE

Virginia   Anacostia

Md.

MASSACHUSETTS

Government Printing Office

G PL.

G STREET

G ST.

F ST.

National Postal Museum

Union Station

395

Union Station

F   STREET

GROFF COURT

ACKER PLACE

Thurgood Marshall Federal Judiciary Building

E   ST.

LEXINGTON PLACE

Judiciary Square
M

MCCULLOUGH CT.

NEW JERSEY AVENUE

D ST.

D   STREET

MASSACHUSETTS   STREET

3RD

4TH   5TH   6TH

D

MARYLAND AVE.

Department of Labor

LOUISIANA AVENUE

C ST.

Union Station Plaza

Robert A. Taft Memorial

Russell Senate Office Building

Dirksen Senate Office Building

Hart Senate Office Building

JUSTICE CT.

AVENUE

Stanton Park

C ST.

MASS. AVE.

CONSTITUTION

DELAWARE AVENUE

FIRST   STREET

MARYLAND AVENUE

Sewall-Belmont House N.H.L.

FREDERICK DOUGLASS CT.

A   STREET

PENNSYLVANIA AVE.

U.S. Capitol

Ulysses S. Grant Memorial

Capitol Reflecting Pool

Supreme Court of the U.S.

TERRACE CT.

MILLER'S CT.

E. CAPITOL ST.

NORTHEAST
SOUTHEAST

To Lincoln Park

MARYLAND AVE

Thomas Jefferson Bldg.

Folger Shakespeare Library

John Adams Building

LIBRARY CT.

A   STREET

.S. Botanic Garden

LIBRARY OF CONGRESS

INDEPENDENCE

AVENUE

Bartholdi Park

Rayburn House Office Building

Longworth House Office Building

Cannon House Office Building

James Madison Building

PENNSYLVANIA

AVENUE

Eastern Market

WASHINGTON

O'Neill House Office Building

Capitol South
M

C

ST.

CAROLINA

Seward Square

C STREET

ederal enter SW
J

DELAWARE AVE.

RUMSEY CT.

D   ST.

D   ST.

3RD   2ND

IVY   ST.

JERSEY ST.

FIRST ST.

NORTH   STREET

Folger Park

2ND   STREET

STREET

STREET   STREET

M
Eastern Market

E   STREET

S. CAROLINA AVE.

Marion Park

395

SOUTH CAPITOL ST.

VIRGINIA AVENUE

DUDDINGTON PLACE
F STREET

Garfield Park

E   ST.

3RD

4TH   5TH   6TH

7TH

G   ST.

SOUTHEAST   FREEWAY

VIRGINIA   AVE.

VIRGINIA   AVE.

SW   SE

0   200 yards
0   200 meters

U.S. Capitol

U.S. Capitol

www.aoc.gov

🅐 Map p. 51

✉ Capitol Hill, between
Independence &
Constitution Aves.

☎ 202-225-6827

🚇 Metro: Capitol South
or Union Station;
Bus: 34, 35, 36, 91

ONE OF THE MOST RECOGNIZED LANDMARKS IN THE
world, the marble white U.S. Capitol, rising in domed and columned
splendor at the Mall's east end, defines the center of Washington.
South, East, and North Capitol Streets and the Mall radiate out from
the Capitol in the cardinal directions, dividing the city into quadrants. In this vaulted location, Presidents are inaugurated, national
issues debated, and new laws made.

**Paintings by
John Trumbull
(1756–1843)
hang in the
echoing cavern
of the Capitol's
Rotunda,
depicting impor-
tant moments
in the American
Revolution.**

EVOLUTION

The Capitol you see today looks almost nothing like its original conception. From the laying of the
cornerstone by George Washington
in 1793 to the placing of the statue
of "Freedom" atop the dome in
1863, some half dozen major
designers and architects put their
visions and efforts into the final
image. Erecting an edifice as important as the Capitol was about as
easy as enacting a controversial new
law. The egos of architects, engineers, and congressmen often
clashed; funding grew scarce at
times; and disputes drove major
players into resigning their posi-
tions. Like the nation's early history,
the history of the Capitol is one of

false starts, compromises, and ultimate triumph.

Pierre Charles L'Enfant stub-
bornly refused to come up with an
architectural plan for the Capitol,
declaring that he had it "in his
head." His dismissal in 1792 led to a
national competition to design the
building, the winning architect to
receive $500 and a city lot. The 16
known entries were so poor that the
contest had to be extended. An amateur architect named William
Thornton finally came up with a
winning design—a Pantheon-like
dome flanked by symmetrical wings
for the Senate and the House.
Though greatly modifying and
extending the design over the years,
later architects generally followed

this basic layout; they also incorporated the Corinthian pilasters, seven-bay portico, balustrade, and other neoclassic details Thornton had envisioned. The beauty of his plan lay in the fact that it was both grand and simple, as George Washington said, yet also flexible enough to accommodate a growing nation.

In 1800 the government moved from Philadelphia to Washington, and President John Adams addressed the Congress in the Capitol's brick-and-sandstone north wing, the only completed part of the building. During these early years, Thornton resigned, and two out of the three other architects were fired over their attempted design alterations. Fortunately, in 1803 the government hired the brilliant British architect Benjamin Henry Latrobe, and his collaboration with President Thomas Jefferson, himself an amateur architect, made for substantial progress.

Then in August of 1814, British troops marched on Washington, and torched many buildings, including the Capitol. The fire destroyed much of the building's interior, though the walls remained standing. For the next few years, Latrobe worked at restoring the damage. Cost overruns and a dispute about vaulting the ceilings of the House and Senate Chambers finally led to his resignation. Boston architect Charles Bulfinch stepped in. Quieter and more conservative than Latrobe, Bulfinch ingratiated himself with Congress and President James Monroe. Bulfinch served until 1830, completing the building with a copper-covered wooden dome and an east portico.

By 1850, an expanding Congress had outgrown its chambers, necessitating the addition of new grand wings to the original building. The Capitol expansion project was still underway when the Civil War broke out. Construction went on, culminating in the addition of the current cast-iron dome, which replaced a leaky, wooden predecessor. On Dec. 2, 1863, the magnificent nine-million-pound dome, rising from a circular portico, was crowned with "Freedom," the 19.5-foot-tall bronze figure of

Tulips highlight the beauty of the Capitol at night. The nation's leading landscape architect, Frederick Law Olmsted, designed the grounds in the 1870s.

a woman dressed in flowing robes. A 35-gun salute (for each of the states, including those that had seceded) greeted "Freedom's" ascent. An interesting historical footnote concerns her headgear. The original plan had her in a liberty cap, worn by freed slaves in ancient Greece. Then Secretary of War Jefferson Davis—president of the Confederacy by the time the statue was placed atop the Capitol—objected, saying the cap was "inappropriate to a people who were born free." A helmet with eagle feathers was substituted.

In the 1870s, renowned landscape architect Frederick Law Olmsted added terraces to the north, south, and west sides. Congress again outgrew the building in the early 20th century, scattering to the nearby Senate and House office buildings. A major addition in 1958–62 added 32 feet to the east front, leaving the sandstone west facade as the only original exterior not covered with a marble addition.

VISITING

At the heart of the Capitol, the **Rotunda** soars 180 feet to a round ceiling fresco, "The Apotheosis of Washington" (1865), by Italian-American artist Constantino Brumidi. A berobed George Washington stares down from on high, surrounded by a swirl of clouds and figures that represent the 13 Colonies and American democracy. Much closer to the floor, a 300-foot-long frieze, begun by Brumidi but not completed until 1953, encircles the Rotunda. The frieze depicts more than 400 years of American history from Columbus to the Wright brothers.

On the Rotunda's west side hang the four huge scenes from the American Revolution painted by Washington's aide-de-camp John Trumbull. Across from them, on the east side, are canvases portraying the discovery and settlement of the United States. A small white marble stone marks the center of the Rotunda's floor; here eminent Americans such as Abraham Lincoln and

John F. Kennedy have lain in state.

One room south of the Rotunda is the **National Statuary Hall,** where the House of Representatives met from 1807 to 1857. In 1864 Congress first invited each state to send a bronze or marble statue of two prominent citizens. The weight of the statues and the space they take up have long since necessitated that some be placed elsewhere. Among notables on site are Henry Clay (Kentucky), Daniel Webster (New Hampshire), Robert E. Lee (Virginia), and King Kamehameha I (Hawaii).

North of the Rotunda is the **Old Senate Chamber,** which served the Senate from 1810 to 1859 (except between 1814 and 1819, when senators had to meet across the street after the British burned the Capitol). Here such famous men as Clay, Webster, and John C. Calhoun hotly debated the issues of slavery and economics prior to the Civil War. During one memorable speech in 1856, an infuriated congressman named Preston Brooks invaded the chamber and attacked Senator Charles Sumner, who had been speaking against slavery for five hours, with a cane. Today the Senate uses this chamber for closed-door conferences, including a 1999 session on the impeachment trial of Bill Clinton.

Rembrandt Peale's famous portrait of George Washington (1823) hangs on the chamber's east wall, above the Vice President's dais.

On the first floor, directly beneath the Rotunda, awaits the **Crypt.** George and Martha Washington were to be entombed here, but family members objected, so the two remain at Mount Vernon, in Virginia. Ringing the room, 40 Doric sandstone columns help support the Rotunda. Gutzon Borglum, who carved Mount Rushmore, created the marble head of Lincoln displayed here. The statue's missing left ear symbolizes the slain President's incomplete life.

North of the Crypt, through the small Senate Rotunda and to the right, stands the **Old Supreme Court Chamber.** The Senate originally met in this vaulted room designed by Latrobe; the Supreme Court used it from 1810 to 1860. In the early 1970s, restorers armed with mid-19th-century descriptions returned the chamber to its earlier appearance. Half of the furnishings, including justices' desks and chairs, are original.

On the first floor of the north wing, the colorful Brumidi Corridors boast a wealth of frescoes and other paintings by Constantino Brumidi, who worked in the Capitol for 25 years in the late 1800s.

Capitol views

One of the earliest travel books about America was written by Frances Trollope, mother of English writer Anthony Trollope and herself a prolific novelist. In her popular *Domestic Manners of the Americans* (1832), written after a three-year journey to the fledgling United States, she found much to disparage. But she was impressed by the Capitol:

"None of us, I believe, expected to see so imposing a structure on that side the Atlantic. I am ill at describing buildings, but the beauty and majesty of the American capitol might defy an abler pen than mine to do it justice. It stands so finely too, high, and alone.... The view from the capitol commands the city and many miles around, and it is itself an object of imposing beauty to the whole country adjoining." ■

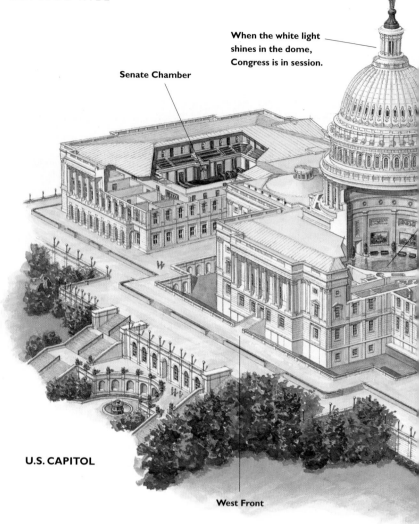

When the white light shines in the dome, Congress is in session.

Senate Chamber

U.S. CAPITOL

West Front

Sometimes called the Michelangelo of the Capitol, Brumidi had done some restoration work on the Vatican, and he based his designs for the corridors on its Raphael loggia. The historical scenes and heroes, as well as the depictions of flora and fauna in trompe l'oeil frames, provide a rich summary of early America. Later paintings include the first moon landing and a tribute to the crew who died in the 1986 explo-

sion of the *Challenger* space shuttle.

On the other side of the Crypt, in the south wing, are the **First Floor House Corridors;** they contain some of the National Statuary Hall collection as well as murals by contemporary American artist Allyn Cox. The Capitol engulfed in flames in 1814 and wounded Union soldiers lying in a makeshift hospital in the Rotunda are among the scenes depicted here.

The heart of American democracy, the U.S. Capitol is also the geographic center of Washington; the city's four quadrants radiate from the middle of the building.

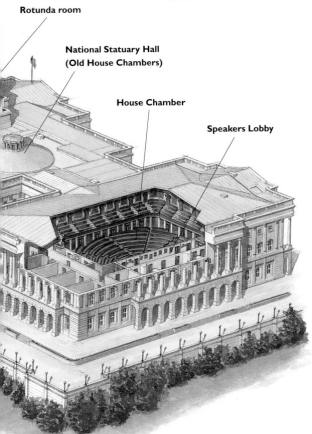

Rotunda room

National Statuary Hall
(Old House Chambers)

House Chamber

Speakers Lobby

The **Congressional Chambers** are located in the Capitol's wings (the House south, the Senate north). The 435 House representatives are not assigned specific seats, though Democrats traditionally sit to the Speaker's right, Republicans to the left. The same arrangement holds for the more stately Senate, but here desks are based on seniority.

The only way to see the House or Senate in session is to contact your representative or senator for special passes before coming to Washington. (Congress is usually in recess during August and in the fall during elections.) Many congresspeople have tour information on their individual websites. Your member of Congress can also provide a pass for a VIP tour of the Capitol building, which is more comprehensive than the ones offered to the public. ■

Politics at work

In the summer of 1787, following the successful rebellion of the 13 Colonies against England and the loosely structured "Confederation" period, 55 leaders from the newly independent states met in Philadelphia's State House (now Independence Hall) to revise the the Articles of Confederation, the country's first constitution. Trying to strike a delicate balance between sufficient government power to rule a nation yet guarantee adequate liberty for its citizens, the delegates decided to toss out the Articles and create a new document. The result: the Constitution of the United States of America—the fundamental law of the U.S. federal system and a landmark document of the Western world.

This constitution, having been the product of secret deals and silent compromises, could not become the law of the land by fiat, so the Founders asked that it be ratified by the people of the 13 independent states. There were many heated state conventions, some producing violence, other producing eloquent words, that have helped Supreme Court Justices determine the meaning of this concise blueprint for the government we have today—living up to its preamble: "We the People of the United States of America…"

From the beginning Congress met to air differences and reach hard fought compromises. The reason the capital is in Washington, for instance, is because of the very public Compromise of 1790, in which northern congressmen and senators got their southern counterparts to approve funding our first national debt in return for placing the nation's capital in the south on the Potomac River, not far from George Washington's home. From the First Congress came the traditions of national debt and logrolling. And anyone who has tuned into

C-SPAN knows that political debate and compromise continue to be integral ingredients in making laws.

You can see the fireworks first-hand in Washington several different ways. The most obvious is go to the Capitol, where you can hear your senator give a speech or watch a debate about a current issue on the floor of the House. Before leaving home contact your representative or senator for special passes. Many congresspeople have information on their websites. You can also call your politician's office (202-224-3121). And when you stop in to pick up your gallery tickets, maybe you'll have a chance for a chat with your hometown legislator.

Right: "Senate Hearing" by William Gropper (1897–1977): Making fun of gasbag politicians is a 200-year-long tradition, but discord was intentionally designed in the Federalist Papers to allow a voice to different groups.

While the work done on the Congress floor is well publicized, much of the real work goes on behind the scenes in committees and subcommittees—the first place where most bills being nominated as future laws are discussed and debated and picked apart. Most days the legislature is in session, a dozen or more committees and subcommittees meet—most of which are open to the public. Here you can watch the future of high definition television being decided, hear an EPA administrator grilled about pollution enforcement, listen to debates about space exploration, or attend the confirmation hearing for a newly nominated federal judge. To find out what committees your local elected officials are on, visit *www.house.gov* or *www.senate.gov*.

If a bill is good and has powerful friends on the committee, it will be recommended to the House or Senate for debate and vote. Of the some 10,000 bills introduced every year, only about 10 percent ever make it to the floor of either the House or Senate to be voted on.

If passed, the bill is sent to the other chamber, referred to committee, and so on. If the bill makes it through the tortured path to passage in that chamber, then a "Conference" committee is set up to settle differences between the two bills, if there are any. The Senate and House vote again on the revised bill, and if that bill still passes then it goes to the President for his signature—or veto.

Regardless of how a bill turns out, the process is both interesting and fun to watch. You will be observing how that blueprint for a government hashed out in a steamy room centuries ago works every day on issues great and small. ■

Supreme Court

Supreme Court

www.supremecourtus.gov

🅰 Map p. 51

✉ 1st & E. Capitol Sts., N.E.

☎ 202-479-3000 or 202-479-3211

🕐 Closed Sat.–Sun.

🚇 Metro: Capitol South or Union Station; Bus: 96

THIS IMPOSING NEOCLASSIC BUILDING OPPOSITE THE Capitol makes a simple yet powerful statement with its wide marble stairway and its lofty portico rising on 32 Corinthian columns.

An architrave just below the pediment bears the inscription "Equal Justice Under Law," an echo of Justice John Marshall Harlan's famous dissenting opinion in 1896 in *Plessy v. Ferguson*: "In view of the Constitution, in the eye of the law, there is in this country no superior, dominant, ruling class of citizens. There is no caste here.... [A]ll citizens are equal before the law."

Here the nation's highest tribunal arbitrates cases involving the Constitution or the nation's laws. In this court of final appeal, decisions have been handed down that have profoundly influenced the country. In 2000 the Court showed its muscle again by effectively settling the controversial U.S. presidential race.

Surprisingly, the Supreme Court did not have its own building until 1935. Before then it sat in various places within the Capitol. In 1929 Chief Justice William Howard Taft, the only U.S. President (1909–1913) to serve on the Court (1921–1930), urged Congress to authorize the erection of a Supreme Court building. The neoclassic edifice designed by Cass Gilbert was constructed with 27,400 pieces of marble. Every feature lends a sense of gravity and dignity, from the 6.5-ton bronze doors to the seated marble giants out front— "Contemplation of Justice" (left) and "Guardian of Law" (right).

VISITING

You enter through the main (west) entrance on the building's second floor, which leads to the **Great Hall** and its long line of busts depicting former chief justices. At the end of the hall lies the actual **courtroom.** When the Court is not in session, you can visit the chamber, and learn about court procedure and the building's architecture, by attending a free lecture there, given on the half hour.

There is much for the eye to feast on in the nation's most important courtroom. Behind the raised mahogany bench stand the chairs of the nine justices, their height varying according to how tall the justice is (so that they all appear the same height when seated). Along the sides of the room rise 24 veined marble columns, above which sculpted marble panels depict such lawgivers as Moses, Confucius, and Napoléon. Above these friezes stretches the bright red and blue ceiling coffered with hand-carved wood and plaster rosettes and lined with gold.

When the court is in session (*Oct.–April Mon.–Wed.*), you can listen to oral arguments by lining up on the plaza in front of the building. Seating begins at 9:30 a.m. and 12:30 p.m. Some cases attract big crowds, with people even sleeping outside the court to ensure a place inside. You may have a better chance with the other line—for those who just want to hear a three-minute sample of the case. Seating begins at 10:00 a.m. and 1:00 p.m.

More than 7,000 petitions asking the Supreme Court to overturn a lower-court ruling arrive every year. Only 100 to 120 make it to the argument stage. Each side is given 30 minutes to argue its case; the justices then write their opinions. You can access these and other Court information via the internet.

Go down a flight of stairs to the ground level, where you'll find a small theater in the **Lower Great Hall;** a 24-minute film details the workings of the Court and includes interviews with current justices. The hall also has several exhibits on the Supreme Court. On the south side the famous Warren Court (1953–1969), presided over by Chief Justice Earl Warren, still sits in session, in a cast stone and aluminum sculpture. The Warren Court's progressive opinions included the outlawing of school segregation.

At the hall's east end rises a statue of the great fourth Chief Justice, John Marshall, who served 1801–1835. He is considered responsible for our system of constitutional law, including the doctrine of judicial review (*Marbury* v. *Madison*, 1803), by which the Court can declare acts of Congress unconstitutional. Follow signs for a view of two amazing marble-and-bronze freestanding spiral staircases; the ascending ovals make the five-story building appear twice as tall as it really is. ■

**Opposite:
The neoclassic
Supreme Court
Building, with its
open courtyard
of Georgia marble,
was completed
in 1935.**

Library of Congress

Library of Congress
www.loc.gov

🗺 Map p. 51

✉ 1st St. &
Independence Ave.,
S.E.

☎ 202-707-8000

🕐 Closed Sun.

🚇 Metro: Capitol South;
Bus: 34, 35

AFTER EXTENSIVE RENOVATION FROM 1986 TO 1997, THE Library of Congress—the world's largest library—has emerged as one of the most breathtaking buildings in the city. Inside and out, the Italian Renaissance-style Thomas Jefferson Building (main building) dazzles the eye with its opulent yet tasteful cornucopia of sculpture, murals, mosaics, and architectural flourishes. Whether you come here for serious research or just to wander around, you'll leave understanding why this temple of learning was considered, at its opening in 1897, the most beautiful public building in America.

Originally housed in the U.S. Capitol, the Library began in 1800 as a reference collection for Congress. After the British burned the Capitol in 1814, destroying the books, Thomas Jefferson sold his personal library of 6,487 volumes—one of the country's most extensive—to Congress. Larger than the original collection, Jefferson's contained law books, as well as works of literature, history, science, architecture, and philosophy. As he wrote at the time, "There is, in fact, no subject to which a member of Congress may not have occasion to refer." His unbounded interest in everything has set the tone for the Library ever since.

The Library suffered a second devastating blow in 1851 when fire destroyed two-thirds of the collection. Though most titles have since been replaced, almost 900 remain missing. The Library is now conducting a worldwide search for copies of the books.

Ainsworth Rand Spofford, Librarian of Congress from 1864 to 1897, took Jefferson's eclectic philosophy seriously and began amassing a huge collection, including two copies of every copyrighted work in the country. The flood of material led to the construction of the Thomas Jefferson Building, the first of the Library's three buildings.

Though the Library does not hold every book published in the U.S., it does acquire some 10,000 of the 22,000 items received every day.

You can request books at the central desk, then read them at one of the tables in the octagonal Main Reading Room.

In all, the Library now holds some 120 million items, including more than 18 million books, 4.5 million maps, and the papers of 23 U.S. Presidents. It takes 530 miles of shelves to hold all this material.

Through the years the Library has been an invaluable resource for legislators, students, scholars, and filmmakers. To help preserve this collection and make it freely available, the National Digital Library Program is placing much of it on the internet *(www.loc.gov)*.

VISITING

You can take one of the daily tours of the **Jefferson Building;** or pick up a self-guided tour brochure at the visitor center just inside the west side's ground level entrance. The nearby theater shows a 12-minute film on the Library's history. Farther down the corridor lie three galleries of American popular culture.

On the next floor is the **Great Hall,** where visitors feel as if they have entered a Mediterranean palazzo. Grand staircases lead up through carved marble arches; brilliant mosaics and paintings honor music, poetry, astronomy, and other disciplines; and columns and sculptures add to the vertical effect, as if to emphasize man's lofty aspirations. In the east corridor two Library treasures rest behind glass cases: the **Giant Bible of Mainz** and the **Gutenberg Bible,** both made in Germany in the mid-1450s. On the second floor, an arcade makes a square around and above the Great Hall, offering unobstructed views of the first floor and the high ceiling. More artwork graces this floor. The **Treasures Gallery** (south end) holds rotating exhibits on American history and culture from the Library's permanent collection.

From here, the east stairway leads up to the **Visitors' Gallery,** which has a wonderful view of the

Main Reading Room, the sanctum sanctorum. A splendid coffered dome rises to a cupola 160 feet above the floor. Farther down, 16 bronze statues in balustrades represent such luminaries as Beethoven and Newton. Below, library patrons work at concentric circles of desks.

To use the library, you need a reader's pass, available at the **Madison Building,** across Independence Avenue. The Madison opened in 1980 and holds photos, prints, and a film archive; on the third floor, the **Mary Pickford Theater** *(202-707-5677)* screens free classic films. The 1939 deco-style **Adams Building,** behind the Jefferson on Second, has a business and science reading room. ■

A grand marble staircase in the Library of Congress's exquisite Great Hall

Folger Shakespeare Library

Folger Shakespeare Library
www.folger.edu

🅰 Map p. 51
✉ 201 E. Capitol St., S.E., between 2nd & 3rd Sts.
☎ 202-544-4600
🕐 Closed Sun.
Ⓜ Metro: Capitol South; Bus: 96

The Folger's Reading Room evokes an Elizabethan great hall.

THIS UNIQUE LIBRARY HOLDS THE WORLD'S LARGEST collection of William Shakespeare's works. Originating from a gift by Henry Clay Folger, the library opened in 1932 and now houses 280,000 books and manuscripts; 27,000 paintings, drawings, prints, and engravings; and many musical instruments, costumes, and films.

In 1879 a lecture on the Bard by Ralph Waldo Emerson fired the interest of Folger, then a 22-year-old student at Amherst College. A decade later, he bought his first Shakespeare folio. With the money he made in the oil business (as president of the Standard Oil Company of New York), he went on to buy thousands of rare books, manuscripts, and paintings. In the early 1900s, he began casting about for a site to build a library; he finally chose one adjacent to the Library of Congress (see pp. 62–63). But just after the cornerstone was laid, in 1930, he died; his wife, Emily, saw the project to completion.

The bold lines of this art deco-inspired neoclassic marble building make it a fitting presence among its neighbors. Nine bas-reliefs on the north side depict scenes from the Bard's plays. A statue of Puck (from *A Midsummer Night's Dream*) graces a fountain on the west side. On the east lawn lies an **Elizabethan flower and herb garden.**

For more details on the Folger, take one of the daily tours, which start at the docent's desk directly inside the library's entrance. Or wander on your own through the wood-paneled 30-foot-high **Great Hall,** which displays a copy of the Bard's first folio and changing thematic exhibits from the library's collection. You may peer through an iron gate into the adjacent Tudor-style **Reading Room,** where a stained-glass window depicting the "Seven Ages of Man" (*As You Like It*) adorns the west end. A Shakespeare bust is mounted on the east wall. The room is open to scholars and graduate students for research.

At the building's eastern end, the **Folger Theatre** offers an intimate venue for seeing the Bard's plays or hearing 16th-century music performed or readings by award-winning authors. The oak columns, tiered balconies, and sky canopy contribute to the atmosphere of an Elizabethan courtyard. ∎

The newly revamped garden as seen from across Independence Avenue

United States Botanic Garden

HAVE YOU EVER WANTED TO LOUNGE BENEATH THE COOL palms of an oasis or hike among the cactuses of a desert? Have you wondered what it would be like to step back millions of years? If you have, you can't leave the Hill without visiting the U.S. Botanic Garden.

Congress established the garden in 1820 for the collection, growing, and distribution of important plants. In the following decades, parts of the facility fell into disrepair. Then in 1997, the botanic garden began a 33.5-million-dollar renovation. The newly reopened garden (2001) has been expanded and updated, and 70 percent of its 3,000-plant collection is new.

Among the new plants is the guarana tree, a creeping shrub native to Brazil. From the berries, Brazilians prepare a popular national drink. You'll find the tree in the **Garden Court,** which features "economic plants," used to produce fibers, food, and cosmetics.

To take a walk in a tropical rain forest, wander over to the new 93-foot-high **Palm House;** a mezzanine puts you on the jungle canopy level. You can even visit an abandoned plantation here. For a drier experience, try the **World Desert.** Look for *Lithops otzeniana,* a succulent newcomer with green translucent leaves in the shape of tiny pig's feet. For a rest from the desert go next door to the **Oasis.**

To learn about healing specimens, such as ephedra and aloe, stop in at the **Medicinal Plants** area. Or for sheer beauty there is the **Orchid House** and its 12,000 flowering plants. One place you shouldn't miss is the **Garden Primeval,** where you'll see the world as it appeared when dinosaurs roamed the land. ∎

U.S. Botanic Garden

www.aoc.gov/WSBG/usbg_overview.htm

🅜 Map p. 51
✉ 245 1st St., S.W.
☎ 202-225-8333
🕐 Closed Sun.
Ⓜ Metro: Federal Center S.W.; Bus: 32, 35

More places to visit on Capitol Hill

BARTHOLDI PARK
Frédéric-Auguste Bartholdi, Statue of Liberty creator, sculpted the park's 30-foot-high, cast iron central fountain for the Centennial Exposition of 1876 in Philadelphia; it was moved here in 1934. Three sea nymphs stand on toe, appearing to hold the large upper basin, while water jets from the mouths of fish and turtles. Various theme gardens surround the fountain. Map p. 51 ✉ Independence Ave. & 1st St., S.W. 🚇 Metro: Federal Center SW

CAPITAL CHILDREN'S MUSEUM
Children love this 25-year-old museum with hands-on educational fun such as lab demonstrations, giant soap bubbles, a walk-through cave, television and radio studios, and a maze. Map p. 51 ✉ 800 3rd St., N.E. ☎ 202-675-4120 💲 $$ 🚇 Metro: Union Station

EASTERN MARKET
This 1873 block-long building holds scores of bustling stalls selling everything from meats and cheeses to seafood and baked goods. On Saturdays farmers sell vegetables, fruits, and flowers; this is also festival day, with its street performers, artists, and clothes designers. A flea market operates on Sundays. Map p. 51 ✉ 7th & C Sts., S.E. ☎ 202-546-2698 🕐 Closed Mon. 🚇 Metro: Eastern Market

NATIONAL POSTAL MUSEUM
The former Washington City Post Office

One of the many fresh fruit and produce stands at Eastern Market

Building makes an elegant home for this museum. Marble columns and a coffered ceiling in the entrance hall strike an impressive note. The 90-foot-high atrium features suspended prop planes and a railway car, illuminating ways mail was once carried. State-of-the-art galleries here explore such topics as the history of mail service and stamp collecting. Map p. 51 ✉ 2 Massachusetts Ave., N.E. (just W of Union Station) ☎ 202-357-2291 🚇 Metro: Union Station

SEWALL-BELMONT HOUSE
Robert Sewall built this two-story brick house in 1799–1800. In the 20th century, Alva Belmont helped purchase it for the National Woman's Party, headquartered here since 1929. The house contains memorabilia of women's rights leaders. Map p. 51 ✉ 144 Constitution Ave., N.E. ☎ 202-546-3989 🕐 Closed Sun.–Mon. 🚇 Metro: Union Station

UNION STATION
Completed in 1908 and beautifully restored in the 1980s, this grand beaux arts-style building is worth visiting just for its architecture. Faced in white Vermont granite, the station's huge Romanesque arches give way to a triumphal, echoing Main Hall where 36 larger-than-life Roman legionnaires preside on the gallery level. A barrel-vaulted ceiling with gold-leaf coffers soars 96 feet high. There are more than 130 shops and restaurants. Map p. 51 ✉ 40 Massachusetts Ave., N.E. ☎ 202-289-1908 🚇 Metro: Union Station ∎

The vast expanse of the Mall, with its Smithsonian museums and stately monuments, is the Washington everyone comes to see. But this is also a laidback place for picnicking, afterwork softball and soccer games, and just taking a stroll.

National Mall

Annual Smithsonian Folklife Festival, a summer highlight on the Mall

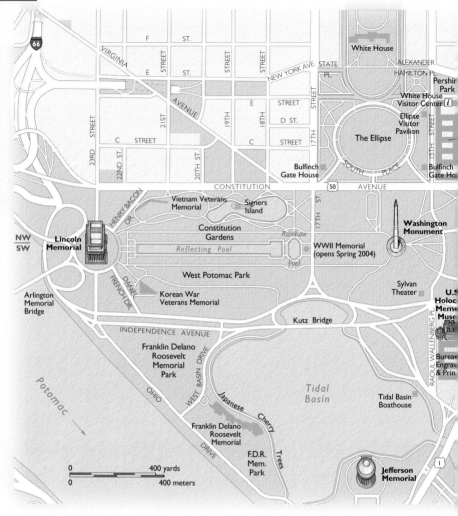

National Mall

LINED AND DOTTED WITH THE MOST SIGNIFICANT GROUP OF MUSEUMS AND monuments in the country, the National Mall is a long avenue of green grass edged by shade trees. You could spend a week, and more, visiting this world-famous tourist mecca.

One day hundreds of colorful kites are flying near the Washington Monument, on another a crowd is shouting and waving banners, and on yet another day the Mall is just a peaceful stretch of green. From the U.S. Capitol to the Lincoln Memorial, America's grand promenade extends for more than 2 miles between Constitution and Independence Avenues. Walkers, joggers, soccer players, and Frisbee throwers regularly take to the inviting lawns.

In summer, thousands flock to the Smithsonian Folklife Festival (late June–early July), the Fourth of July celebration, and the Sylvan Theater's outdoor concerts. Numerous

other events are held on the Mall, including a kite festival *(late March–early April)* and the Black Family Reunion *(Sept.)*. The Mall is also the stage for rallies by many national groups. Whatever the season, people come not just to watch but to participate.

Pierre Charles L'Enfant's city plan of 1791 included a "vast esplanade" lined with magnificent residences. But by the end of the 1800s, the Mall was very different from his vision: Coal piles, sheds, tracks, and a railroad station made it less than appealing. In 1901 the MacMillan Commission recommended reviving L'Enfant's plan. Tracks and debris were removed, vistas were opened up, and marshy areas were filled. With the addition of the Lincoln Memorial, the Mall stretched to the Potomac River, making it the east–west axis of a memorial park area. The White House and Jefferson Memorial form the north–south axis, with the Washington Monument in the middle.

By the late 1980s, the Mall's eastern part held nine Smithsonian museums and two National Gallery of Art buildings. In 2004 the National Museum of the American Indian opens near the National Air and Space Museum. ■

Smithsonian Institution

The Smithsonian Institution started with an 1829 bequest of more than $500,000 from British scientist James Smithson. No one knows exactly why Smithson, who had never visited the United States, left his estate to the U.S. "to found at Washington…an establishment for the increase and diffusion of knowledge."

His bequest may have been in reaction to the refusal of British society to recognize his use of his father's name. The illegitimate son of a duke, Smithson took his mother's name, Macie, until 1802, when at age 37 he began publishing scientific writings. Another reason could be that perhaps he admired America's democratic ideals.

According to Smithson's will, his estate would go to the U.S. if his nephew died without heirs, which he did in 1835. The U.S. Congress accepted the bequest in 1836, and in 1838 the British courts approved the transaction and sent 105 bags of gold sovereigns off to the U.S. For the next eight years, Congress argued about what to do with the gift. In 1846, President Polk signed the act establishing the Smithsonian as a trust administered by a Board of Regents and Secretary.

The Smithsonian is now the world's largest research and museum complex, with 16 museums and galleries, the National Zoological Park, and various research stations. Nine museums and galleries are located on the Mall: the Smithsonian Castle, Freer Gallery of Art, Arthur M. Sackler Gallery, National Museum of African Art, Arts and Industries Building, Hirshhorn Museum & Sculpture Garden, National Air and Space Museum, National Museum of Natural History, and National Museum of American History (the National Gallery of Art is also on the Mall, but it is not associated with the Smithsonian). Four more—the Renwick Gallery, Smithsonian American Art Museum, National Portrait Gallery, and National Postal Museum—are nearby in the downtown area, and the Anacostia Museum lies across the Anacostia River. New York holds the Cooper-Hewitt National Design Museum and the National Museum of the American Indian, though the latter will soon have a presence on the Mall, due to open in 2004.

The Smithsonian also offers a year-round schedule of music, theater, dance, film programs, lectures, and Discovery Theater performances for young people. In summer, the Smithsonian Folklife Festival takes over the Mall in a celebration of international cultures, complete with craftspeople and musicians.

SMITHSONIAN CASTLE

The Smithsonian's first building, the Norman-style red-sandstone Castle was designed by James Renwick, Jr. Ten years after its completion in 1855, fire damaged the structure, but it was rebuilt, then renovated and enlarged in the 1880s. Until the addition of the Arts and Industries Building in 1881, the Castle housed everything—a science museum, art gallery, lecture hall, research labs, offices, and living quarters for the secretary and his family. Today it functions as the Smithsonian's information center and holds administrative offices.

As you enter the Castle, turn left to enter the **crypt room,** which has a small exhibit on James Smithson, including a marble urn containing his ashes. The main room has an information desk, touch-screen monitors in six languages, scale models of Washington, electronic wall maps, and two theaters that show a 24-minute overview of the Smithsonian. In the back, off Independence Avenue, lies a lovely Victorian-style garden with benches. The Castle's historic **Commons** restaurant is open to the public (202-357-2957, *reservations recommended*). ■

Smithsonian Institution
www.si.edu
🅜 Map pp. 68–69
✉ Smithsonian Castle, 1000 Jefferson Dr., S.W.
☎ 202-357-2700
🚇 Metro: Smithsonian; Bus: 13A, 52

The 4-acre Enid A. Haupt Garden on the south side of the Castle

Freer Gallery of Art

Freer Gallery of Art

www.asia.si.edu

Map p. 69

Jefferson Dr. &
12th St., S.W.

202-357-2700

Metro: Smithsonian;
Bus: 13A, 52

DATING FROM THE FOURTH MILLENNIUM B.C. TO MODERN times, the objects in the Freer make a comprehensive sweep of Asian art. The collection, donated by Detroit businessman Charles Lang Freer (1856–1919), now numbers more than 28,000 individual works and is considered among the finest in the world. It is complemented by a large collection of 19th- and 20th-century American pieces, including many works by James McNeill Whistler.

Opened in 1923, the Italian Renaissance-style building has a pink granite exterior and polished white marble floors. Its galleries surround a hallway where large windows look out onto a refreshing inner courtyard. The lighting and exhibit space combine to lend a refined, contemplative atmosphere. Of the 19 galleries, 16 are devoted to Asian art, including Indian sculpture, Japanese lacquerware, Chinese paintings, Korean ceramics, and Islamic metalware. The Freer does not host traveling exhibitions or lend any of its objects; the gallery rotates pieces from its permanent collection.

Among the Asian works are the 10th-century Indian bronze "Queen Sembiyan Mahadevi as the Goddess Parvati" **(Gallery 18)** and a 12th-century wood sculpture,

"Bosatsu," from the late Heian period of Japan **(Gallery 17).**

American treasures include the exquisite **Peacock Room,** which is a must-see. Whistler painted the room, called "Harmony in Blue and Gold," for a rich London shipowner. Recently restored to its original elegance, the room features antique gilded leather walls, a metal ceiling painted in a feather pattern, and a painting known as "The Princess in the Land of Porcelain." The opposite wall has a painting of two peacocks, a reference to a quarrel between Whistler and his patron over the fee. Freer bought the room intact from a London dealer and installed it in his Detroit home; it was moved to Washington in 1919.

The Freer's lower level connects to the Arthur M. Sackler Gallery. ∎

Artist James M. Whistler painted the sumptuous Peacock Room as though it were an enormous lacquer box.

Arthur M. Sackler Gallery

HOUSED ALMOST ENTIRELY BELOW THE GROUND, THIS 1987 museum has at its core the Asian collection of research physician and medical publisher Arthur M. Sackler. Among its many treasures are Chinese bronzes and jades, Persian manuscripts, ancient Iranian silver, and works from Tibet and Japan. The museum exhibits items from its growing permanent collection as well as from other collections in the United States and elsewhere. Visiting the Sackler and the Freer, which are administered jointly, gives you a comprehensive overview of traditional and modern Asian art.

Arthur M. Sackler Gallery
www.asia.si.edu

 Map p. 69

📧 1050 Independence Ave., S.W.

☎ 202-357-2700

🚇 Metro: Smithsonian; Bus: 13A, 52

The **first level**—one level below ground—contains works from a variety of cultures. Many of the rooms display only a half dozen or so objects in glass cases, with subtle lighting and just enough information to keep you interested but not overwhelmed. Wander through them and see a beaten brass incense burner from 13th-century Syria; a ceramic, gazelle-shaped drinking vessel from 4th-century B.C. Iran; and a hall of 10th- to 14th-century granite deities from India.

In the **Arts of China galleries,** also on the first level, the Ancient Chinese Art section displays 12th- to 13th-century B.C. jade knives crafted by incredibly skillful artisans—not a fact that one always associates with pieces from the Neolithic period. Another section, the Arts of Six Dynasties and Tang in China, holds Tang dynasty tomb guardians adorned with brilliant horns and flames. The guardians look as fierce and original as they must have 13 centuries ago.

The **second level** of the gallery holds rotating exhibits; recently, for instance, there was a fascinating show of photographs that were taken in India from 1840 to 1911.

Do not overlook the **third level** of the Sackler, where displays of contemporary Japanese bowls and vases, colorfully glazed, are enhanced by a small pool and bubbling fountains.

From the third level visitors can find access to the **S. Dillon Ripley Center,** which features temporary exhibits, and continue on to the National Museum of African Art. ■

Terra-cotta festival statues from India dating from 1984–85

National Museum of African Art

**National
Museum of
African Art**
www.nmafa.si.edu

⬛ Map p. 69

✉ 950 Independence
Ave., S.W.

☎ 202-357-2700

🚇 Metro: Smithsonian;
Bus: 13A, 52

LIKE THE SACKLER, THIS ADJACENT MUSEUM'S UNDER-ground, climate-controlled levels showcase excellent works of art in quiet, carpeted, low-lit rooms. Because most African art objects are created from organic materials that do not hold up well over a long time, much of the art here is from the 19th and 20th centuries.

The National Museum of African Art concentrates on the traditional arts of sub-Saharan Africa, with particular emphasis on royal Benin, central African ceramics, and such utilitarian objects as headrests and stools. There are also masks and figurines, as well as everyday personal objects, often imbued with religious and cultural significance.

You'll find the major portion of the exhibition on the **first level** underground. Arranged in geographical groupings, three different exhibits display samples of the permanent collection of more than 7,000 objects. The **Art of the Personal Object exhibit** demonstrates how functional items such as bowls, baskets, and snuff containers were used in daily life in parts of eastern and southern Africa. The **Images of Power and Identity exhibit** shows religious and ceremonial objects. A wonderfully elaborate toothed-crocodile headdress, bearing spiral horns, casts shadows on the floor, while beautiful wooden masks from the Ivory Coast and Liberia sit within their glass cases and grimace inscrutably. Colorful instruments,

Face mask from Democratic Republic of Congo (early to mid-1900s)

drums, figures, and totems catch the attention of visitors: With just a little bit of imagination, you can practically see and hear an initiation ceremony taking place right in front of you. To help your imagination, old black-and-white photos show the context of many of the objects. You see, for example, a tall wooden figure decorated with glass beads, cowrie shells, brass, and fabric. Beside it is a picture of King Njoya (*R.* 1886–1933) of Bamum, Cameroon. He is shown standing next to his palace, which was actually an elaborate three-story grass hut; examine the pillars holding up the palace roof and you'll notice a number of wooden figures similar to the one on display. You may also notice a 1950s photo of a Belgian Congo tribal chief wearing an ivory pendant; in an adjacent display case is the exact same kind of pendant.

The third exhibit, **Kerma & Benin: Two Ancient African Cities,** has pottery from an archaeological discovery of the ancient Nubian empire of 2500–1500 B.C., and a display on the West African city of Benin, A.D. 1300–1897. You almost feel like an explorer yourself, wandering the maze of rooms and making great finds.

Don't miss the temporary exhibits on the first level, as well as on the **second level.** Levels one and three both offer access to the adjoining Arthur M. Sackler Gallery. ■

Hirshhorn Museum & Sculpture Garden

IN A WHITE, HATBOX-SHAPED BUILDING, THE HIRSHHORN exhibits modern works of art. A substantial gift (nearly 12,000 works between 1974 and 1981) from philanthropist Joseph H. Hirshhorn (1899–1981) forms the core of the rotating collection. The 82-foot-high building surrounds an open courtyard featuring a bronze fountain, while across Jefferson Drive on the north lies a lovely recessed sculpture garden. Designed by Gordon Bunshaft, the museum was considered daring when it opened in 1974; it has since become an accepted fixture of the National Mall and the Smithsonian.

Hirshhorn Museum & Sculpture Garden
www.hirshhorn.si.edu
- Map p. 69
- Independence Ave. & 7th St., S.W.
- 202-357-2700
- Metro: L'Enfant Plaza; Bus: 36, 54

Two circular floors contain permanent and special exhibits, and a basement level holds permanent works by contemporary artists from the second half of the 20th century to the present. Start on the **third floor** and work your way around counterclockwise from the escalator to follow a more or less chronological progression. Paintings hang in the outer galleries; sculpture graces the inner galleries, where picture windows overlook the courtyard.

Early 20th-century art is represented by a number of greats, including Marsden Hartley, Thomas Hart Benton, Thomas Eakins, Childe Hassam, Maurice Prendergast, and John Sloan. Also of particular note are the quiet, brooding urban scenes of Edward Hopper. Continuing around, you encounter a trompe l'oeil painting by Salvador Dalí entitled "Skull of Zurbaran" (1956) and a playful Rene Magritte, "Delusions of Grandeur II" (1948).

Halfway around the third floor, pause for a spectacular wide-angle view of the entire Mall. Elsewhere on this floor are works by Joan

The Hirshhorn's circular courtyard often serves as a setting for receptions.

What was there before

Before the Hirshhorn took shape on the Mall, the U.S. Army Medical Museum (now the National Museum of Health & Medicine; see p. 190) occupied the site from 1887 to 1968. More than 25,000 specimens of diseased or wounded flesh and bones were kept here, and morbidly fascinated tourists could see preserved gunshot wounds, a vertebra from John Wilkes Booth, and disfigured and diseased organs. Over the years the tastes of the public changed, and the museum was moved to the Walter Reed Army Medical Center at 6900 Georgia Avenue, N.W. Meanwhile, the Hirshhorn delivers its own provocative, if not gross-out, punch. ■

Miró, Max Ernst, Willem de Kooning, Jackson Pollock, Roy Lichtenstein, Man Ray, and Mark Rothko. In short, you can hardly think of a major 20th-century artist not on display. Among noteworthy sculptures are George Segal's haunting "Bus Riders" (1962), cast from live models in plaster-soaked gauze bandages, and Robert Arneson's grotesque "General Nuke" (1984), with a missile nose and bloody snarl. One gallery on the third floor, **Directions,** brings the work of some of the world's most exciting emerging artists to Washington, D.C.

The **second floor** features temporary exhibits and, in the inner walkway, European sculpture from 1850 to 1935. Among the latter are small pieces by Degas, Rodin, Matisse, Picasso, and Brancusi. On the **basement level** you'll find pieces by living or recent artists such as Andy Warhol, Christo, and Julian Schnabel. Exhibits are rotated in this large space, but you can count on seeing several installations that vary from silly to thought provoking.

Outside, the highlight of the **sculpture garden** is the Rodin group, "Monument to the Burghers of Calais" (1884–89). The dark, robed figures, striking anguished poses, are in stark contrast to the heroic sculpture found throughout Washington. Abstract works by Claes Oldenburg, Henry Moore, David Smith, and Alexander Calder make whimsical, modernist statements. Shaded benches offer a chance to contemplate the artwork at leisure. ■

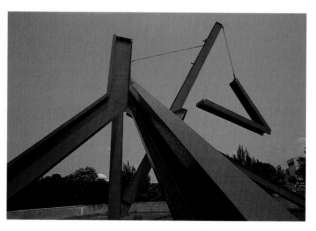

An angular ode to modern art: "Are Years What? (for Marianne Moore)" (1967), composed of industrial I-beams with a suspended, moving V element, is considered one of Mark di Suvero's greatest works.

National Air and Space Museum

THE EXCITEMENT OF AERONAUTICAL AND SPACE-FLIGHT technology draws more than nine million annual visitors to the National Air and Space Museum. Four tremendous marble-covered blocks, joined by glass-fronted bays, distinguish the exterior. Inside, 23 galleries on two floors cover nearly 4 acres of exhibit space. Even though the museum attracts large crowds, it has plenty of elbow room and a lot of air space for the dramatic display of rockets and airplanes.

National Air & Space Museum
www.nasm.si.edu

▲ Map p. 69
✉ Independence Ave. & 7th St., S.W.
☎ 202-357-2000
🚇 Metro: L'Enfant Plaza; Bus: 36, 54

The Smithsonian's involvement in air and space goes back to 1857, when it began using balloons to collect weather data. Later, during the Civil War, the first secretary of the Smithsonian, Joseph Henry, won President Abraham Lincoln's support for making military observations from balloons. The third secretary, Samuel Pierpont Langley (1887–1906), was an astronomer and airplane pioneer. He experimented successfully with heavier-than-air craft on the Potomac in the 1890s, but the first actual manned, controlled flight was made by the Wright brothers in 1903.

During the first half of the 20th century, the Smithsonian participated in or funded major rocket research and astrophysical observation projects. In 1971, Apollo astronaut Michael Collins was appointed director of the new

A mural showing the Milky Way galaxy highlights the "Explore the Universe" exhibit.

Lindbergh

Perhaps more than any other aviator, Charles Lindbergh (1902–1974) captured the public's admiration. Son of a Minnesota congressman, he spent many of his early years in Washington, D.C. Later he attended a Wisconsin college but dropped out to enroll in a Nebraska flying school. For a few years he was a stunt flyer and an airmail pilot. Then he competed for a $25,000 prize offered to the first person to fly from New York to Paris nonstop.

On May 20, 1927, the aviator took off in the *Spirit of St. Louis*, named for the city where he received financial backing. Because the large fuel tank partially blocked his view, Lindbergh relied on a periscope or tilted the plane to see forward. He flew for 33.5 exhausting hours before landing at Le Bourget Field near Paris and receiving a warm welcome by a cheering crowd of 100,000.

Back in Washington, Lindbergh stayed a few days at the Patterson House on Dupont Circle with President Coolidge, who lived there while the White House was being renovated. Later that year the U.S. Congress awarded him a Medal of Honor. The following year he gave his plane to the Smithsonian, where it is prominently displayed in the Milestones of Flight gallery.

In 1929, Lindbergh wed Anne Morrow, and together they made several flights to chart airline routes. When their son was kidnapped and killed in 1932, the unending publicity drove them abroad. Lindbergh advocated neutrality at the outbreak of World War II, leading to criticism by President Roosevelt, yet he quietly served as an aircraft consultant and flew on combat missions over the Pacific. He described his famous transatlantic flight in thrilling detail in *We* (1927) and *The Spirit of St. Louis* (1953), the latter winning a Pulitzer Prize. ∎

Charles A. Lindbergh (1902–1974), with the *Spirit of St. Louis*

National Air and Space Museum, and construction began the next year. The Wright Flyer and other aircraft that had been on display in the Arts and Industries Building were moved to the new museum, and in 1976 it opened to the public.

There is more to come. The **Steven E. Udvar-Hazy Center** is scheduled to open December 2003. Located near Dulles Airport in Virginia, the facility will be even bigger than the building on the Mall. It will display aircraft from the museum's preservation, restoration, and storage facility in Suitland, Maryland, including the *Enola Gay* and a prototype of the shuttle *Enterprise*.

Opposite: The *Spirit of St. Louis* took Charles Lindbergh across the Atlantic in 1927; 35 years later, Mercury Friendship 7 carried John Glenn into Earth orbit.

VISITING

A drawback to so large a space is that, depending upon where you are, you may have to walk the equivalent of a city block to get to a rest room or dining area. If you're with children, or anyone who tires easily, you'll have a more enjoyable time if you carefully plan your visit (see the floor plan on pp. 80–81). If you decide to split up, determine a specific place and time to meet; otherwise you could spend a long time trying to locate members of your party. Purchase tickets to the IMAX and planetarium shows first, then tour the galleries that most interest you. Plan to spend about half a day for a quick

overview of the whole museum or a thorough look at a few galleries.

Almost all the aircraft and most of the spacecraft are the genuine articles. Some space vehicles, of course, stay in space; in those cases backups, test vehicles, or authentic reproductions are shown. Labels highlight the differences.

FIRST FLOOR

Just inside the Mall entrance, the outstanding **Milestones of Flight gallery** holds aviation's greatest hits. A museum in itself, this is a gallery where almost everyone will want to linger. From the ceiling hangs the wood-and-fabric plane that Orville Wright flew into history in 1903 at Kitty Hawk, North Carolina. Near that first piloted airplane hangs the *Spirit of St. Louis,* in which Charles Lindbergh made the first solo, nonstop flight across the Atlantic in May 1927.

Another place of honor is given to Chuck Yeager's sleek orange Bell X-1, which in 1947 became the first aircraft to break the sound barrier. Nearby is the Mercury Friendship 7, the capsule in which John Glenn became the first American to orbit Earth in 1962. Then there's the Apollo 11 Command Module, which carried the first humans to the moon and back in 1969.

Examples of space probes are pretty close to the real thing: The Viking Lander, for example, is a copy used to simulate what Vikings 1 and 2 did on Mars from 1976 to 1982. Finally, you can touch a four-billion-year-old moon rock. Collected in 1972 during the Apollo 17 mission, the iron-rich volcanic shard was found in the Taurus-Littrow Valley. Touch this talisman and think about all that was accomplished in 70 years of air and space history.

Past the museum shop, to

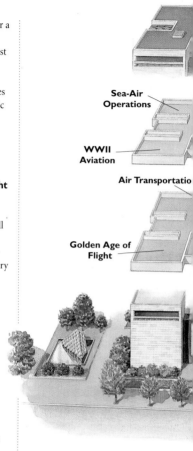

Sea-Air Operations

WWII Aviation

Air Transportatio

Golden Age of Flight

the right, you come to the **Air Transportation gallery.** Its several planes from the 1920s and '30s illustrate strides in commercial aviation. Across the hall just to the right is the **Golden Age of Flight.** Scratchy recordings of old torch songs set the tone for this exhibit of the glamour days, and a small theater continuously runs historic footage. Here you can see Howard Hughes's single-prop H-1 racer, in which he set a speed record of 352 mph in 1935. That same year the nearby *Gamma Polar Star* made the first transantarctic flight. Also on display is a Beech Staggerwing, a biplane flown by aviation pioneer Edwin Eugene Aldrin, the father of

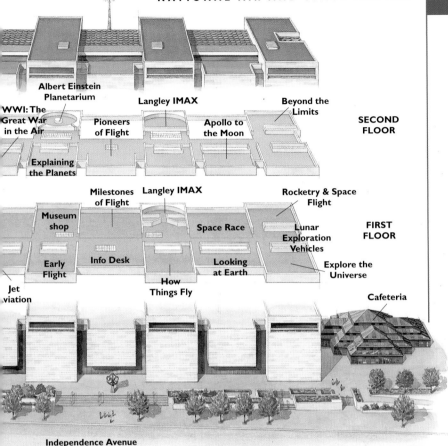

SECOND FLOOR

- Albert Einstein Planetarium
- WWI: The Great War in the Air
- Langley IMAX
- Pioneers of Flight
- Apollo to the Moon
- Beyond the Limits
- Explaining the Planets

FIRST FLOOR

- Milestones of Flight
- Langley IMAX
- Rocketry & Space Flight
- Museum shop
- Space Race
- Lunar Exploration Vehicles
- Early Flight
- Info Desk
- Looking at Earth
- How Things Fly
- Explore the Universe
- Jet Aviation
- Cafeteria

Independence Avenue

astronaut Edwin "Buzz" Aldrin. In the adjacent **Jet Aviation gallery,** you can trace the development of jet technology. The plane with its wings folded up is a 1945 FH-1 Phantom, the first type to take off from and land on an aircraft carrier.

The **Early Flight gallery** is set up in the style of a 1913 aeronautical exhibition. An 1894 Lilienthal glider with batlike ribbed wings hangs at the entrance, while farther along a mannequin makes a sales pitch for a Bleriot monoplane. Also here is a worn-looking 1909 Wright Military Flyer, the world's first military plane.

Step across the Independence Avenue entrance hall, pausing to admire the two tremendous murals. On one wall, Robert T. McCall's 1976 "The Space Mural: A Cosmic View" traces space history from the Big Bang to lunar exploration and beyond. On the opposite wall, Eric Sloan's "Earthflight Environment" (1976) shows a western landscape beneath a sky filled with the kinds of weather pilots must fly through.

Children will especially take to the adjoining **How Things Fly gallery,** which contains about 50 hands-on exhibits. Visitors can learn about lift, drag, air pressure, wave action, and other principles of flight. Discover what's the best material for insulating a spacecraft from friction heat; climb into the

Praised by pilots for its agility, a World War II Italian fighter plane—one of two remaining Macchi C.202s—hangs above a North American P-51 Mustang, a superb American fighting machine of the same vintage.

cockpit of a Cessna 150; watch a live demonstration on why things fly or don't fly. Next door, the **Looking at Earth gallery** holds a de Havilland DH-4 surveying plane, a Lockheed U-2 spy plane, and model satellites. You can touch a screen to view a Landsat image of any state.

At the east end of the first floor is the shiny Mylar-covered Lunar Module 2, a duplicate of one used on Apollo 5. The drop tests during that mission, evaluating the landing gear, were so successful that this backup version was never used. It's the same kind of craft that went to the moon with Apollo 11.

The popular **Rocketry and Space Flight gallery,** on the northeast corner of the first floor, harbors boosters and missiles from the space race. Especially interesting are the suspended Apollo and Soyuz docked together and a bell-shaped Soyuz landing module autographed by Russian cosmonauts. You also can stare up at a 42-foot-tall test vehicle of the Hubble Space Telescope; its 8,500

pounds make it only one-third the weight of the actual telescope. You can walk through (from the upper level) a backup of the Skylab space station. Launched in 1973, its working counterpart fell to Earth in 1979, breaking up and landing in Australia and the Indian Ocean.

The first floor is also where you enter the **Langley IMAX Theater** *(fee).* Here you'll see amazing films projected on a five-story-high screen with seat-rumbling effects. "To Fly!" is the long-running classic.

At lunchtime, you can catch a bite at the newly renovated two-story restaurant, where high glass ceilings and gantrylike scaffolding lend a space-age atmosphere.

SECOND FLOOR
On the second floor, you can visit the **Einstein Planetarium** *(fee)* and see multimedia presentations on the planets and stars.

The **Sea-Air Operations gallery** next door holds carrier aircraft from 1911 to the present,

including a 1930s F4B-4, a World War II FM-1 Wildcat, an SBD Dauntless dive-bomber, and an A-4 Skyhawk from the 1950s and '60s. Walking around the upper and lower decks, you can watch videos on the major Pacific aircraft carrier battles of World War II and learn about carrier missions in the atomic era. Across the hall, go into **World War II Aviation** to learn more about the air history of World War II. Continue down the south side of the floor to the next exhibits.

The glory days of air fighting are examined in unromanticized detail in the **Great War in the Air gallery,** which tells the story of World War I aviation. On display are a German Fokker D.VII, a British Sopwith Snipe, and others.

Next, the **Exploring the Planets gallery** includes a duplicate of the Voyager spacecraft and a meteorite that might have come from Mars. In **Pioneers of Flight,** you'll find several famous aircraft: Here are Amelia Earhart's Lockheed Vega, in which she became the first woman to fly solo across the Atlantic in 1932; the Lindberghs' 1930s Tingmissartoq, used for charting airline routes; and the Gossamer Condor, which made the first human-powered flight.

The **Where Next, Columbus? gallery** examines exploration possibilities of the future and includes a simulated Martian landscape and a hydroponic garden. The heady years of manned spaceflight are examined in the **Apollo to the Moon gallery,** while **Flight and the Arts** offers exhibits on aeronautics and spaceflight in art, film, and popular culture. Across the hall, design your own aircraft in **Beyond the Limits.** On display are a lightning-fast Cray-1 supercomputer, a robotic airplane, and the brains of a Minuteman intercontinental ballistic missile.

If you're curious about how planes and spacecraft are restored, call the **Paul E. Garber Facility** *(301-238-3407)* in Suitland, Maryland, to inquire about tours. ■

National Gallery of Art

National Gallery of Art

www.nga.gov

Map p. 69

Constitution Ave. between 3rd & 7th Sts., N.W.

202-737-4215

Metro: Archives; Bus: 36, 54

ONE OF THE COUNTRY'S TOP ART MUSEUMS, THE NATIONAL Gallery of Art holds a comprehensive collection of Western master-pieces. The West Building exhibits European painting and sculpture from the 13th to 19th centuries; American art; and prints, drawings, decorative arts, and temporary shows. The newer East Building, or East Wing, contains modern and contemporary art.

In the 1920s, financier Andrew Mellon began collecting great art with the idea of establishing a museum in Washington. In 1931 he completed a purchase of 21 paintings from Russia's Hermitage Museum, including Raphael's "Alba Madonna." Mellon died in 1937, the same year that construction began for the new

museum designed by John Russell Pope and funded by the A.W. Mellon Educational and Charitable Trust.

Other major donors soon added to the holdings—including 375 Italian paintings and 18 sculptures from Samuel H. Kress, founder of a chain of five-and-dime stores. In March 1941, President Roosevelt

In 1999 the National Gallery Sculpture Garden was opened across Seventh Street from the gallery. A gift from the Morris and Gwendolyn Cafritz Foundation, the garden contains 17 works of 20th-century sculpture.

WEST BUILDING

Entering the West Building from the Constitution Avenue, Seventh Street, or Fourth Street entrance puts you on the ground floor, from which you must go upstairs to the main floor. Entering from the Mall, you begin on the **main floor,** where European and American paintings are exhibited in 93 rooms. Between the two T-shaped wings of the building, the spectacular **Rotunda,** ringed by Tuscan marble pillars, rises to a high oculus above a central fountain graced by a statue of Mercury. The dome is strongly reminiscent of John Russell Pope's other great Washington structure, the Jefferson Memorial.

Extending from either side of the Rotunda, the **West Sculpture Hall** contains works in bronze, while the **East Sculpture Hall** has works in marble. Each hall ends in a garden court, where free concerts are often held. The halls and courts are surrounded by galleries: Gallery 1 is on the far, northwest side of the rotunda, and Gallery 93 is on the far, northeast side. The galleries generally proceed chronologically, with nationalities grouped together. Many of the rooms have portable information plaques that provide more background on the works.

Galleries 1–15 hold **13th- to 15th-century Italian paintings.** Representing the early Florentine and central Italian Renaissance, these works range from Byzantine iconography to the beginnings of the high Renaissance. One of the most famous paintings in the museum hangs here: Leonardo da

Rising from the plaza between the East and West Buildings, glass tetrahedrons act as skylights for a lower concourse.

presided over a dedication ceremony attended by nearly 9,000 guests.

The holdings continued to grow, and in the late 1960s, architect I.M. Pei was hired to create a plan for a new building to accommodate the collection. Opened in 1978, the East Building had to fit a trapezoidal site, mesh with the neoclassic West Building, and be an appropriate receptacle for modern art. The resulting marble-faced monolithic surfaces, acute angles, and glass hyphens make it not only visually arresting but also a fitting counterpart to the nearby 1970s buildings—the Hirshhorn and the Air and Space Museum. An underground concourse connects the two buildings.

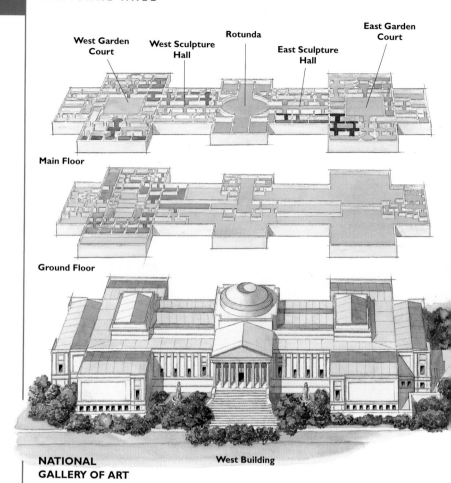

West Garden Court

West Sculpture Hall

Rotunda

East Sculpture Hall

East Garden Court

Main Floor

Ground Floor

NATIONAL GALLERY OF ART

West Building

Vinci's "Ginevra de' Benci," a 1474 oil on wood. The only Leonardo painting in the Western Hemisphere, this portrait is of a pretty, pale-faced, flat-eyed young woman; like the Mona Lisa, her expression is inscrutable and no-nonsense. Other masters on display are Giotto ("Madonna and Child," ca 1320–1330), often considered the first great Italian painter; Fra Filippo Lippi ("Adoration of the Magi," ca 1445); and Botticelli ("Giuliano de' Medici," ca 1478), famous for "The Birth of Venus" in Florence and for efforts to express the spirit of classicism.

You'll find **16th-century Italian and Spanish works** in Galleries 16–28. Here is art from the northern Italian Renaissance, distinguished by allegorical and religious scenes within a colorful, sensual, pastoral setting. Especially outstanding are paintings by the Venetian master Tiziano Vecelli, or Titian, whose lovely "Venus with a Mirror" (1555) is vibrant with life. Raphael's "Alba Madonna" (1510) hangs here, as do works by Tintoretto, one of the great Mannerist painters. Don't neglect to pause in Gallery 26 for Bernardino Luini's "Fresco Cycle," with the "Story of Procris and Cephalus" (1520–22).

WEST BUILDING GALLERIES

12th- to 15th-century Italian

16th-century Italian and Spanish

17th- and 18th-century Italian, Spanish, and French Baroque

15th- to 16th-century Netherlandish and German

17th-century Dutch and Flemish

18th- and 19th-century Spanish

18th- and early 19th-century French

19th-century French

British

American

Special Exhibitions

Photography

Prints and Drawings

Non-Exhibition Space

Sculpture

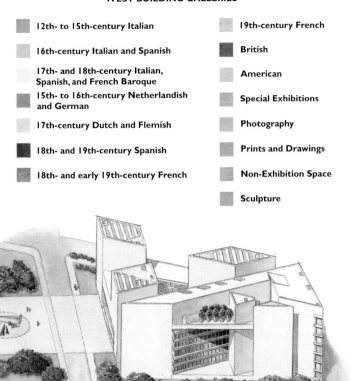

East Building

America's only Italian Renaissance fresco series recounts a myth in nine pastoral scenes around a villa-like room floored with mosaic tiles from third-century Tunisia. Gallery 28 has several works by El Greco.

Galleries 29–34 and 36–37 display **17th- to 18th-century Italian, Spanish, and French Baroque** paintings. Among the artists are Tiepolo—a Venetian master known for his handling of chiaroscuro, the interplay of light and shadow—and Velázquez, whose use of color foreshadowed Impressionism. Look for Georges de la Tour's "The Repentant

Magdalene" (1640) and Jacopo Manfredi's tavern scene, "Bravos Drinking and Making Music" (1615). Continuing into Galleries 35, 35A, and 38–41A, **15th- to 16th-century Netherlandish and German** painters include Albrecht Dürer (the "Leonardo of the North") and Matthias Grunewald, whose relatively few works, mostly of religious subjects, were enough to secure his reputation as one of the greats of his time.

Among the most popular areas of the museum, Galleries 42–51 feature **17th-century Flemish and Dutch** paintings. From

Self-portrait by Vincent van Gogh

Rubens's "Daniel in the Lions' Den" (1613–15) to Rembrandt's "Portrait of a Man in a Tall Hat" (1663) and his dark "Self-Portrait" (1659), the possibilities of realism are pushed to an intensity that would influence art for generations. In "The Mill" (1650), Rembrandt demonstrates his expert handling of chiaroscuro. Other works include Vermeer's miniature "The Girl with the Red Hat" (1665), Jan Steen's lively "The Dancing Couple" (1663), and the black-hatted and white-collared "Dutchmen" by Frans Hals.

Walk now to the east side of the rotunda, where Gallery 52 contains **18th- and 19th-century Spanish** paintings, notably by Francisco de Goya. **French art** from the **18th and early 19th centuries** lines the walls of Galleries 53–56, much of it in a florid style depicting lighthearted sophistication in French society. Among the treasures are Antoine Watteau's "Italian Comedians" (1720), Boucher's "Madame Bergeret" (1746), and Fragonard's "A Young Girl Reading" (1776).

British works fill Galleries 57–59, 61, and 63. Painters represented here include Hogarth, Reynolds, Romney, Gainsborough, Constable, and Turner. The land-scapes of Constable and seascapes of Turner are particularly worth noting. **American** paintings are on view in Galleries 60A–B, 62, and 64–71. Gilbert Stuart's portraits of early U.S. Presidents vie for attention with the big mid-19th-century landscapes of Bierstadt, Cole, and Church. Other works are by Homer, Whistler, Bellows, Ryder, Sargent, and Cropsey. Galleries 72–79 are reserved for **special exhibitions.**

Impressionist and other 19th-century French painting is on exhibit in Galleries 80–93. These rooms are filled with the light and color of leading exponents Renoir and Monet, and the idiosyncratic styles of Cézanne and van Gogh. Also on display are Parisian nightlife scenes by Degas and Toulouse-Lautrec. Among the great works are Renoir's "Girl with a Watering Can" (1876), Manet's "The Railway" (1873), and Monet's "Woman with a Parasol—Madame Monet and her Son" (1875).

The ground floor showcases **photography and sculpture,** as well as **prints and drawings** by luminaries such as Michelangelo, Leonardo, Manet, and Cézanne. From here you can reach the East Building via a belowground concourse, or enter it from Fourth Street.

EAST BUILDING

The towering walls and angles of the East Building (or East Wing) are marvels in themselves. Gracing the entrance, Henry Moore's curvy bronze "Knife Edge Mirror Two Piece" (1977–78) mimics the shape of the building, in rounded form. The building itself consists of two triangular shapes, the one on the north exhibiting works of modern art and the other holding offices.

At the ground floor information desk you can check on current exhibits and the tour schedule. This floor opens to a soaring atrium, the focal point of which is an untitled mobile by Calder. A selection of small French paintings is usually on view; these lovely "postcards" of French people and scenes are by Impressionist and Postimpressionist greats. The **mezzanine** and **upper levels** hold several large exhibition rooms for permanent and temporary exhibits. On display are works that trace the evolution of modernism, and the artists include Picasso, Braque, Miró, Mondrian, Arp, Magritte, Stella, O'Keeffe, Lichtenstein, Kandinsky, Brancusi, and Giacometti.

Take the winding staircase to the **tower level** to view the Matisse

cutouts (1950s), huge colorful paper collages the artist created near the end of his long life. The **concourse level** also boasts extensive exhibit space for large canvases and installations.

SCULPTURE GARDEN

Opened in 1999, the 6-acre Sculpture Garden lies across Seventh Street from the West Building. Its 17 works include "Puellae" (1992), featuring 30 headless, shriveled, 3-foot-tall girls—Polish-born sculptor Magdalena Abakanowicz's eerie depiction of a Holocaust story. You can't miss Louise Bourgeois's 9-foot-tall "Spider" (1997), part of the artist's series that explores childhood memory and loss. Another large piece, "Aurora" (1992–93) by Mark Di Suvero, illustrates elegance and balance on a massive scale.

A café serves sandwiches, salads, and drinks. ■

Opposite: Jan van Eyck's "The Annunciation" (1434–36, oil on wood transferred to canvas) was probably once the left wing of a triptych. Below: Claes Oldenburg and Coosje van Bruggen's "Typewriter Eraser, Scale X" (1999, stainless steel and fiberglass), found in the Sculpture Garden, depicts one of Oldenburg's favorite childhood playthings from his father's office.

National Museum of Natural History

National
Museum of
Natural History

www.mnh.si.edu

🅰 Map p. 69

✉ 10th St. &
Constitution Ave.,
N.W.

☎ 202-357-2700

🚇 Metro: Federal
Triangle,
Smithsonian;
Bus: 13A, P2

DINOSAUR FOSSILS, SPARKLING GEMS, A GIANT SQUID, AN insect zoo, and rare Native American artifacts—these are the kinds of things that make this such a popular museum. The Smithsonian's National Museum of Natural History explores in wondrous detail the natural world and our place in it. Housed in a green-domed beaux arts building from 1904, this was the third Smithsonian building, erected to hold the institution's bursting collection.

The teeming variety of nature continues to assert its importance: More than 87 percent of the Smithsonian's entire population of artifacts, specimens, and works of art belongs to this museum alone. That's more than 124 million individual specimens and artifacts. Though most people won't see these specimens, researchers from around the world use the collection to carry out various systematic studies. Think of all the millions of beetles, butterflies, mosquitoes,

sponges, mollusks, mineralogical samples, birds' eggs, microscopic organisms, and Native American baskets stored in drawers and on shelves. Much of the collection is kept in the museum's Suitland, Maryland, support center.

VISITING

You can easily spend a day wandering through the museum, getting sidetracked from whatever it was you had set out to see. If you have only a few hours, pinpoint a couple

exhibits and plot your route (maps available at information desks at both entrances). Entering from the Constitution Avenue side puts you on the **ground floor,** which has a **highlights** exhibit, a sampler of the treasures awaiting you within. Before you head up to the two exhibit floors, walk to the back of this floor, past the Atrium Café and Museum Shop, to the **Birds of D.C.** exhibit. Many people miss this compendium of taxidermed eastern birds, on display since the 1920s. Along with bald and golden eagles, swans, and warblers, the extinct Carolina parakeet and passenger pigeon are represented.

First floor

If you enter the museum from the Mall side, you'll step into the grand Rotunda, one of the city's great interior spaces. The eight-sided Rotunda rises to a dome 125 feet from the floor; columned galleries offer splendid views from above.

But the sight in the middle of the Rotunda is what grabs most people's attention: Standing 13 feet 2 inches at the shoulder, the **African bush elephant** weighed 12 tons when it was killed in 1954. It is the largest mounted specimen of Earth's largest land animal, and its grassy savanna display has recently been revamped with sound effects and other mounted animals. The snarling fox, croaking frogs, and so forth offer many surprises.

From the Rotunda you can trace the evolution of life on Earth by starting with the **Early Life** exhibit, just to the right of the Mall entrance. It contains one of the oldest known fossils—a mass of fossilized microbes 3.5 billion years old—and presents a short animated film that outlines the origins of life. The rare fossils of 530-million-year-old soft-bodied animals, among the museum's most important finds, were discovered in 1909 by geologist Charles Walcott, the Smithsonian's

Crowds pass in and out of the Rotunda on their way to galleries, often pausing to view the mounted African elephant; the enormous animal was about 50 years old when killed in 1954.

A model of a salt crystal, enlarged nearly 1.5 billion times, bedazzles visitors to the Hall of Geology, Gems, and Minerals.

fourth secretary.

The adjacent **Dinosaurs** exhibit showcases the skeleton of an 80-foot-long *Diplodocus*, a family member of the largest land animals ever. The **Ancient Seas** area displays the curving, partially reconstructed skeleton of a 30-foot whale that swam the ocean about 39 million years ago. Before moving on to the next area, watch scientists and artists at work in the glassed-off **Fossil Lab.** One major task they perform is to ready plaster casts for display by painting them to look exactly like the real fossils.

Just around the corner, the **Ice Age Hall** explores the beginnings of human influence on the world of animals and plants. Casts and composite skeletons of a woolly mammoth, mastodon, and giant ground sloth illustrate the large creatures that went extinct more than 10,000 years ago. Pleistocene survivors include a mounted wolverine, musk ox, and badger. You can't help pausing before the diorama of a Neanderthal burial, a

re-creation of a ritual performed 70,000 years ago. In a compelling, intimate scene, the deceased lies bound in the fetal position while his family and a shaman look on.

The other exhibits on this floor explore various cultures. The new **African Voices** sports a jazzy look with world-beat music and touch terminals. By contrast, the older **Asian and Pacific Cultures Galleries** have the same terrazzo floors and glass display cases they have had for decades. But there is something comforting about the older displays, and their longevity attests to their excellence; the totems and stone discs and vivid dioramas free the imagination to wander to faraway lands. Likewise, the **Native Cultures of the Americas Hall,** with dried scalps, eagle-feather bonnets, buffalo-hide shields, and ivory carvings, is a perennial favorite.

The northwest hall features **Arts of the Americas,** including brilliant Zuni pottery and Mexican papier-mâché figures. In the far corner, the **Discovery Room** (*closed Mon.*) holds a number of animals, fossils, shells, and minerals that visitors can handle. Also in this part of the museum, a 400-seat **IMAX Theater** (*fee*) shows large-format 2-D and 3-D films on a screen 66 feet high.

Second floor

On the second floor, many people head directly for the **Janet Annenberg Hooker Hall of Geology, Gems, and Minerals.** Here you can learn how a meteorite impact may have wiped out the dinosaurs, build a virtual volcano, touch a piece of limestone scarred by Ice Age glaciers, see fluorescent minerals, view a mock-up vertical mine shaft, and watch a film on plate tectonics. You will definitely want to ogle the dazzling **National Gem Collection,** starring the 45.5-carat Hope Diamond, the largest blue diamond in the world. Other outstanding riches include a thousand-diamond diadem given by Napoleon I to his wife Empress Marie Louise; a pair of Marie Antoinette's earrings; and the world's largest perfect quartz sphere, a magically clear 107-pound globe from China. Just beyond lies a hall of sparkling crystals in a myriad of colors, shapes, and sizes, including such oddities as twinned and twisted crystal formations.

Continuing on this floor, the **South America: Continent and Culture Hall** has life-size tableaus, detailed murals, and a number of weapons, tools, and other artifacts to present the life and history of four South American regions: the wide Patagonian grasslands, the lush tropical rain forests, the dry Pacific coastlands, and the high Andean mountain valleys.

Turn the corner and you'll see an interesting exhibit on the giant squid. Two preserved specimens, including a 9-foot female that washed ashore on Plum Island, Maine, in 1980, are the only ones in the world on display in a museum. Earth's largest invertebrate animals, giant squid live from about 650 to 2,300 feet beneath the surface of the ocean. Scientists have never studied them alive, because no one knows exactly where in the ocean they live.

The next-door **Western Cultures** exhibit covers the rise of Western civilization from the end of the Ice Age to about A.D. 500. Helping to tell the story of the emergence and spread of Western culture are a reconstructed Ice Age cave with flint tools; early Egyptian pottery; reconstructed Bronze Age tombs from Jordan's Bab-edh-Dhra, the City of the Dead (3000 B.C.); an Egyptian coffin; and a mummified bull.

Walk around to the **Hall of Bones and Reptiles,** where you can see mammal skeletons varying in size from the pocket mouse to the huge, extinct Steller's sea cow. The adjoining **O. Orkin Insect Zoo** is a storehouse of delights for anyone who appreciates the most abundant animals on Earth. Live exhibits, accompanied by buzzing and chirping sound effects and video information stations, give this exhibit an edge. Watch live bees, water striders, darkling beetles, centipedes, tarantulas, and whip scorpions. Labels indicate which species, such as scorpions and tarantulas, are "insect relatives." It's interesting, and somewhat worrisome, to try out the touch-panel house diorama; flashing lights indicate where insects might live—silverfish in the bathroom, carpenter ants in the floor, and roaches in the kitchen. You also can walk through a simulated rain forest with giant cockroaches and cave arthropods. ∎

National Museum of American History

National Museum of American History

www.americanhistory.si.edu

🏛 Map p. 69

✉ 10th St. & Constitution Ave., N.W.

☎ 202-357-2700

🚇 Metro: Federal Triangle; Bus: 13B, 52

THE NATIONAL MUSEUM OF AMERICAN HISTORY COLLECTS, cares for, and preserves more than 17 million artifacts, which together create a vast and fascinating mosaic of life in the United States. Dedicated to "inspiring a broader understanding of our nation and its many peoples," this bonanza of American history reflects the trends and events in the country's multifarious history.

The building was called the National Museum of History and Technology from its opening in 1964 until 1980, when the name was changed to more accurately reflect the museum's scope of interests and responsibilities. The museum now focuses on technology and culture as a way of presenting history.

VISITING

With so many different kinds of exhibits spread over three sprawling floors—more than 30 exhibit areas on nearly twice the floor space of the National Air and Space Museum—you'll have a difficult time taking in the whole museum in one gulp. If you have the time, spend a few hours on one floor, then come back another day and look at the displays on a different floor. You can also just hit a few highlights. The first floor concentrates on science and technology, while the second floor focuses on cultural, social, and political history. The eclectic collection of the third floor includes musical history, coins, ceramics, armed forces history, printing and graphic arts, and a wonderful exhibit on the Presidency of the United States.

A museum visitor delivers an impromptu inaugural presidential address.

First floor

The Constitution Avenue entrance puts you on the first floor, the Mall on the second. Starting from the Constitution Avenue side, the first exhibit you come to after a stop at the information desk is **Material World;** an array of everyday objects made from 1700 to the 1980s illustrates the various kinds of materials we use. Of particular note is a sleek dragster made of stainless steel, titanium, gold, and Lexan. Behind this exhibit, don't overlook the **Palm Court** ice-cream parlor, featuring a marble soda fountain and wooden display cabinets that were once part of an 1890s Georgetown confectionary shop.

The labyrinth of galleries on the east side of the first floor focuses on agriculture and transportation. *(Construction work will affect much of this area through 2002.)* Go back in time in the agriculture section to see a big red International Harvester driven 1,800 miles to Washington in 1979 as part of the American Agricultural Movement; a monster 1924 Huber Steam Tractor; and an 1886 combine that was pulled by 20 horses. In the corner of the **Maritime** area is a 1920 Marine Steam Engine, complete with churning sound effects, while model ships galore are all about. Next door, the huge **Railroads Room** features a gleaming 1926 locomotive—titled the 1401 Engine—with a realistic huffing-puffing sound track. There is also an 1898 electric streetcar once used on the Seventh Street line in Washington.

Over 40 vehicles are on display in the **Road Transportation Gallery,** including an early 19th-century Conestoga wagon, a 1938 Chevrolet Good Humor ice-cream truck, a 1913 Model T Ford, an 1818 bicycle, and an 1869 Roper steam velocipede—an early motorcycle.

The adjacent **Engines of Change** exhibit explores the industrial revolution in America and the ways in which work-saving machines have changed our lives. At the front of this gallery, the 1836 *John Bull* is the world's oldest operable locomotive. The adjoining **On Time** exhibit looks at the ways Americans have measured, used, and thought about time in the past 300 years. It contains a wonderful collection of ingenious timepieces, from sundials to atomic clocks.

Over on the west side of the first floor, the emphasis is on science. The extensive **Science in American Life** takes on issues in society affected by science. One corner, for example, examines the effect of the birth control pill on

the sexual revolution. Other displays trace the ripples cast by experimental psychology, nylon, and atomic testing. Videos, interactive terminals, historical photographs, newspaper articles, and artifacts offer a variety of ways to delve into these fascinating topics, so if you feel overwhelmed by the avalanche of material, you can decide how deeply you want to plunge. In the **Hands On Science Center** *(closed Mon.)* visitors can do exper-

Magazine photographs and campaign buttons in the "First Ladies" exhibit

1875   1900   1925

BUCHANAN · LINCOLN · JOHNSON · GRANT · HAYES · GARFIELD · ARTHUR · CLEVELAND · HARRISON · CLEVELAND · McKINLEY · ROOSEVELT · TAFT · WILSON · HARDING · COOLIDGE · HOOVER · ROOSEVELT

A primer on the nation's leaders anchors the popular "American Presidency" exhibit.

iments to learn about testing for radioactivity, conserving textiles, and protecting against ultraviolet rays.

The adjacent **Information Age** exhibit walks you through the history of telecommunications and computers. Starting with Samuel Morse's telegraph (invented 1835–37) and Alexander Graham Bell's original telephone (from 1876), you move on to the early computers—including a 1946 machine that takes up as much space as a modern-day office. The exhibit traces computer evolution from such behemoths to desk-size models that offer virtual reality; interactive activities explore the worlds of television, military coding, and more.

Second floor
The **Star-Spangled Banner,** which has been at the Smithsonian

since 1907, was taken down from its wall in 1998 and moved to a second-floor lab, where visitors can watch ongoing preservation work. The flag will be on display again in 2003. In 1814 this flag flew over Fort McHenry when the British Navy attacked Baltimore. In the early light of dawn, Francis Scott Key, on a ship in the Chesapeake, saw that the flag was still flying and was inspired to write a poem that eventually became the lyrics to the national anthem. What the British couldn't bring down, decades of exposure to light and air pollution have, however. You can watch the conservators working meticulously in a glassed-in lab, vacuuming the flag and removing it from a linen backing put on in 1914.

The exhibit next door, **Field to Factory,** explores the massive migration of blacks from the rural

South to the industrialized North from 1915 to 1940. Here visitors can view outfits and booklets of the Ku Klux Klan and read stories from black-run newspapers of the 1920s.

On the same side of the museum is the popular exhibit **First Ladies: Political Role and Public Image;** it showcases evening gowns worn by the Presidents' wives. The exhibit also chronicles the changing role of the First Lady and delves into social and political accomplishments.

Across the hall, **After the Revolution: Everyday Life in America** takes a look at the first generation of people to live in a new nation, the United States of America. The exhibits lead from rural to urban settings and explore the lives of early American families.

Now go on to one of the newest major exhibits: **Within These Walls.** Using a house that stood from colonial days through the mid-1960s in Ipswich, Massachusetts, this exhibit showcases 200 years of American history. The Georgian-style, timber-frame house is the largest artifact in the museum. It serves to highlight the lives of five ordinary families who dwelled in the house and lived through great changes and events in our nation's past.

Third floor

There's much to choose from up here, but the exhibit that probably appeals to everyone is **The American Presidency: A Glorious Burden,** which opened in November 2000. The portable desk on which Jefferson drafted the Declaration of Independence, the hat Lincoln wore the night he was assassinated, Washington's general officer's uniform, and many other objects capture the spirit of the men responsible for leading the nation from its infancy to the present. Among the subjects explored are impeachment (including the proceeding against Bill Clinton), the Supreme Court, Congress, assassinations, the press, and life in the White House. One popular corner lets visitors deliver inaugural addresses using a teleprompter. At another display, you can push buttons to hear songs about the Presidency composed by George Gershwin, Alice Cooper, and others.

Another fun, if small, exhibit on this floor—**Icons of Popular Culture**—displays such items as a pair of Dorothy's ruby slippers, the Lone Ranger's mask, Indiana Jones's leather jacket, and Michael Jordan's basketball jersey.

Among the many other third-floor exhibits is a fascinating one on **Printing and Graphic Arts;** it features tools and equipment of the printing trades, a printshop, a newspaper shop, and a foundry. ■

A wreath adorns the black-granite wall of names at the Vietnam Veterans Memorial.

A walk around the monuments

The western end of the Mall, where you'll find the city's most significant monuments and memorials, is a delightful place for walking. A 3-mile loop taking you past a half dozen major memorials makes for a wonderful morning or afternoon; benches along the way offer rest stops. About two blocks from the start is the Smithsonian Metro stop. Parking during cherry blossom season *(late March–early April)* is nearly impossible.

Begin at the **Washington Monument ❶,** off 15th Street between Constitution and Independence Avenues. Set on a slight rise, this 555-foot marble obelisk is surrounded by flags from every state in the nation.

Begun in 1848, the monument rose slowly but steadily for five years to 152 feet; at that point funding ran out and building ceased for almost 25 years. Look about a third of the way up to see where the work stopped. Though taken from a nearby Maryland quarry, the more recent marble is of a darker color. The monument is currently in the final stages of a comprehensive restoration effort, which includes installation of a new elevator system and security facility. When the structure reopens, you can ride the elevator to the 500-foot level for one of the best views of the city. If you wish, you can descend the 897 steps past the scores of memorial stones, but only on scheduled tours led by rangers. Visit the ticket kiosk near the monument for same-day tickets, or call *(800-967-2283)* for advance tickets.

From the grounds of the Washington Monument, you can see the Lincoln Memorial directly to the west and the Jefferson Memorial across the Tidal Basin, but your next destination is hidden among the trees of **Constitution Gardens,** a memorial to the founders of this nation. Walk down the hill, cross 17th Street, and take the sinuous trail through lovely landscaping just north of the **Reflecting Pool.** On the pool's east end the **National World War II Memorial** will be constructed by March 2003. On small **Signers Island,** a memorial honors the 56 signers of the Declaration of Independence.

Just west, architect Maya Lin's stunning **Vietnam Veterans Memorial ❷** presents a moving contrast to the classical-style monuments all about. A tremendous black-granite wedge, bermed into the earth instead of standing above it, is inscribed with the names of all the 58,209 Americans who died or were missing in action in the Vietnam War. Polished to a reflective sheen, the walls of the wedge seem to project life as much as honor death. As you walk the path beside the memorial, the names

The FDR Memorial also remembers the Depression-era President's lovable dog, Fala.

of the dead increase dramatically as the walls reach their high point at 10.1 feet. The nearby bronze group of three soldiers, by Washington sculptor Frederick Hart, adds a dose of gritty realism. Dedicated in 1982, the memorial was

🅜 See area map pp. 68–69

▶ Washington Monument

🔁 3 miles

🕐 2 hours

▶ Jefferson Memorial

NOT TO BE MISSED

- Vietnam Veterans Memorial
- Lincoln Memorial
- Jefferson Memorial

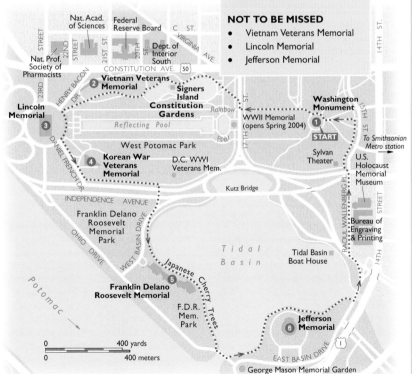

Dedicated in 1995, the Korean War Veterans Memorial honors the 1.5 million Americans who served in the "forgotten war." Private contributions funded the $18 million memorial.

supplemented in 1993 by another bronze group, the **Vietnam Women's Memorial,** in tribute to the women who took part in the war.

Continue on to the magnificent **Lincoln Memorial** ❸. Designed by architect Henry Bacon and sculptor Daniel Chester French, the memorial was built from 1914 to 1922 to honor Abraham Lincoln, President during the Civil War. The 36 Doric columns represent the number of states at the time of Lincoln's death. Inside, facing the Mall, the 19-foot-tall statue of a seated Lincoln was carved from 28 blocks of white Georgia marble. The walls of the memorial are inscribed with words from the Gettysburg Address and Lincoln's second inaugural speech. Especially dramatic at night, the memorial shimmers in the Reflecting Pool. From here you have a straight-line view to the Washington Monument and U.S. Capitol.

Another compelling memorial lies just to the southeast. Dedicated in 1995, the **Korean War Veterans Memorial** ❹ features 19

gray soldiers warily crossing a field of scrubby junipers. Next to this riveting stainless-steel group, a black-granite wall is etched with a mural of those who served, while another wall bears the simple message: "Freedom Is Not Free." Beside a "pool of remembrance" stands a stone carved with the war's toll—the numbers of killed, wounded, missing, and captured.

Walk east toward the **Tidal Basin** and cross West Basin Drive at the second traffic light, in front of the nearly hidden **D.C. WWI Veterans Memorial,** honoring the District's veterans.

The Mall's newest memorial blends into the trees of West Potomac Park on the Tidal Basin's west side. Honoring the 32nd U.S. President, the **Franklin Delano Roosevelt Memorial** ❺ spreads along the water's edge in a series of unroofed, granite-walled alcoves, one for each of his four terms. The effect is less of something grand to stare at than of something spacious to wander through. Dedicated in 1997, the grace-

by John Russell Pope in the style of the ancient Roman Pantheon and completed in 1943. Inside the colonnaded building a 19-foot bronze of Jefferson stands beneath a towering dome. Among the quotes on the wall is one from a letter written in 1800: "I have sworn upon the altar of God eternal hostility against every form of tyranny over the mind of man." A lower lobby has exhibits, a gift shop, and a bookstore.

Behind the monument on Ohio Drive, the **George Mason Memorial Garden** opens in spring 2002. In keeping with the quiet patriot's love of his garden at Gunston Hall (see p. 224), the setting is a classical landscape designed as a peaceful, contemplative place.

Complete the walk by rounding the Tidal Basin and heading up 15th Street to the flag-encircled Washington Monument. ■

No more monuments

Since the early 1900s, when more and more monuments and museums began sprinkling the Mall, there has been a rising concern about overcrowding. Controversy raged throughout the 1930s, for instance, over the placement of the Jefferson Memorial: Critics worried about losing some of the famous cherry trees, a gift from the city of Tokyo in 1912. A new site was chosen and the final design was reduced to about half the original size. More recently, the FDR Memorial was altered in the 1990s in response to various groups. There was also an enormous flap in 2001 over the placement of the National World War II Memorial. While some 450 veterans' groups support this new memorial, opponents fear that the sweeping views up and down the Mall will be lost.

Despite the efforts of many people— including an official Joint Task Force on Memorials—to stop "monument sprawl," plans and proposals are pushing ahead for even more construction. A memorial to Martin Luther King, Jr., was announced in September 2000, and others being considered include ones honoring the Black Patriots of the American Revolution, and the John Adams family. ■

ful memorial was criticized at first by disability advocacy groups who claimed that it showed only the public Roosevelt. Paralyzed by polio from the age of 39, Roosevelt was confined to a wheelchair, but during carefully staged public appearances, he stood for his speeches by propping himself up and holding on to a son or an aide. Many, including his wife, Eleanor, have declared that his inspiring optimism and strength were a direct result of his disability. In 2001 a statue of FDR in his wheelchair was added to the memorial, opposite the information center. From here, you walk through the landscaped plazas, past statuary, waterfalls, and shade trees. Sculptures of a breadline, a man listening to a fireside chat, and a rural couple are reminders of FDR's challenging era.

On the south side of the Tidal Basin stands the impressive **Jefferson Memorial** ⑥. The view from here, across the Tidal Basin with its gulls and paddleboats and springtime cherry blossoms, is not to be missed. Dedicated to the author of the Declaration of Independence and third U.S. President, the structure was designed

U.S. Holocaust Memorial Museum

U.S. Holocaust Memorial Museum
www.ushmm.org

🅰 Map p. 69

✉ 100 Raoul Wallenberg Pl. (15th St.), S.W., just S of Independence Ave.

☎ 202-488-0400

🚇 Metro: Smithsonian; Bus: 52

OPENED IN 1993, THIS MUSEUM SERVES AS A MEMORIAL TO the millions of people murdered during Nazi rule in Germany from 1933 to 1945. The architecture—windowless recesses, brickwork guard towers, and obscured windows—suggests some of the themes and images documented within. Inside, the skylit first-floor atrium is overshadowed by heavy steel trusses. A factory-like brick wall on one side is where visitors enter and ascend, via a cargo-style elevator, to see the permanent exhibition, starting on the fourth floor.

The Holocaust Museum's first floor sets a somber tone for a visit to the galleries above.

VISITING

Pick up timed passes at the desk on the first floor, or call *(800-400-9373)* for advance passes. The exhibition is self-guided and takes two to three hours. Because there are several films, audio programs, and a lot of text on the three-floor exhibit, you may want to make a selective tour. The **Meyerhoff Theater** on the concourse level shows a 14-minute orientation film. Most of the exhibits are not recommended for children under 11; it's also a

good idea to prepare older children for what they are about to see.

On the **fourth floor,** which covers the spread of Nazism from 1933 to 1939, visitors are funneled through hallways from one exhibit area to the next. The dim, quiet halls, with grated ceilings, reflect the museum's somber content. A theater, grim photographs, and monitors displaying silent footage bespeak the early years of the Third Reich and the start of its sanctioned violence toward Jews, Poles,

Gypsies, homosexuals, political dissidents, the handicapped, and others.

On the **third floor,** the years 1940–45 are examined in grisly detail through displays on ghettos, deportations, slave labor, and extermination camps. Among the powerful artifacts are a cobblestone floor from a Warsaw ghetto, clothing, and a cemetery gate from Karnow where Jews were routinely shot. A walk-through tower is lined with family photos from a shtetl, a Jewish village; you later learn that this entire village of 4,000 was destroyed in 1941, bringing 900 years of continuous history to an abrupt and complete end. Perhaps most telling are the shelfloads of victims' belongings—rusty scissors, can openers, graters, razors, toothbrushes—and the huge piles of old shoes. There are bunks from Auschwitz and a scale model that shows how the gas chambers and crematoria worked. Video monitors show unsettling images such as

medical experiments, executions, and malnourished children. The monitors are shielded by walls so young children cannot see them; adults can elect not to watch.

Efforts at resistance and the ultimate liberation of survivors are documented on the **second floor.** In the **Hall of Remembrance,** an eternal flame honors victims of the Holocaust; visitors may light candles in their memory.

The **first floor** recounts the Holocaust from a child's point of view; this hands-on gallery is suitable for children eight years and older. Downstairs, the **concourse level** has changing exhibitions and a **Wall of Remembrance** honoring the estimated 1.5 million children who died. Outside the museum, it's a relief to look across the Tidal Basin to the Jefferson and FDR Memorials and remember those who stood against tyranny and won. As one FDR Memorial donor put it, a man in a wheelchair beat Hitler. ■

More places to visit around the National Mall

ARTS AND INDUSTRIES BUILDING

The Smithsonian's second oldest building, this brick-and-sandstone edifice beside the Castle was completed in 1881 to exhibit items from the first world's fair—the 1876 Centennial Exposition in Philadelphia. The original home of the National Museum, the building was the first showcase for many objects before the new Smithsonian museums were built. Changing exhibitions from the Smithsonian collection and traveling exhibits are now on view here. ◪ Map p. 69 ✉ 900 Jefferson Dr., S.W. ☎ 202-357-2700 🚇 Metro: Smithsonian

BUREAU OF ENGRAVING & PRINTING

One of the popular standards of Washington tourism, the bureau is the place to see a lot of money—up to 38 million dollars—being printed daily. To replace worn-out bills and keep up with economic growth, this facility and a similar one in Fort Worth, Texas, churn out about 7 billion notes a year in denominations from $1 to $100. The 24 high-speed presses run 24 hours a day, 5 days a week, with nearly 50 percent of that time spent turning out $1 bills. On 40-minute tours you

Visitors can tour streets near the National Mall in old-fashioned style.

can see 32-note currency sheets rolling through production and 4,000-note "bricks" being prepared for distribution to the 12 Federal Reserve Banks around the country. You'll also learn about the latest techniques to prevent counterfeiting. A visitor center on the premises sells uncut sheets of legal tender and other currency-related novelties. www.moneyfactory.com ◪ Map p. 69 ✉ 14th & C Sts., S.W. ☎ 202-874-3188 or 202-874-2330 🕐 Closed Sat.–Sun. Call for summer and winter tour hours; obtain free tickets from booth on west side of the building 🚇 Metro: Smithsonian; Bus: 13A, V7

VOICE OF AMERICA

Since 1942 this government-operated news service has been on the airwaves. Now broadcasting in 53 languages to 91 million listeners worldwide, the VOA strives to present accurate news and the "policies of the United States clearly and effectively." All programs are produced here in more than 40 radio studios and 3 TV studios. On 45-minute tours visitors see 1940s murals by Ben Shahn and witness the polyglot buzz of activity in radio studios and newsrooms. www.voa.gov ◪ Map p. 69 ✉ 330 Independence Ave., S.W. ☎ 202-619-3919 🕐 Tours Mon.–Fri. 10:30, 1:30, 2:30. Call for reservations. 🚇 Metro: Federal Center, S.W. ∎

Although a certain famous residence at 1600 Pennsylvania Avenue gets most of the attention, the neighborhood around the White House overflows with art galleries, historic houses and hotels, churches, museums, and other stops of note.

White House & around

The south portico of the White House

White House & around

A LOCUS OF POLITICAL POWER THAT IS ALSO A MAJOR TOURIST ATTRACTION, the home of the Chief Executive is a living museum of the Presidency in downtown Washington. The immediate environs are rich in history, culture, and political excitement.

In 1791 a surveyor and an engineer picked the site for a presidential "palace," as the latter called it. The surveyor was George Washington, the engineer was Pierre Charles L'Enfant, and the site was a cornfield above a tidal marsh where hunters shot ducks and geese.

Just a mile from the site of the future Capitol, the manse they envisioned would be about four times the size of the current White House.

Thomas Jefferson, Secretary of State at the time, persuaded Washington to hold a competition for the design. Unimpressed by the

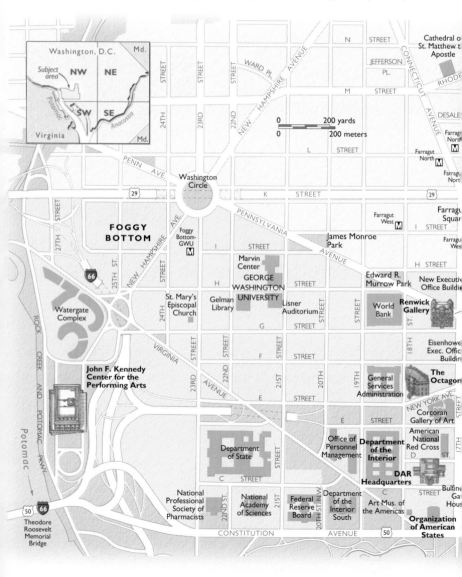

mundane entries that resulted, Washington urged Irish-born architect James Hoban to have a go. Hoban's entry, selected in 1792, was an adaptation of the Duke of Leinster's palace near Dublin. Regrettably, Washington—then on the verge of his second term as President—would not live to see the structure completed.

The next President, John Adams, moved into the partially completed mansion on November 1, 1800, only to lose his reelection bid less than a month later. Jefferson, his successor, spent the next eight years in the Presi-

dent's House (it was not called the White House until 1901), opening it to the public and establishing it as a national symbol. President James Madison enjoyed no such stability: The British burned the building to the ground in 1814, forcing Madison to abandon the President's House for temporary quarters nearby.

After Abraham Lincoln's assassination in 1865, some lobbied to move the President to a more secluded location, in Rock Creek Park. President Ulysses S. Grant, who had served as Lincoln's commanding officer, nixed that idea.

By the turn of the 20th century, it was clear that the White House—Theodore Roosevelt's designation for it—enshrined the American presidential legacy. Indeed, each President has left his stamp on the place: Rutherford B. Hayes put in the first telephone, Benjamin Harrison installed electric lights, and Theodore Roosevelt hung a moose head above the fireplace in the State Dining Room.

The presidential neighborhood grew in tandem with the White House. In the 1810s, St. John's Church, Decatur House, and a number of posh, federal-style residences were built around President's Park (renamed Lafayette Square in 1824). By 1900—when the Treasury Building, Old Executive Office Building, Corcoran Gallery, Renwick building, Blair House, the Octagon, and Willard Hotel had all gone up around 1600 Pennsylvania Avenue—the area was a thriving mix of government buildings, art galleries, hotels, and residences.

From west of 20th Street to the Potomac River, the Foggy Bottom neighborhood is a busy mix of 19th-century row houses, apartment buildings, and major institutions: the State Department, World Bank, Kennedy Center, and George Washington University. The breweries and gasworks that once filled this bottomland with foggy vapors were gone by the mid-20th century, when the area began to morph into a middle-class neighborhood.

From its tidy lawns and ornate facades to its clean sidewalks and crisply suited Secret Service agents, the White House area maintains and inspires a polished decorum. Until World War II, you could walk to the front door of the White House and leave your calling card. Security then moved outward to the fence line, and in 1995 Pennsylvania Avenue in front of the building was closed to traffic. ■

White House

White House

www.whitehouse.gov

🅰 Map p. 107

✉ 1600 Pennsyl-
vania Ave., N.W.

☎ 202-456-7041

🕐 Closed Sun.–Mon.

🚇 Metro: McPherson
Square or Metro
Center; Bus: 42,
G8

**The dignified
north portico
basks in the glow
of early evening.**

THE OLDEST PUBLIC BUILDING IN THE DISTRICT OF
Columbia, the White House has been the home of every U.S. President except George Washington. In this most famous of residences,
the President signs bills into law, meets with national and international leaders, entertains guests, and does his best to lead a private
family life. Despite more than 200 years of expansions and renovations, the White House has kept its essential appearance and design.

Washington's designers intended
the executive mansion to be one of
two focal points of the new Federal
City (the Capitol would be the other). Nine blueprints were submitted
to a competitive design panel;
among those rejected was a plan
put forward anonymously by Thomas Jefferson.

The winning design—the work

of Irish-born architect James Hoban—honored the stately symme-
tries of Georgian manor houses in
the British Isles. Not that it lacked
detractors: Benjamin Henry Latrobe, who worked on the White
House in the early 1800s and is
considered the country's first professional architect, assailed Hoban's
concept as "a mutilated copy of a

House, muddy boots and all; while President Jackson slipped away to a nearby hotel, his aides filled tubs with juice and whiskey and set them on the lawn to coax the crowds outside. The Inaugural open houses continued until 1885, when Grover Cleveland replaced them with a parade, which he watched from the relative safety of a grandstand in front of the White House.

During the War of 1812, the British retaliated for the American burning of public buildings in Canada by burning down the President's House and other city landmarks in 1814. When British soldiers arrived at the hastily vacated executive mansion on the night of August 24, 1814, they found Dolley Madison's dinner still on the table (a few of them sat down and polished it off). Shortly after midnight, the soldiers threw flaming javelins into the mansion. By morning it was a smoldering shell. The house was rebuilt within its original walls over the next few years.

By the mid-20th century, the White House had reached a serious state of structural decline: The walls and floors could no longer support the alterations and additions of previous decades. From 1948 to 1952, Harry and Bess Truman lived in Blair House, across Pennsylvania Avenue, while the White House was gutted. Everything from furniture to paneling was taken out; a new basement was dug, new foundations were laid, and a steel framework was installed. The basic house was still there, but it was now much safer. Since then, each First Family has added its own decorative touch: The Kennedys redesigned the Rose Garden, while the Reagans contributed a new set of Lenox china.

VISITING
Self-guided tours of the White House were suspended in the wake

badly designed original near Dublin."

Nonetheless, the cornerstone of the President's House (George Washington's preferred term for it) was laid in October 1792, a year before work began on the Capitol. The pale sandstone for the white-painted walls came from Aquia Creek, on the Virginia side of the Potomac. Eight years later, with President John Adams nearing the end of his term, the house was finally ready for occupation.

Jefferson, the third President, held the first Inaugural open house in 1805 and forged the tradition of throwing the house open to public tours. The custom got out of hand in 1829, when some 20,000 well-wishers tromped through the White

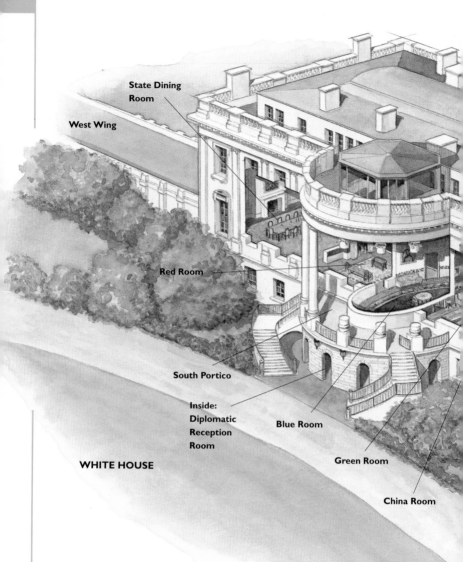

State Dining Room

West Wing

Red Room

South Portico

Inside:
Diplomatic
Reception
Room

Blue Room

Green Room

China Room

WHITE HOUSE

of the events of September 11, 2001. The following account assumes they will resume at some point with their former popularity—6,000 visitors per day during the 10 a.m. to noon touring hours (*Tues.–Sat.*).

Though the house is well worth seeing, doing so requires some work—especially in the spring and summer high season. Arrive close to noon on a winter weekday and you may be able to walk right in. All tours start at the southeast gate.

From mid-March until about Labor Day, you must pick up free timed tickets at the **White House Visitor Center** in the Commerce

East Room

Library

East Wing

Visitor entrance

Vermeil Room

Department lobby (*SE corner of 15th & E Sts., 202-456-7041*). The tickets are available starting at 7:30 a.m. for that day only, though lines often form before 7; one person can obtain up to four tickets. Tours are sometimes canceled without notice, so call the night before.

The visitor center contains some noteworthy exhibits: porcelain acquired by the Monroes, early 19th-century White House furniture, a typewriter used by Woodrow Wilson. A 30-minute orientation video offers good background.

Another option—**a reserved tour**—is available by contacting your Congressperson or Senator

The Red Room's French Empire-style furniture dates back to the early 1800s.

eight to ten weeks in advance. These tours, with a maximum of 70, last 25 to 35 minutes and focus on White House history and art.

While waiting in line at the Visitors Entrance on East Executive Avenue, you'll hear an audio program on the house and its history broadcast from speakers inside the fence. Looking through the gate, you can see part of the mansion's lovely 18-acre grounds. Once you get inside, your pace will hinge on the size of the crowd; expect to spend 15 to 20 minutes.

After passing through security, you enter a corridor on the ground floor with information panels on White House architecture and glass-walled views of the modern sculpture and well-groomed plant-

ings in the **Jacqueline Kennedy Garden.** Next, peer into the roped-off **Library**, filled with federal-style furniture. Across the hall, the **Vermeil Room** has portraits of recent First Ladies and a collection of gilded silver known as vermeil.

The rooms you can actually walk through are up on the State Floor. The first one you enter—the expansive **East Room**—is also the largest in the house: It hosts press conferences, receptions, award ceremonies, and concerts. Among the weddings held here were those of Nellie Grant, Alice Roosevelt, and Lynda Bird Johnson. Imagine skid marks on this floor; the energetic children of Theodore Roosevelt are said to have roller-skated across it. The furnishings include a decorated

concert grand piano, a 1938 gift from the Steinway company.

Continue around to the **Green Room,** used by Jefferson as a dining room but now functioning as a reception parlor. The window affords a great view beyond the Ellipse (an open greensward just north of Constitution Avenue) to the Jefferson Memorial. Much of the Green Room's furniture came from the workshop of Duncan Phyfe in the early 1800s. The green watered-silk wall coverings were chosen by Mrs. Kennedy.

The elegant and oval **Blue Room** contains several pieces of furniture bought by James Monroe, who refurbished the room after the 1814 fire. Presidents still receive guests here. First Ladies frequently entertain in the adjacent **Red Room,** furnished as an American Empire parlor of 1810 to 1830.

Some 130 guests can be seated in the gracious **State Dining Room,** which boasts painted oak paneling from a 1902 renovation. Out in the **Cross Halls,** the floors are of Tennessee marble (no skating here!). A carpeted marble staircase leads to the second and third floors, open only to the First Family and guests. Famous rooms up there include the Lincoln Bedroom and the Queen's Bedroom. The West Wing *(not open to public)* holds the Cabinet Room, numerous staff and reception rooms, and the President's Oval Office (built in 1909) and its adjoining Rose Garden. The White House also contains an indoor tennis court, jogging track, swimming pool, movie theater, bowling lane, and billiard room. The total number of rooms in the house: 132.

Your tour will exit the front door beneath a columned portico, then follow the walkway to the front gate. As photos are forbidden inside, many people pause here before leaving to get a shot. Through the viewfinder you may discover that the White House looks not at all palatial—a mansion, yes, but at heart just a home. ■

President and Mrs. Bush arrive at a State Dinner with Mexican president Vicente Fox and his wife, Martha Sahagun.

A stroll around the White House

Walking in the area around the White House will give you a concentrated taste of Washington's core. Yet the knots of tourists, security officers, and limousines that buzz around the executive mansion like drones around a queen bee are only part of the picture. Because local laws bar skyscrapers, you can enjoy long, green views across the Ellipse and the Mall. The area is also dotted with house museums, art galleries, benches for idling, and restaurants for both tourists and power brokers.

Once you've visited the White House, you tend to forget it's there, as do the locals who go about their business in the area, treating the structure as nothing more than an attractive backdrop. Since virtually no one sees the First Family come and go, it's easy to overlook that the President of the United States is living in splendid isolation in that beautiful historic house. The occasional presence of television crews and reporters is a reminder that "presidential privacy" is something of an oxymoron. (With local sidewalks often closed by security, call 202-619-7256 for updates on restricted areas.)

Roller hockey on traffic-free Pennsylvania Ave. in front of the Old Executive Office Building

Starting at the White House Visitor Center (see p. 111), you can view exhibits and pick up tickets for the **White House** ❶ (see pp. 108–113). The section of Pennsylvania Avenue in front of the White House is closed to traffic, so stroll along here to take good, unobstructed pictures. The park just north of the White House, **Lafayette Square** ❷, is a perfect place to sit with a sandwich and people-watch.

As a public park in full view of the White House, the square is also strategically ideal for demonstrating for or against something. Activists for causes such as nuclear disarmament have maintained a peaceful vigil here since 1981; it's easy to engage the protesters in conversation to find out what they hope to accomplish. In the middle of the square is Clark Mills's statue of Andrew Jackson on a rearing

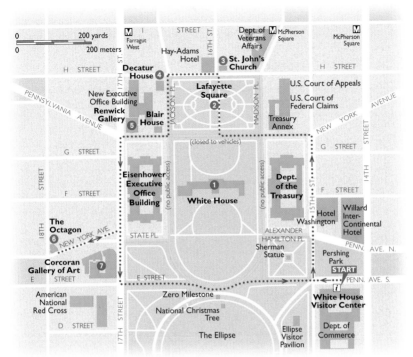

horse. Statues of foreign-born Revolutionary War heroes occupy the four corners: Marquis de Lafayette, Baron Friedrich von Steuben, Thaddeus Kosciusko, and Comte de Rochambeau. Many of the federal-style row houses along the square are White House offices, saved from the wrecking ball by Jackie Kennedy's determination to preserve the historical character of the square.

Across H Street from the square stands the gold-domed **St. John's Church** ❸ (see p. 128), "church of the Presidents." Catercorner from here, at Jackson Place and H Street, **Decatur House** ❹ (see p. 127) was built in 1818 for naval hero Stephen Decatur. Head south and turn right on Pennsylvania Avenue to see the 1810 white brick **Blair House,** where foreign dignitaries often stay; Robert E. Lee was offered command of the Federal Army here in 1861. On November 1, 1950—about midway through the Trumans' four-year stay at Blair House while the White House was being renovated—a policeman was killed on the street defending the President from an assassination attempt.

🅰 See area map pp. 106–107
▶ White House Visitor Center
↔ 1.5 miles
🕐 3 hours
▶ Corcoran Gallery of Art

NOT TO BE MISSED
• White House
• Lafayette Square
• Corcoran Gallery of Art
• Renwick Gallery

In that block, the **Renwick Gallery** ❺ (see p. 117), a Smithsonian museum, shows off its mansard roof and redbrick-and-sandstone exterior opposite the even more flamboyant **Eisenhower Executive Office Building** *(202-395-5895, call for tour information).* A massive piece of architecture originally named the Old Executive Office Building, the EEOB is one of the country's finest Second Empire-style structures. Built from 1871 to 1888 (just after the Renwick), the granite pile shocked locals who had expected a neoclassic temple to house the State, War, and Navy departments. It now holds various presidential agencies, including the National Security Council, the Office of Management and Budget, and the Office of the Vice President.

Head south on 17th Street and turn right on New York Avenue. The historic **Octagon** ⑥ (see p. 122) stands on the corner of 18th Street. Go back to 17th and turn right; on your right is the **Corcoran Gallery of Art** ⑦ (see pp. 118–19), housed in an attractive beaux arts building. From here, walk east on E Street, between the South Lawn of the White House and the Ellipse. *Marine One*, the President's helicopter, lands on the South Lawn, site

of the annual Easter Egg Roll. The National Christmas Tree, planted during the Carter Administration, stands on the Ellipse near the Zero Milestone, whence city distances are measured. On the corner of E and 15th Streets, a bronze William Tecumseh Sherman sits astride a horse, its tail raised toward the South, on the spot where he reviewed victorious Union troops. He faces the Greek Revival **Department of the Treasury** *(202-622-0896, call for tour information)* and its statue of Alexander Hamilton; sadly, the building blocks the view from the White House to the Capitol.

Cap the day at the rooftop bar of the 1918 Hotel Washington *(15th & F, May–Oct.)* for its views of the White House and Mall. ■

The Willard

While you're in the vicinity of the White House, peek inside the Willard Hotel *(202-628-9100)*, a Washington landmark since the 1850s at 1401 Pennsylvania Avenue. Nathaniel Hawthorne called the Willard the "center of Washington" for its role as the heart of political lobbying in the 19th century. The hotel has hosted Presidents, foreign heads of state, and a gaggle of celebrities from Mark Twain to Harry Houdini to Mae West.

In 1901 the venerable hostelry was rebuilt as a 12-story beaux arts hotel under the guid-

ance of Henry Hardenbergh, architect of New York's famous Plaza Hotel. Closed in 1968 when much of Pennsylvania Avenue hit the skids, the Willard reopened in grand style in 1986, a crowning achievement of the Congressionally created Pennsylvania Avenue Development Corporation.

The restored Willard boasts scagliola marble columns, polished wood paneling, glittering chandeliers, and other trappings of opulence. Shops, a bar, a café, and an elegant restaurant provide multiple opportunities to splurge. ■

Renwick Gallery

KNOWN AS MUCH FOR ITS ARCHITECTURE AS FOR ITS ART-work, the Renwick occupies a building designed in 1859 by James Renwick, architect of the Smithsonian Castle. Sandstone pilasters and garlands embellish the redbrick facade, while decorative iron-work crowns the tripartite mansard roof. The Second Empire-style building functioned as a military warehouse during the Civil War.

Upon its completion in 1874, the Renwick served as the original Corcoran Gallery until that collection moved to a new building nearby. The building then became the home of the U.S. Court of Claims from 1899 until 1964, when it was slated for demolition.

The Renwick came under the aegis of the Smithsonian Institution in 1965. Now a department of the Smithsonian American Art Museum, the Renwick offers changing exhibits of American crafts and decorative arts, as well as selections from its permanent collection of 20th-century American crafts.

The museum's centerpiece, the sumptuous (and recently refurbished) **Grand Salon,** awaits you at the top of a red-carpeted staircase. Plush poufs (circular settees), brocade sofas, and dark red walls covered with 19th-century paintings confer the air of a Victorian picture gallery. Among the pieces on display here are several fine portraits of Native Americans by George Catlin. There is also a handful of Western landscapes by Thomas Moran, including an 1893-1901 "Grand Canyon of the Yellowstone," but these will be returned to the Smithsonian American Art Museum after the latter's reopening in 2004. Lectures, concerts, and receptions are also held in the Grand Salon.

The smaller **Octagon Room,** opposite the Grand Salon, holds works by such iconic American painters as George P. A. Healy, Winslow Homer, and others. Additional rooms on this upper level contain fun, daring contemporary works in fiber, clay, wood, metal, glass, and mixed media. Exhibits from the permanent collection are rotated twice a year. The **first floor** holds short-term exhibits from the Renwick's own holdings or from those of other museums. ∎

Renwick Gallery
http://nmaa-ryder.si.edu/collections/renwick/main.html

Map pp. 106–107

17th St. & Pennsylvania Ave., N.W.

202-357-2700 or 202-357-1300

Metro: Farragut West; Bus: 34, N2

Grand indeed is the Renwick's 90-foot-long Grand Salon.

Corcoran Gallery of Art

Corcoran Gallery of Art

www.corcoran.org

- Map p. 106
- 500 17th St., N.W., between E St. & New York Ave.
- 202-639-1700
- Closed Tues.
- $ Wed., Fri., Sat., Sun.; free Mon. (all day) & Thurs. after 5 p.m.
- Metro: Farragut West; Bus: 80

Philanthropist William Corcoran founded his art gallery "for the purpose of encouraging American genius."

WASHINGTON'S OLDEST ART MUSEUM (AND THE THIRD oldest in the country), the Corcoran Gallery holds a distinguished collection of American and European artworks. It is the largest non-federal art museum in Washington, D.C.

The Corcoran started out three blocks north, in the building now called the Renwick Gallery (see p. 117), which was built to hold the collection of banker-philanthropist William Wilson Corcoran (1798–1888). When the collection outgrew its available space, an architectural competition resulted in the hiring of New York architect Ernest Flagg. His stately beaux arts-style building, the first of its kind in the city, was completed in 1897. Bronze lions flank the entrance to the symmetrical white marble building; the green copper roof caps an architrave inscribed with the names of such great artists as Rembrandt and Velázquez. Neither one of them, curiously, is represented inside.

Twin skylit atriums on the **first floor** draw the viewer in. A gift shop and auditorium lie off the north atrium, a café and numerous galleries off the south atrium. **Gallery I** generally holds temporary exhibits of contemporary American art. The smaller galleries contain excellent examples of 19th- and 20th-century art, including works by Renoir, Corot, Eakins, Homer, Cassatt, and Whistler. John Singer Sargent's 1878 "Oyster Gatherers of Cancale" and Edward Hopper's cool blue sailing scene, "Ground Swell" (1939), are attention grabbers.

The Corcoran is the place to learn that not everyone is cut out to be an artist—and that's a good thing. Samuel Morse's 1822 "Old House of Representatives," showing democracy in action as a routine business, was considered insufficiently dramatic for its time; discouraged, the painter went off and invented the telegraph.

Gallery 8 showcases the white-and-gold **Salon Doré**, an 18th-century room from Paris's St.-Germain quarter. Part of a sizable gift from industrialist and U.S. Senator William A. Clark (1839–1925) of Montana, the gilded room glitters with Corinthian pilasters, huge framed mirrors, and a ceiling mural.

Paintings on the **second floor** display a broad range of American styles, from the colonial period to the early 20th century. Among masterworks here are the magnificent "Washington Before Yorktown" (1824–25) by Rembrandt Peale and Frederic Church's "Niagara" (1857), described by a critic as the "finest oil picture ever painted on this side of the Atlantic."

Partly spurred by his rivalry with Church, Albert Bierstadt named his "Mount Corcoran" (1876–77) after the museum's benefactor in a bid to sell it to him (the plan worked; it's now part of the permanent collection). Also notable is his "Last of the Buffalo" (1889), which captures the essence of a West that was coming to an end: It shows an Indian spearing a buffalo as it rams his horse.

Art go boom!

With attendance exploding in the 1990s (from 100,000 visitors per year to nearly 900,000) and its collection expanding (from 12,000 to more than 16,000 pieces), the Corcoran needs to add a new wing. In 1999 the museum asked award-winning architect Frank O. Gehry, known for his innovative use of metals and indigenous

stone, to design the addition. The stunning new wing—its groundbreaking scheduled for 2003—will add 110,000 square feet of space for galleries, classrooms, offices, a restaurant and shop, and a center of art and technology for children. ■

Elsewhere on this floor are works by 20th-century artists Rothko, Sloan, Henri, Frankenthaler, and Warhol. Temporary and traveling exhibits of recent and current art often occupy much of the gallery space on this level. ■

Albert Bierstadt's "Last of the Buffalo" is one of the Corcoran's finest works.

It's a spooky little town

Intrigue. Mystery. Romance. Spies and spy catchers have captured the imagination of the moviegoing public for years, but in Washington—home of the CIA, the FBI, and the Pentagon—such cinematic proxies are redundant: The streets are alive with secret agents seeking or supplying classified information in nonstandard ways. Every now and then an agent is nabbed, exposing an underworld in which backyard barbecuers such as Aldrich Ames or Robert Hanssen turn out to have led lives of treachery and deceit.

"Rebel Rose" Greenhow and daughter

Spying caught on in Washington during the Civil War, when amateur agents on both sides of the Mason-Dixon Line scoured the capital city for war-related information. Thomas Nelson Conrad, a former Georgetown College headmaster, sat in Lafayette Park across from the White House for hours, meticulously noting President Lincoln's comings and goings. Conrad hoped to kidnap the President, then exchange him for prisoners of war. The Confederacy rejected his plan as infeasible.

The most romantic figure in Washington's espionage history may be the Rebel Rose. Intelligent, beautiful, and duplicitous, Rose O'Neal Greenhow (1815?–1864) haunted Washington's loftiest social circles before the Civil War, befriending Presidents, senators, and tycoons. When war broke out and men left for battle, spying became women's work.

None was more deft than Greenhow. Inside her modest house at 398 16th Street, N.W. (no longer standing), she plied unsuspecting targets with oysters, wild turkey, and champagne, pumping them for information all the while.

At one dinner party, Greenhow learned that the Federals were planning to move into Virginia. By quickly passing a coded message to Confederate Gen. Pierre G. T. Beauregard inside a woman's hair bun, she enabled him to reposition some of his troops—and, ultimately, to win the First Battle of Bull Run.

Soviet KGB colonel Vitaly Yurchenko made world headlines when he strolled into the U.S. Embassy in Rome in August 1985 and stated he wished to defect. Among the tidbits he had to share: NSA analyst Ronald Pelton had served as a double agent since 1980 and CIA officer Edward Lee Howard since 1984.

But Yurchenko was not a happy decamper. His ex-girlfriend, now the wife of a Russian diplomat stationed in Montreal, had no plans to leave her husband. Worse, the good colonel was relegated to a prisonlike existence in the United States, where his CIA case officers insisted on escorting him everywhere.

On November 2, 1985, Yurchenko and his CIA handler repaired to Georgetown's Au Pied de Cochon restaurant. At some point Yurchenko stepped out for a breath of fresh air and grabbed a cab to the Soviet embassy, where he rescinded his defection. Four days later he was on a plane to the Soviet Union, leaving the intelligence community debating whether he had been a legitimate defector or a KGB plant. A plaque has been installed in the booth where Yurchenko's "Last Supper" took place (the exact table is in dispute).

Following in the forked footsteps of Greenhow and Yurchenko came career CIA officer Aldrich Ames, who in 1994 was accused of exposing U.S. intelligence assets inside the former Soviet Union. The info swap occurred at Chadwick's, at 3205 K Street in Georgetown; the blue mailbox that Ames chalkmarked to signal a "dead drop" still receives letters on R Street at 37th. For his tipoffs, Ames received more than 2.7 million dollars from the Soviets—and life in prison from the Americans.

At this chummy beer-and-burger joint on Georgetown's K Street, the traitorous Aldrich Ames revealed to Russian agents the names of 20 CIA operatives working within the Soviet bloc; 10 were executed as spies.

TO WATCH A SPY

The Clandestine Capital emerges from the shadows in several formal ways. A few times each month, an unlikely team of former FBI, CIA, and KGB agents offer their popular **SpyDrive tour** of 30 espionage sites (866-779-3748, *www.spydrive.com*). Another spy tour is offered by the **Cold War Museum** (*www.coldwar.org*). Founded in 1996 to preserve Cold War history, this traveling exhibit is in search of a permanent home. The $30million **International Spy Museum** (*800 F St., N.W., www.spymuseum.org*), set to open in 2002, will house one of the world's largest collections of espionage paraphernalia, plus interactive exhibits and a store. Or go to the source: The CIA's Langley HQ (*www.cia.gov*) has a museum and store. —*Barbara A. Noe* ■

The Octagon

The Octagon
www.archfoundation.org/
octagon

🏛 Map p. 106

✉ 1799 New York Ave., N.W.

☎ 202-638-3221 or 202-638-3105

🕐 Closed Mon.

💲 $

🚇 Metro: Farragut West, Farragut North; Bus: 80

A gem of early Washington history, the redbrick Octagon stands bravely in the shadow of austere modern buildings. The neighborhood's first private residence, it was built about the same time as the White House. Its longevity owes much to its designer, William Thornton, also the first architect of the Capitol (see pp. 52–57).

The house was completed in 1801 for entrepreneur/political aspirant/urban pioneer John Tayloe III, who wanted to be near the power center of the new Republic. The location and stylish architecture paid off when the British burned the President's House in 1814 and the Madisons took shelter in the Octagon, just a five-minute walk from the executive mansion. Less than six months later, Madison signed the war-ending Treaty of Ghent in an upstairs parlor.

The Tayloes moved back in, grateful for the space; they raised 15 children. After Mrs. Tayloe's death in 1855, the Octagon was rented out as a girls' school, then a naval office, then a tenement house. The American Institute of Architects, whose modern headquarters looms just behind the Octagon, bought and restored the building in 1902.

Guided tours cover the structure's history and architecture. Take one to learn that "Octagon" is a misnomer: The house has only six sides, plus a curved front pavilion. ∎

The Octagon was not named for the shape of its staircase.

DAR Headquarters

Daughters of the American Revolution
www.dar.org

🏛 Map p. 106

✉ 17th & D Sts., N.W.

☎ 202-628-1776

🕐 Closed Sat.

🚇 Metro: Farragut West; Bus: 13B

This robust beaux arts building was built between 1905 and 1929 to serve as the headquarters of the Daughters of the American Revolution. Visitors may tour 33 **period rooms** that showcase early American decorative arts.

Highlights include an 18th-century Georgia tavern, an 1850s California whaling station, and a parlor furnished with pieces from the White House of James and Elizabeth Monroe. A museum displays exhibits drawn from the DAR's collection of 33,000 pieces of textile, ceramic, silver, glass, and furniture.

Built in the 1920s on the building's west side, **Constitution Hall** is a 3,800-seat horseshoe-shaped auditorium designed by John Russell Pope (the hand behind the National Gallery of Art, Jefferson Memorial, and National Archives). All kinds of concerts and lectures are held here, but Constitution Hall is best (or worst) known for the one that never took place: After the DAR's 1939 refusal to let black contralto Marian Anderson perform, Eleanor Roosevelt bravely stepped in, and Anderson sang at the Lincoln Memorial instead. ∎

Organization of American States

BLENDING CLASSICAL AND SPANISH COLONIAL ELEMENTS, this striking white building is headquarters for the Organization of American States, a regional alliance of nations promoting peace and economic cooperation among its 35 member countries from the Americas and the Caribbean.

Dedicated in 1910, the building was the work of architects Paul Cret (also the designer of the Folger Shakespeare Library; see p. 64) and Albert Kelsey. Just inside the elaborate triple-arched entryway, a lush villa-like courtyard boasts an octagonal Aztec-style fountain and overflows with tropical plants.

Upstairs, the large **Hall of the Americas** auditorium is graced by Tiffany stained-glass windows and a vaulted ceiling. In the back, a walkway through an Aztec garden leads to the **Art Museum of the Americas,** roofed in red tile, which must be entered from the 18th Street side. In several attractive wood-floor galleries, the museum offers temporary exhibits from its permanent collection, plus traveling shows of Latin American and Caribbean art and photography.

After your visit inside, head for the triangular park across 18th Street to view the raised-sword equestrian statue of Simon Bolívar the Liberator. It was presented to the United States in 1958 as a gift from Venezuela. ∎

Organization of American States

www.oas.org

🅰 Map p. 106

✉ 17th St. & Constitution Ave., N.W.

☎ 202-458-3000

🕑 Closed Sat.–Sun., museum open Tues.–Sun.

🚇 Metro: Farragut West; Bus: S1, 80

The OAS courtyard offers a whiff of the tropics.

John F. Kennedy Center for the Performing Arts

John F. Kennedy Center for the Performing Arts

www.kennedy-center.org

- Map p. 106
- Rock Creek Pkwy., N of Theodore Roosevelt Mem. Br.
- 202-416-8340
- Metro: Foggy Bottom–GWU; Bus: 80

ONCE MALIGNED AS AN UNSIGHTLY PILLBOX BY THE Potomac, the Kennedy Center has since earned the affection of Washingtonians as the city's premier bastion of culture. The center was designed by architect Edward Durrell Stone as a living memorial to President Kennedy, and its 1971 opening elevated the city from a cultural backwater to a leader in the live arts. The world's foremost opera singers, pianists, jazz musicians, dancers, and actors have performed on the stages of the Kennedy Center. The National Symphony Orchestra and the Washington Opera, both based here, have achieved recognition. Among the many groups that have performed at the center are the Metropolitan Opera, La Scala opera company, the Bolshoi ballet, and the Berlin Philharmonic.

As a national memorial, the building and grounds of the Kennedy Center are maintained by the National Park Service. A presidentially appointed board of trustees oversees the operation of the center, which is supported both by ticket sales and by private donations.

VISITING

Free guided tours are offered daily; call for times. You may also wander about on your own, but some theaters are closed to the public during rehearsals. Tickets *(purchase at box office or call 202-467-4600 or 800-444-1324)* must be purchased for most performances. The Millennium Stage program, however, offers free daily performances by ensembles in the Grand Foyer.

The Kennedy Center is at its best at night, when floodlights envelop its white Carrara marble in a vibrant glow. The north entrance opens into the **Hall of States,** its soaring ceiling lined with state flags; at the south entrance the **Hall of Nations** contains the flags of countries with diplomatic ties to the

2,450-seat **Concert Hall,** renovated in 1997, is home to the National Symphony; the 1,100-seat **Eisenhower Theater** is named for the President who signed legislation for a National Cultural Center; and the spectacular 2,300-seat **Opera House** completes the trio of big performance spaces. Just inside the north entrance, off the Hall of States, the 250-seat **American Film Institute** presents classic films and live performances. On the Roof Terrace level, the 500-seat **Terrace Theater** is a delightful venue for jazz combos, solo recitals, chamber music, and dramatic performances. For a cozier setting, take in an experimental or family show at the 350-seat **Theater Lab.** An Education Resource Center on this level offers a list of seminars, workshops, and art displays.

The Kennedy Center (left) sits serenely beside the Potomac River. Inside (below), patrons hurry to a performance of the Washington Ballet.

United States. Both halls lead to the **Grand Foyer**—at 630 feet one of the longest rooms in the world. This royal, red-carpeted space is outfitted with floor-to-ceiling mirrors and 18 crystal chandeliers donated by Sweden. Halfway down the hall you'll find Robert Berks's big, emotive bronze bust of Kennedy.

Seeing a performance is the reason to come here—and the best way to take in the auditoriums. The

Up on the **Roof Terrace,** walk out onto the patio for a view of the memorials, the Potomac, some Arlington high-rises across the river, and the distant form of the hilltop Washington National Cathedral. This promenade is always the place to be—especially on July 4th. ■

The National Geographic's state-of-the-art broadcast studio, inaugurated in 2001 to launch the National Geographic Channel in the U.S., forms part of the Society's complex.

More places to visit around the White House

NATIONAL GEOGRAPHIC SOCIETY

The National Geographic Society's magazines, books and guidebooks (including this one), maps, films, and classroom materials—all aimed at "the increase and diffusion of geographic knowledge"—are conceived and produced here at the organization's headquarters. Plenty of events, exhibits, and slide-illustrated lectures are also offered for visitors. Revamped in 2001, **Explorers Hall** features interactive displays that reveal little-known details about dinosaurs, undersea exploration, and other natural history topics. New 3-D models of the Grand Canyon, Mount Everest, and Afghanistan are part of a permanent collection on display. Temporary exhibits often highlight the work of National Geographic photographers and recent discoveries by National Geographic researchers. Explorers Hall also houses the National Geographic Store, which offers the Society's entire product line of books, magazines, games, videos, and educational products for sale.

Map p. 107 17th & M Sts., N.W. 202-857-7588 Metro: Farragut North, Farragut West

B'NAI B'RITH KLUTZNICK NATIONAL JEWISH MUSEUM

This comprehensive museum of Jewish art, history, and culture documents the life and festival cycles of Judaism. Named for the B'nai B'rith service organization and Chicago attorney Philip Klutznick, the collection includes 18th-century German and Italian berith knives, a silver phylactery (ca 1800) from Poland, 18th-century bronze Sabbath lamps, and a case of shining silver Torah finials and crowns. A 1790 letter from George Washington to Moses Seixas, a sexton of the Touro Synagogue in Newport, Rhode Island, promises that the U.S. government "gives to bigotry no sanction; to persecution no assistance."

Map p. 107 1640 Rhode Island Ave., N.W. 202-857-6583 Closed Sat. Metro: Farragut North, Dupont Circle

CATHEDRAL OF ST. MATTHEW THE APOSTLE

This redbrick 1890s cathedral, with its ribbed copper dome, is a commanding downtown presence. The funeral Mass of John F. Kennedy was held here in 1963; outside, three-year-old John Jr. bravely saluted his father's casket, creating an indelible image. A cavernous interior, embellished with mosaics, a skylit dome, flickering votive candles, and paintings and statues, forms a haven for prayer or meditation. ⓐ Map p. 106 ✉ 1725 Rhode Island Ave., N.W. ☎ 202-347-3215 Ⓜ Metro: Dupont Circle

CHARLES SUMNER SCHOOL

Its handsome M Street exterior rivets the gaze on this redbrick building, opened in 1872 as a school for African American children (and named for the abolitionist senator from Massachusetts). Now an archive and museum of the District's public schools, the Sumner School also hosts concerts, lectures, films, and art exhibitions.
ⓐ Map p. 107 ✉ 1201 17th St., N.W. ☎ 202-442-6060 🕐 Closed Sun. & July–Aug. Ⓜ Metro: Farragut North, Dupont Circle

DECATUR HOUSE

For his triumphs in the War of 1812, Commodore Stephen Decatur earned enough to build this three-story federal-style house on Lafayette Square. Benjamin Henry Latrobe designed the redbrick town house, completed in 1818, but Decatur never really got to enjoy the place: He was killed in a duel with a fellow officer 14 months after moving in. His wife rented the house to the likes of Henry Clay and Martin Van Buren. Guided tours cover the period-furnished rooms of the first floor and the lavish Victorian rooms of the second,

The Decatur House dining room contains period furnishings and table settings.

which still seem to pulse with the vibrant presence of a later owner, Mrs. Truxtun Beale, who presided over a salon for ambassadors and politicians in these quarters.
ⓐ Map p. 107 ✉ 748 Jackson Pl., N.W. ☎ 202-842-0920 🕐 Closed Mon. 💲 $ Ⓜ Metro: Farragut West

DEPARTMENT OF STATE

What must foreign heads of state think when they arrive at the door of this drab 1961 building to meet with the Vice President or Secretary of State? Most of them aren't given the time to form a negative opinion; they are whisked to the eighth floor, where they step into a sparkling geode of elegance.

The designers of the **Diplomatic Reception Rooms** may have calculated this dismay-cum-delight effect on visiting dignitaries. Perhaps you'll experience a similar sensation when you visit the Department of State's suite of rooms decorated with one of the country's finest collections of early American furnishings. A 45-minute tour—which reveals such surprises as Paul Revere silver, George Washington's Chinese porcelain, and Francis Scott Key's side chairs—takes in eight of the reception rooms. *(Tours were interrupted after the attacks of Sept. 11, 2001; call 202-647-3241 for updates.)* Elsewhere you'll come across portraits of George and Martha Washington by Rembrandt Peale, paintings by Gilbert Stuart and John Singleton Copley, and Chippendale furniture from Philadelphia, New York, and Boston. The rooms on the south side—among them the breathtakingly grand State Dining Room—give impressive views of the Mall and its monuments.
ⓐ Map p. 106 ✉ 23rd and C Streets, N.W. ☎ 202-842-0920 🕐 Closed Mon. 💲 $ Ⓜ Metro: Farragut West

DEPARTMENT OF THE INTERIOR MUSEUM

Tucked inside the Department of the Interior, this small, quiet museum has a particularly good exhibit on Native Americans, including a gallery of Edward S. Curtis photos. Displays chronicle the Interior Department's 1930s origins, when it comprised the National Park Service, U.S. Fish and Wildlife Service, U.S. Geological Survey, and the Bureaus of Mines,

More places to visit around the White House

Indian Affairs, Reclamation, and Land Management. Drawings, homestead claims, handmade maps, exploration tools, and videos tell the story of the country's settlement.
Map p. 106 ✉ 1849 C St., N.W. ☎ 202-208-4743 🕐 Closed Sat.–Sun. Ⓜ Metro: Farragut West, Foggy Bottom–GWU

HAY–ADAMS HOTEL

The elegant Italian Renaissance-style Hay–Adams, one of Washington's finest small hotels, fronts the north side of Lafayette Square, offering a good view of the White House. Built in the 1920s, the hotel occupies the site of residences owned by statesman John Hay and historian Henry Adams. Stop in for afternoon tea, fine dining, or the nighttime piano bar.
www.hayadams.com Map p. 107 ✉ 16th & H Sts., N.W. ☎ 202-638-6600 Ⓜ Metro: Farragut West, McPherson Square

The bronze of Albert Einstein at the National Academy of Sciences

NATIONAL ACADEMY OF SCIENCES

Free concerts and art exhibits are often held in this think tank. Otherwise it is best known to visitors for its outdoor bronze of Albert Einstein, seated on white granite among a glade of elms and hollies. Robert Berks, who sculpted the similarly mudpie-style JFK bust in the Kennedy Center, uses proportion to emphasize his subject's amazing head. A 28-foot-wide sky map swirls at Einstein's feet.
Map p. 106 ✉ 2101 Constitution Ave., N.W. ☎ 202-334-2000 Ⓜ Metro: Foggy Bottom–GWU

ST. JOHN'S CHURCH

Every U.S. President since James Madison has found some occasion to worship at St. John's Episcopal Church. The yellow stucco building, with its white wood bell tower and bright gold dome, was completed in 1816 after a design by Benjamin Henry Latrobe, who also helped conceptualize the Capitol, the White House, and neighboring Decatur House. A national historic landmark, the church is open weekdays from 9 a.m. to 3 p.m. for meditation and prayer. A skylit dome and memorial stained-glass windows brighten the interior, where a brass plate marks the President's Pew—No. 54.
Map p. 107 ✉ 1525 H St., N.W. ☎ 202-347-8766 🕐 Closed Sat. Ⓜ Metro: Farragut West, McPherson Square

ST. MARY'S EPISCOPAL CHURCH

Originally St. Mary's Church for Colored People, this handsome building was the city's first house of worship for black Episcopalians. The congregation pooled its money to hire famous architect James Renwick, only to learn that his design would break their budget. Around again went the collection plate. With the extra $3,000 thus raised, a simple yet lovely church was built; the first services were held in 1887. The altar triptych depicts two saints of African descent; the center window is Tiffany stained glass. A national historic landmark, the church boasts working gas lights and iron radiators.
Map p. 106 ✉ 730 23rd St., N.W. ☎ 202-333-3985 🕐 Closed Sat. Ⓜ Metro: Foggy Bottom–GWU ■

With its eclectic mix of entertainment venues, hotels, historic structures, museums, retail establishments, and federal and private office buildings, downtown offers something for everyone.

Downtown

Detail at the entrance to the National Building Museum

Downtown

WASHINGTON'S DOWNTOWN HAS BEEN LOCATED JUST NORTH OF THE MALL since the city's founding in 1791. Sprung from the intersection of Pennsylvania Avenue and Seventh Street, where the city's main street met the main northern thoroughfare, the area has since sprawled to 14th Street and Louisiana and Massachusetts Avenues. Booming with new vitality, downtown buzzes with new restaurants, shops, theaters, and galleries, making all the more reason to come visit its clutch of long established museums.

Throughout the 1800s, boutiques, hotels, and theaters thrived downtown, catering to the area's residents. The turn of the 20th century, however, brought the exodus of affluent merchants and residents to the suburbs, thereby opening up the downtown area to successive groups of lower income citizens. Then came the assassination of Martin Luther King, Jr., in 1968, instigating riots and the large-scale abandonment of commercial ventures. As buildings fell into miserable disrepair and the crime rate exploded, the area became one to avoid.

The outlook soon changed. In 1972, Congress created the Pennsylvania Avenue Development Corporation to plan the revitalization of Pennsylvania Avenue—the neglect-

R.I. AVE.
VERMONT AVE.
STREET
Mary McLeod Bethune Council House N.H.S.
N STREET
National City Christian Church
M ST.
Thomas Circle
To Metropolitan A.M.E. Church
GREEN CT.
L STREET
MASSACHUSETTS AVENUE
12TH STREET
11TH STREET
9TH ST.
STREET
L STREET
Washington Convention Center (opens March 2003)
Mt. Vernon Square (opens Spring 2003)
City Museum of Washington, D.C.
NY. AVE.
29
13TH STREET
29
K STREET
Franklin Square
14TH STREET
STREET
McPherson Square M
National Mus. of Women in the Arts
NEW YORK AVENUE
Washington Convention Center
I ST.
MASSACHUSETTS AVENUE
I ST.
H ST.
Friendship Arch
New York Avenue Presbyterian Church
G ST.
H STREET
G PL.
Metro Center M
CHINATOWN
Smithsonian American Art Museum
MCI Center
National Building Museum
H STREET
13TH ST.
12TH STREET
11TH STREET
Metro Center M
Nat. Portrait Gallery M
Gallery Place-Chinatown M
G ST.
F STREET
Metro Center M
Petersen House
Ford's Theatre N.H.S.
International Spy Mus. (opens Spring 2002)
Gallery Place-Chinatown
Judiciary M Square
National Theatre
Warner Theatre
E ST.
PENNSYLVANIA QUARTER
5TH STREET
Judiciary Square
4TH STREET
3RD STREET
2ND STREET
Judiciary Square
PENN. AVE. N.
Freedom Plaza
PENN. AVE. S.
J. Edgar Hoover FBI Building
1 50
Shakespeare Theatre
1 50
E ST.
Judiciary Square
D ST.
Wilson Building
14TH STREET
PENNSYLVANIA AVE.
Old Post Office
Market Square
INDIANA AVE.
Federal Triangle M
Ronald Reagan Building & International Trade Center
i
Dept. of Commerce
U.S. Navy Mem. & Naval Heritage Ctr.
Archives-Navy Memorial M
To Surratt Boardinghouse
John Marshall Park
C STREET
Mellon Auditorium
E.P.A.
Internal Revenue Service
Dept. of Justice
AVENUE
Federal Trade Commission
CONSTITUTION
1 50 AVENUE
National Archives

Washington, D.C.
NW NE
Subject area
SW SE
Md.
Potomac
Virginia
Anacostia
Md.

Vendors and courting couples are often spotted on downtown sidewalks.

ed streetscape was unbefitting for what many consider to be America's Main Street. Initially, the PADC focused on renovating Pennsylvania Avenue's historic buildings: the Old Post Office, the Willard Hotel, and the National and Warner Theatres. Each successful venture encouraged the next, as city planners and developers saw the possibility of returning downtown into a dynamic commercial district and residential neighborhood.

Coupled with renovation, new construction brought the Washington Convention Center (1982); Market Square (1984, *N of the Archives*); the Lansburgh (1992, *8th & E Sts.*), a residential/retail/cultural arts venue complex; and the new convention center (scheduled to open in 2003, *N of Mt. Vernon Sq.*). In the last few years, 3.5 billion dollars have been invested in the area's development, in-

cluding 30 new restaurants.

The most important development, however, was the arrival of the MCI Center in 1997. This entertainment and sports arena showcases a year-round parade of sports events and concerts; its presence alone has upped annual downtown visitation from three to eight million people.

All this new life complements several museums that often have been overshadowed by those on the nearby Mall, including the National Museum of Women in the Arts, the Smithsonian American Art Museum, the National Portrait Gallery, the National Building Museum, and the National Archives.

Amid the modernization rush, tiny Chinatown clings to its heritage. Once clustered on the north side of Pennsylvania Avenue in the 1880s, the enclave established its distinctive appearance after moving to the H Street area in the 1930s, where it remains today. The area features Cantonese, Szechuan, and Hunan restaurants, as well as traditional pharmacies selling all kinds of unusual remedies. ∎

Ford's Theatre National Historic Site

Ford's Theatre National Historic Site
www.nps.gov/foth
🅰 Map p. 130
✉ 511 10th St., N.W.
☎ 202-426-6924
🚇 Metro: Metro Center; Bus: D6

Petersen House
✉ 516 10th St., N.W.

A WORKING THEATER AND A MUSEUM TO ONE OF THE nation's most tragic dramas, Ford's Theatre has a morbidly compelling quality. John Wilkes Booth shot President Abraham Lincoln here on April 14, 1865, five days after Lee's surrender at Appomattox. Lincoln's untimely death pushed to legendary heights the historical greatness he had achieved by keeping the Union from falling apart.

The theater closed shortly thereafter, serving as an office building and later as a storage facility. Acquired by the National Park Service in 1933, it was restored to

Scene of the crime: The Presidential Box is on permanent display at Ford's.

its original 1865 splendor and reopened to the public in 1968. The theater now hosts a full program of contemporary American plays.

The ornate interior boasts the authentically re-created **Presidential Box** with American flags, lace curtains, red velvet wallpaper, plush seats, and the original settee. You

can walk up to the balcony for a look. No one sits there anymore—which is just as well, since it's apparently the only bad seat in the house.

When the theater is not in use, Park Service officials offer short informative talks on the night's events. Booth, a disgruntled actor, shot Lincoln in the head and then jumped down to the stage, breaking a small leg bone; he supposedly shouted "*Sic semper tyrannis*" (thus always to tyrants) and hobbled off. He fled on horseback through the southern Maryland countryside, only to be caught 12 days later and shot dead.

The **museum** downstairs contains several noteworthy artifacts, including the .44-caliber derringer Booth used in the shooting, the hunting knife he used to stab one of Lincoln's box companions, and the clothes Lincoln was wearing (look for his custom-made black overcoat from Brooks Brothers).

Continue following the night's events across the street at the **Petersen House,** where Lincoln was taken. Never regaining consciousness, the President died the next day. Peek into the parlor where Mary Todd Lincoln waited through the night, the back parlor where Lincoln's secretary of war began investigating the murder, and the period-furnished bedroom in which Lincoln died. A weary sadness pervades these cramped quarters, the empty boots and jacket suggesting an owner that will never return. ■

National Museum of Women in the Arts

THIS WELL-DESIGNED MUSEUM FOCUSES SOLELY ON THE work of women artists. Founder and art collector Wilhelmina Cole Holladay felt that women were often completely overlooked in standard art history texts. Determined to correct the imbalance, her resulting museum, which opened in 1987, showcases and promotes the talent of women artists from the Renaissance to the present.

Notable in itself, the Renaissance revival building began as a Masonic temple in 1907, served as a movie theater in the 1960s, and, after being threatened with demolition in the early 1980s, was purchased by Holladay in 1983. Restored to its former glory, the grand hall shines with polished marble floors and decorative plasterwork. On the mezzanine level's north side, added during the restoration, you can still see a Masonic cartouche with the letter *M* worked in.

Begin your visit by touring the permanent collection on the third floor, which chronicles women's artistic achievements from the 16th century to modern times. In the **Renaissance Gallery** here look for Lavinia Fontana's 1580 "Portrait of a Noblewoman"; Fontana was the first widely known woman to

sustain a career as an artist. The lovely "Portrait of Princess Belozersky" (1798) by French artist Élisabeth Vigée-Lebrun, depicting a bright-eyed woman with brown ringlets and a gypsy scarf, hangs in the **18th-century Gallery.** The **19th-century Gallery** houses "Sheep by the Sea" (1869) and other works by Rosa Bonheur (1822–1899), famous for her straightforward depictions of animals, as well as "The Bath" (1891) and others by Impressionist Mary Cassatt (1844–1926). Georgia O'Keeffe (1887–1986) and Helen Frankenthaler (1928–) are among those represented in the **20th-century Galleries.**

Special exhibits are found on the first and second floors as well as on the mezzanine level. The fourth floor holds an 11,000-volume library and research center. ■

National Museum of Women in the Arts
www.nmwa.org
🅰 Map p. 130
✉ 1250 New York Ave., N.W.
☎ 202-783-5000
$ $
🚇 Metro: Metro Center; Bus: S2, 13A

Audrey Flack's "Hannah: Who She Is" (1982, oil on canvas) depicts the artist's daughter as a woman/goddess.

Pennsylvania Quarter

**Pennsylvania
Quarter**

 Map p. 130

⊠ 5th to 8th & G to
I Sts.

 Metro: Gallery
Place—Chinatown;
Bus: 70

THE SHINING STAR OF DOWNTOWN'S REVITALIZATION,
the Pennsylvania Quarter neighborhood, also called the Seventh
Street corridor, is quickly becoming Washington's hippest hangout.
With an explosion of luxury apartment complexes, trendy restaurants,
theaters, and galleries joining a panoply of established and future
museums, the once neglected area teems with life both night and day.

**Chinese
influences along
Seventh Street**

The real success story of the
Pennsylvania Quarter begins with
the abandoned Lansburgh department store. In 1992 this imposing
building was rehabilitated into a
mixed-use complex housing 385
luxury residential units, retail space,
and a cultural arts venue. The combination of location, amenities, and
cultural flavor attracted people
(former attorney general Janet
Reno and actor Harry Hamlin have
been among its residents); and new
businesses moved into the commercial spaces.

The Lansburgh's reigning

tenant, the nationally renowned
Shakespeare Theatre *(450
7th St., 202-547-1122)* moved to
Seventh Street from its Capitol
Hill quarters in 1992. Devoted
to presenting the Bard's works—
as well as those of his contempo-
raries and of the playwrights he
influenced—the theater is considered one of the nation's most prestigious. Its noted company of
classical actors has included Dixie
Carter, Hal Holbrook, Stacy Keach,
Kelly McGillis, Jean Stapleton, and
Richard Thomas. In fall 2003, the
well-established repertory **Woolly**

Mammoth Theatre opens across the street.

With the Lansburgh's success, other cultural and entertainment venues were drawn to the area. The most important contributor to revitalization is the colossal **MCI Center** *(7th & F Sts., 202-628-3200)*, which draws thousands of visitors on any given day. Opened in 1997, the 20,000-seat arena hosts circuses, ice skating events, and concerts. It's also home to the Washington Wizards and Mystics basketball teams (men and women, respectively) and the Washington Capitals hockey team. Sports aficionados enjoy the memorabilia and interactive games at the center's **MCI National Sports Gallery** *(202-661-5133)*.

Keeping in step with the quarter's new face, many of its museums—including the **National Portrait Gallery** (see pp. 137–38), the **Smithsonian American Art Museum** (see p. 136), and the **National Archives** (see pp. 140–41)—are undergoing extensive renovations.

And more museums are planned. The **International Spy Museum** *(www.spymuseum.org)*, which tells the inside story of international spies and espionage, is just opening at 800 F Street. Starting in 2003, the **City Museum of Washington, D.C.,** housed in the beautiful 1903 beaux arts-style former Carnegie Library sitting on Mount Vernon Square at Eighth and K Streets, will relate the city's history from its earliest days. The **Newseum,** an interactive museum devoted to newsmaking, will occupy its new home at the corner of Sixth and Pennsylvania in 2005.

Sandwiched amid all this growth, Washington's small **Chinatown** continues to thrive *(6th to 8th Sts. & G to H Sts.)*. Established here since the 1930s, it has a distinctive appearance and atmosphere. Buildings sport Chinese architectural ornamentation and shops and groceries cater to an all-Chinese clientele; restaurants—Full Kee, Hunan Chinatown, and others—prepare dim sum, tea-smoked duck, crispy whole fish, and other Szechuan and Cantonese dishes. ■

Top: The Friendship Arch recalls the quarter's Chinese legacy with stylized script and fiery dragons. Below: Shakespeare Theatre buzz

Smithsonian American Art Museum

Smithsonian American Art Museum
www.americanart.si.edu
🅰 Map p. 130
✉ 8th & G Sts., N.W.
☎ 202-275-1500
🕐 Closed for renovation until 2004
🅼 Metro: Gallery Place–Chinatown; Bus: 70

McKendree Robbins Long, Sr.'s "Vision from Book of Revelation" (1966) invites contemplation.

WITH SOME 39,000 PAINTINGS, SCULPTURES, PRINTS, DRAW-ings, photographs, and folk art, this museum holds the nation's premier collection of works by American artists. Dating from 1829, making it the nation's oldest federal art collection, the museum has renamed itself several times over the years in an effort to accurately reflect its character. Most recently known as the National Museum of American Art, in October 2000 it was rechristened the Smithsonian American Art Museum.

The museum's home—the stately, neoclassic Old Patent Office Building—is undergoing an extensive renovation that will boost the number of works on display from 5 to 40 percent. When it reopens in 2004, the art will be displayed on three levels, with a special "open storage" gallery allowing you to browse through over 5,000 artworks densely packed in Plexiglas cases. In the interim, the collection remains a strong force in the world of American art: More than 500 of the museum's best paintings and sculptures have been exhibited in 70 cities.

The **19th-century collection** includes paintings by such notables as Albert Pinkham Ryder and Impressionist Mary Cassatt, and sculptures by Daniel Chester French and Augustus Saint-Gaudens. Among the favorites are the luminist scenes of the American West by Albert Bierstadt and Frederic Church, representing the flowering of grand landscape painting. The **20th-century collection** has such famous works as Edward Hopper's "Cape Cod Morning" (1950), Robert Rauschenberg's "Reservoir" (1961), and Georgia O'Keeffe's "Yellow Calla" (1926).

In the realm of folk art, you won't want to miss "The Throne of the Third Heaven of the Nations Millennium General Assembly." After he received a vision, local janitor James Hampton meticulously constructed this ecclesiastical piece for the Second Coming. Wrapping old furniture, jelly jars, and light bulbs in gold or silver tin foil, he is believed to have worked on the piece for 14 years; the throne was discovered in a rented garage upon his death in 1964.

Outside, looking as if about to leap from its pedestal, "Vaquero" (Luis Jimenez, 1980) jazzes up the building's columned front portico on G Street. The acrylic-urethane-fiber-glass-steel sculpture shows a shouting Mexican cowboy, pistol raised, hanging onto a bucking blue horse. ∎

Jo Davidson's 1951 likeness of Franklin D. Roosevelt emerges from a block of marble.

National Portrait Gallery

CELEBRATING THE NATION'S HEROES, INTELLECTS, ROGUES, and famous personalities, the National Portrait Gallery offers a revealing look at America's history through portraiture and sculpture. Currently closed for an extensive renovation, the museum plans to reopen in the fall of 2004.

The gallery's collection includes some 18,500 objects in media ranging from traditional oil-on-canvas and marble to photographs and drawings. Each likeness meets the museum's mandate to depict those "who have made significant contributions to the history, development and culture of the people of the United States."

The expected portraits are here, including at least one of every U.S. President from George Washington to Bill Clinton; they hang in the **Hall of Presidents.** Among the many representations of George Washington look for Gilbert Stuart's now iconic 1796 "Lansdowne" portrait. Painted for the Marquis of Lansdowne, Washington is endowed with a dignity and magnetism that befits the father of our nation.

Throughout the gallery you will also find the faces of writers, military leaders, inventors, captains of industry. Must-see likenesses include an engraving of Pocahontas dating from 1616—one of the oldest portraits in the collection; a photograph of Lincoln's assassin, John Wilkes Booth; an etching of Benedict Arnold; John Singleton Copley's "Self-Portrait" (1780–84); Edgar Degas's "Mary Cassatt" (ca 1880–84); and Jo Davidson's Buddhalike terra-cotta bust of Gertrude Stein. Among the rarest images are David Geary's 1954 color photographs of Marilyn Monroe singing to troops in Korea. Other famous depictions include Civil Rights champions Eleanor Roosevelt and Martin Luther King,

National Portrait Gallery
www.npg.si.edu

Map p. 130

8th & F Sts., N.W.

202-275-1738

Closed for renovation until 2004

Metro: Gallery Place—Chinatown; Bus: 70

Jr., sports figures Casey Stengel and Jack Dempsey, and musicians Duke Ellington and Benny Goodman.

A Civil War collection holds portraits of Jefferson Davis, Ulysses S. Grant, Robert E. Lee, Frederick Douglass, Harriet Beecher Stowe, and the "cracked plate" photograph of Abraham Lincoln, taken in 1865 just two months before he died. The gallery's media collections include a wonderful selection of caricatures by Al Hirschfeld and all the portrait covers of *Time* magazine.

The idea of a national portrait gallery dates back to 1857, when Congress commissioned George P.A. Healy to paint official portraits of all the Presidents for the White House. In the years following World War I, a national portrait gallery was proposed as part of a general art collection then being formed within the Smithsonian Institution. The National Portrait Gallery of the United States was officially opened to the public in 1968.

The collection resides in the Old Patent Office Building, a handsome Greek Revival edifice completed in the mid-19th century. During the Civil War it served as a hospital, with Walt Whitman among those attending the suffering within its walls. Don't miss the spectacular Victorian-style **Great Hall** on the third floor, with its colorful skylight, fluted pilasters, and elaborate ceiling medallions. ∎

Sunlight streams through the Metropolitan A.M.E. Church's stained-glass windows.

Downtown churches

Looking somewhat anomalous among downtown's modern face, several historic churches serve as reminders of the past.

So many Presidents have worshiped at the **New York Avenue Presbyterian Church** (*1313 New York Ave.*) that it's nicknamed the Church of Presidents. The stately redbrick building dates from 1951, but a church has graced this site since 1820. Lincoln, though never a member, used to stand in his pew during prayer.

Several Presidents, including James Garfield and Lyndon B. Johnson, attended services at the **National City Christian Church** (*5 Thomas Circle*). The church's present 1930 neoclassic building, designed by John Russell Pope, boasts a 200-foot-high steeple.

The **Metropolitan A.M.E. Church,** the city's earliest black church congregation, formed in 1822. Its 1886 Victorian Gothic building (*1518 M St.*) has hosted numerous distinguished black preachers, including Rev. Jesse L. Jackson. Parishioner Frederick Douglass frequently spoke from the pulpit as well. ∎

National Building Museum

THE GARGANTUAN REDBRICK PENSION BUILDING IS ONE of Washington's least known architectural treasures. Designed by civil engineer Gen. Montgomery C. Meigs, the 1887 Victorian building was referred to by critics, who thought it an eyesore, as Meigs's Old Red Barn. Though the building was badly deteriorated by the 1960s, a study highlighting its potential as a museum space saved it from proposed demolition. Congress called for its restoration in 1980 to house a museum about architecture, urban planning, engineering, and design.

National Building Museum
www.nbm.org
🅰 Map p. 130
✉ 401 F St., N.W.
☎ 202-272-2448
🚇 Metro: Judiciary Square; Bus: D6

Girdling the entire building, the most striking exterior feature is the 3-foot-high terra-cotta frieze designed by Bohemian-born sculptor Caspar Buberl (1834–1899). Depicting a procession of Civil War infantry, artillery, cavalry, and other units, it is emblematic of the building's original purpose: serving the needs of Union veterans.

The interior is just as impressive. The spectacular **Great Hall** will take your breath away. Standing in the middle of this immense, light-filled, open space, bordered on all sides with four tiers of arcades and high clerestory windows, you feel as if you've stepped into an Italian gallery. Eight Corinthian columns, made of brick but plastered and painted to resemble marble, rise 75 feet high on either side of a central fountain. Meigs modeled aspects of this room after several Roman palaces and churches, including the Palazzo Farnese.

The museum **galleries** ring the Great Hall's first two levels. The museum shop, café, and temporary exhibits are found on the first level, while temporary and permanent exhibits are located on the second.

There are two permanent exhibits of note. Through photos and other artifacts, the small but excellent **Building a Landmark** display presents the building's history and its architect. The **Washington: Symbol & City** exhibit presents a good overview of D.C.'s development, complete with hands-on displays. A push-button map of L'Enfant's original city plan, models of the evolving Mall, and a six-minute video of citizens talking about Washington provide insight into the city. Don't-miss artifacts include the five rejected designs for the U.S. Capitol and a copy of the 1792 letter signed by Jefferson dismissing city planner L'Enfant for his refusal to take orders from the District Commissioners. (Both exhibits reopen in the summer of 2002.) ■

Elegant arcaded galleries and marbleized columns define the cavernous Great Hall, which measures 116 by 316 feet.

National Archives

**National
Archives**

www.archives.gov

🅰 Map p. 130

✉ Constitution Ave.
between 7th & 9th
Sts., N.W.

☎ 202-501-5205

🕐 Closed for renovation
until 2003

🚇 Metro: Archives—Navy
Memorial; Bus: P1,
13A

**"The Constitu-
tion"—a stylized
depiction of
James Madison
submitting the
Constitution
to the 1789
Constitutional
Convention—
looms above the
Charters of
Freedom.**

SERVING AS THE NATION'S MEMORY BANK, THE NATIONAL
Archives contain several billion pages of documents, including the
original parchment copies of the Declaration of Independence, the
U.S. Constitution, and the Bill of Rights. John Russell Pope, architect
of the Jefferson Memorial, designed the distinguished 1935 building
expressly for the purpose of housing these all-important manifestos.
In fact it was Jefferson, author of the Declaration, who first voiced
concern about the deterioration of the national records.

Ringed with 72 massive Corinthian
columns, Pope's grand neoclassic
edifice takes up a whole city block.
Bas-reliefs decorate the pediments
atop the north and south porticos.
The 39 limestone steps that front
the south portico on Constitution
Avenue represent the 39 signers of
the Constitution. The foot-thick
bronze doors at the top of the stairs
soar 40 feet high.

Entering through the street-
level entrance door, you first pass
through a visitor center and intro-
ductory exhibits. Then head directly upstairs to the echoing,

semicircular Rotunda that rises to a
75-foot-high dome. New York artist
Barry Faulkner painted in the early
1930s the two large murals decorat-
ing the Rotunda. "The Constitution," on the right side, depicts
James Madison presenting the document to George Washington. "The
Declaration of Independence," on
the left, shows Thomas Jefferson
submitting the proclamation to
John Hancock, presiding officer of
the Continental Congress.

The low-lit, somber hall beneath
the Rotunda creates the right mood
for viewing the United States' most

important paperwork: the Charters of Freedom. Each sheet of the Declaration of Independence, the U.S. Constitution, and the Bill of Rights lies in a new state-of-the-art case that fiercely protects the document against air and moisture. The cases allow all four pages of the Constitution to be shown at the same time. At night, and in the event of an emergency, the documents are retracted into a deep vault for safekeeping.

Other documents relating to the founding of the United States are displayed in the Rotunda room as well, among them an original 1297 version of the Magna Carta (on loan from the Perot Foundation). A predecessor of the U.S. Bill of Rights, the Magna Carta outlines the English system of trial by jury, equality before the law, and freedom from arbitrary arrest.

Encircling the Rotunda room, the large **Permanent Exhibit Gallery** showcases other treasures from the Archives. The Public Vaults feature rotating selected documents; interactive exhibits let visitors piece together strands of history. Draft records, marriage certificates, birth and death records, and other documents within the Community and Family History Vault and the Military Vault especially illustrate the way that ordinary people's lives are affected by government.

Adjacent to the Rotunda room, the **East** and **West Galleries** mount temporary exhibits drawn from the permanent collections. Past exhibits have covered such diverse topics as the history of photography in the 20th century and the history of gifts given to U.S. Presidents.

OTHER TREASURES

The Archives preserve for posterity more than 18 million maps, aerial photographs, and charts; 9 million still photos; hundreds of thousands of films, videos, and sound recordings; and numerous other data files and artifacts. The National Archives and Records Administration, established in 1934 to oversee what to

save, deems less than 2 percent of the federal records worthy of permanent storage.

Representing more than 200 years of history, the repository is creating a rich paper trail. Among the original treasures are the Louisiana Purchase Treaty, the Emancipation Proclamation, Mathew Brady's Civil War photographs, Robert Peary's polar expedition journals, Dust Bowl photographs, Indian treaties, recordings of FDR's fireside chats, captured German records and Japanese surrender documents from World War II, the check that paid for the territory of Alaska, and Nixon's letter of resignation.

The Archives are popular among scholars, students, historians, and researchers of all kinds, who are welcome to use the research facilities here and in College Park, Maryland. Alex Haley used slave ship manifests in researching his novel *Roots*. Opened in 1994, the Maryland branch is the largest archival facility in the world. ∎

In search of guidance outside the National Archives

Federal Bureau of Investigation

Federal Bureau of Investigation
www.fbi.gov/fbinbrief/tour/tour.htm

◬ Map p. 130

✉ 9th & E Sts., N.W.

☎ 202-324-3447

🕐 Tours offered in a.m. only; closed Sat.–Sun.

🚇 Metro: Archives–Navy Memorial; Bus: 30, 32, 34

Note: As of press time tours were suspended indefinitely. Call ahead.

A special agent shows the correct stance for shooting a firearm, the most popular part of the tour.

A HULKING CONCRETE STRUCTURE COMPLETED IN 1975, the J. Edgar Hoover Federal Bureau of Investigation Building houses the main investigative branch of the Department of Justice, which sits on the other side of Pennsylvania Avenue.

The investigation into federal crimes began with President Theodore Roosevelt's Secret Service agents, although specifically trained operatives did not come under the Department of Justice until 1908. Over the next years the concept of a premier law enforcement agency jelled, officially becoming the Federal Bureau of Investigation in 1935. The man most responsible for shaping the FBI was J. Edgar Hoover, under whose directorship between 1924 and 1972 it gained national importance and power. Hoover is known for engaging in controversial activities, including investigations into the lives of private and public citizens alike. In an effort to increase public awareness of the FBI, he established public tours in 1937.

The popular **one-hour tour** begins with a short film, followed by a walk through exhibits exploring the FBI's history. You'll learn all about its fight against gangsters (don't miss the weapons used by Al Capone and other gangsters); its past and present ten most wanted fugitives; and its famous cases against organized and white-collar crime, counterintelligence, drug operations, and terrorism. The tour visits several analysis laboratories where scientific examinations of DNA, weapons, and crime-scene materials take place. At the end of the tour an FBI agent gives a firearms demonstration.

Tickets are first come, first served; you may also reserve them through your congressional representative. ■

More places to visit downtown

FREEDOM PLAZA

The frequent venue of free concerts, popular rallies, and ethnic festivals, this granite plaza is anchored by an equestrian statue of Casimir Pulaski, the Polish nobleman who fought for America in the Revolution and was mortally wounded at the siege of Savannah. The plaza offers a sweeping view down Pennsylvania Avenue to the U.S. Capitol. Inlaid in bronze on the ground are L'Enfant's 1791 city plan, as are outlines for the Congress House and President's Palace. Among the many etched quotes about the city of Washington gracing the plaza is one by Civil War historian Bruce Catton that may resonate with visitors: "Whatever we are looking for, we come to Washington in millions to stand in silence and try to find it."

 Map p. 130 ✉ Pennsylvania Ave. between 13th & 14th Sts., N.W. Ⓜ Metro: Metro Center; Bus: 32, 34, 36

MARY MCLEOD BETHUNE COUNCIL HOUSE

Now a national historic site, this former residence of educator Bethune (1875–1955), who founded Bethune-Cookman College in Daytona Beach, Florida, and the National Council of Negro Women, stores and displays artifacts pertaining to African American women's history. In addition, the house museum is decorated with Bethune's original furnishings and photographs.

www.nps.gov/mamc Map p. 130 ✉ 1318 Vermont Ave., N.W. ☎ 202-673-2402 🕐 Closed Sun. Ⓜ Metro: McPherson Square; Bus: 52, 53, 54

NATIONAL THEATRE

The sixth theater erected on this site since 1835, the National Theatre can claim to be Washington's oldest continuously operating theater. The current theater replaced an ornate five-story structure in 1922. Sumptuous decor includes dazzling chandeliers and the satin brocaded stage curtain. Unlike most large modern theaters, the mezzanine and balcony are close to the stage, giving the space an intimate feel. Lavish Broadway and pre-Broadway shows are staged here, many

starring illustrious actors of stage and screen. www.nationaltheatre.org Map p. 130 ✉ 1321 Pennsylvania Ave., N.W. ☎ 202-628-6161 Ⓜ Metro: Federal Triangle, Metro Center; Bus: 32, 34, 36

OLD POST OFFICE

This castlelike building was erected in the 1890s as headquarters for the U.S. Post Office. A group of preservationists prevented its demolition in the 1970s, and after several years of renovation it reopened as a spacious pavilion of government offices, retail stores, and eateries. For one of the best views in the downtown area, take the elevator ride 12 floors up to the top of the tower. From here the city is at your feet—you can easily pick out such landmarks as the Washington National Cathedral, the Basilica of the National Shrine of the Immaculate Conception, the U.S. Capitol, and the Mall's monuments and

Performers entertain the lunchtime crowd at the Old Post Office Pavilion.

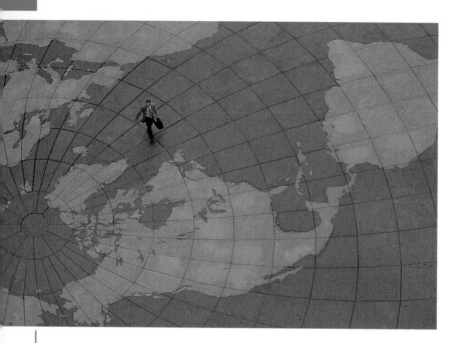

Around the world in more than 80 steps: A 100-foot-diameter map of the world graces the U.S. Navy Memorial plaza.

museums. Directly below on the west side spreads the red-roofed complex of Federal Triangle, home to the Environmental Protection Agency, U.S. Customs Service, and other agencies; these robust buildings stand where a red-light district called Murder Bay flourished in the mid-19th century. www.nps.gov/opot Map p. 130 Pennsylvania Ave. & 12th St., N.W. 202-606-8691 Metro: Federal Triangle; Bus: 13A, 32, 34, 36

U.S. NAVY MEMORIAL & NAVAL HERITAGE CENTER

Situated directly behind the National Archives, this small center contains ship models, artifacts, photographs, a gift shop, and a selective computerized log of sea service personnel, including veterans of the Navy, Marine Corps, Coast Guard, and Merchant Marines. A 242-seat theater screens an exciting DVD film called *At Sea (fee)*. Outside, the circular memorial features a 7-foot bronze statue of "The Lone Sailor" and a correctly oriented granite map of the world. Bronze relief sculptures of famous events in naval history ring the perimeter of the memorial. Bands and choral groups perform here in spring and summer. www.lonesailor.org Map p. 130 701 Pennsylvania Ave., N.W. 202-737-2300 Closed Sun. March–Oct., Sun.–Mon. Nov.–Feb. Metro: Archives–Navy Memorial; Bus: 32, 34, 36

WARNER THEATRE

A block east of the National Theatre, the Warner Theatre started life in 1924 as a silent-movie palace and vaudeville stage. From the mid-1940s to the late 1960s, it only presented movies. Thereafter it functioned mainly as a rock concert venue until shutting down completely. Reopened in 1992, the refurbished theater dazzles the eye with crystal, red velvet, and gold leaf; it now hosts a varied program of established dance and theater companies. www.warnertheatre.com Map p. 130 13th St. between E & F Sts. 202-628-1818 Metro: Federal Triangle, Metro Center; Bus: 32, 34, 36 ∎

Cobbled streets, redbrick row houses, and mule-drawn canalboats elicit Georgetown's historic past. Come evening, the city's young and trendy flock to the neighborhood's buzzing bars, clubs, and restaurants.

Georgetown

Cobblestones of Georgetown

Georgetown

WASHINGTON'S POSHEST SQUARE MILE IS A HIGH-OCTANE COCKTAIL OF cultural refinement and giddy nightlife. While side streets exhibit elegant federal and Victorian architecture, Wisconsin Avenue and M Streets inject excitement with boutiques, bars, and restaurants.

Riggs Bank at the corner of Wisconsin and M marks Georgetown's center.

Georgetown began life as a tobacco inspection and shipment port at the confluence of Rock Creek and the Potomac, the highest navigable point on the river, on a 795-acre tract acquired by Scottish immigrant Ninian Beall in 1703. The Maryland Assembly established a town there in the 1750s and named it for George II. After independence, when the country was planning its federal city, Georgetown had become a thriving trade center, with lordly merchants' houses rising on the hill and artisans' houses and warehouses dotting the riverside. The new city proved a boon to Georgetown's silversmiths, cabinetmakers, and other craftspeople, who did a brisk business fitting the White House and other federal buildings. During the Civil War, Georgetown's significant black community made it an important Underground Railroad stop.

In 1871 the city of Washington annexed Georgetown. By then the little town needed the capital more than the reverse. The advent

of the railroad and steam power had greatly diminished the importance of the C&O canal and thus Georgetown at its eastern end. In the first half of the 20th century, Georgetown lost the cachet of its early years; it functioned primarily as industrial muscle for Washington, its foundry and mills supplying iron, paper, and coal. During Roosevelt's administration, white-collar workers began moving back into Georgetown; then, in 1950, Congress declared it a national historic district, speeding its

restoration and return to fashion.

Rock Creek and the Potomac River form Georgetown's eastern and southern borders; to the west lies Georgetown University and north the hill on which Dumbarton Oaks sits. In these blocks have lived members of such clans as the Washingtons, Lees, and Kennedys. Today diplomats, politicians, journalists, and socialites walk shady brick sidewalks and party in book- and art-filled houses, lubricating the wheels of government, business, and culture. ∎

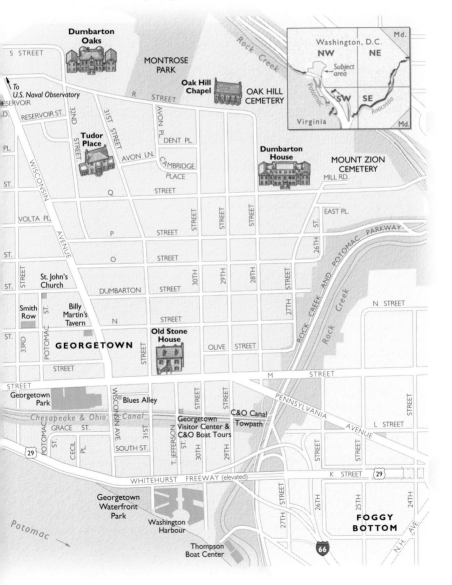

The federal-style town houses of Cox's Row typify the neighborhood's elegant architecture.

Brick sidewalk tour

With its inviting brick sidewalks, tree-lined streets, and historic architecture, Georgetown was made for the leisurely stroller. You can try seeing the city's oldest neighborhood by car, but traffic moves slowly on the narrow streets, some of which are still cobbled and veined with trolley tracks. Better to leave the car behind.

If you drive in, you can find street parking, but it may take a while, especially on the weekends. The network of streets north of M Street is your best bet for parking, though you should pay attention to the signs—most streets are zoned for two-hour parking from 7 a.m. to 9 p.m. (except Sunday). There are several parking lots along M Street and below the canal. Metro buses service M Street and Wisconsin Avenue. You can also walk from the Foggy Bottom–GWU Metro—just over a half mile to the eastern edge of Georgetown.

If you do start from the Metro, you'll head west on Pennsylvania Avenue. Across the bridge, Pennsylvania feeds into M Street, Georgetown's main avenue for shopping, dining, and partying. Spring and summer evenings, the ten-block stretch from here to the Francis Scott Key Bridge is a steady parade of the chic, the casual, and the grungy. While the shops tend to be upscale, the bars, dance floors, and some restaurants cater to a young

crowd, liberally supplied by Georgetown and George Washington Universities. One long-standing favorite restaurant on the east end of M, **La Chaumière** (*2813 M St., 202-338-1784*) features French provincial cuisine; hanging brass pans and a central fireplace give a rural ambience, nicely contrasting with the busyness outside.

Continue west on M to the **Old Stone House** ❶ (*3051 M St., 202-426-6851, closed a.m., & all day Mon.–Tues.*), one of the oldest structures in the city. A craftsman named Christopher Layman built the first floor of the three-story house of local fieldstones in 1765, probably as both home and shop. A legend, later disproved, that George Washington had a headquarters here helped preserve the house. In 1953 the National Park Service acquired the property, restored it, and opened it to the public in 1960. The ground floor has a shop with replicas of 18th-century tools and a kitchen with cast-iron stove. On the second floor, built

Casual posh: Georgetowners relax on shady sidewalks.

by the next owner, you'll find an oak-paneled dining room, a parlor, and bedrooms.

Cross M Street and head downhill on Thomas Jefferson Street to the eastern terminus of the **C&O Canal ❷**, a muddy-bottomed, shallow waterway, bordered by a towpath, that served as a key shipping link in the 19th century. Originally slated to stretch 460 miles to Pittsburgh and connect with the

See area map pp. 146–47

M and 29th Sts. (Metro: Foggy Bottom–GWU)

2 miles

2 hours

St. John's Church

NOT TO BE MISSED

- Old Stone House
- Washington Harbour
- Cox's Row

Ohio River, the Chesapeake and Ohio Canal, begun in 1828, made it only 185 miles up the Potomac to Cumberland, Maryland, where work stopped in 1850. From April through October you can take a scenic ride *(fee)* on a replica 19th-century canalboat, starting from the Georgetown Visitor Center *(1057 Thomas Jefferson St., 202-653-5190)*. A mule-drawn ride is a nice way to while away an hour.

Don't miss the small brick row houses that run along the canal just off Thomas Jefferson Street; they were built after the Civil War as homes for laborers. A few are now Asian take-out restaurants.

Go from the old to the new at the bottom of the hill by crossing K Street under the Whitehurst Freeway; in front of you spreads **Washington Harbour** ❸, a 1980s complex of offices, apartments, shops, and restaurants. At the entrance stands J. Seward Johnson's

realistic sculpture, *Let's Just Skip the Meeting.* You can see why they'd want to play hookey when you wander over to the central pool with its fountains, plantings, and views of the Potomac, Roosevelt Island, the Kennedy Center, Watergate, and the high rises of Rosslyn, Virginia, across the river.

Next head up 31st Street. On your right, just below M, **Cannon's Seafood** has supplied locals with fresh fish since 1937. The alleyway across the street from Cannon's leads to **Blues Alley** *(1073 Wisconsin Ave., 202-337-4141)*, which may look like a dive outside but is actually Washington's swankiest jazz joint. On nights when a big name is in town, you might see 50 people lined up just hoping for no-shows on the reservation list. Definitely call ahead, and expect to pay a hefty cover charge—well worth it for the intimate setting.

Turn right from the alley onto Wisconsin

the new federal city. Gen. Uriah Forrest owned the house then; in 1800–1835 it belonged to William Marbury of the landmark *Marbury v. Madison* case, in which the Supreme Court established the doctrine of judicial review.

For a small detour into cinematic history, cross to the north side of M Street and walk west a short distance. Tucked away near a gas station, an eerily familiar 75-step stone stairway stretches upward. Known as the **Exorcist Steps,** the stairs played a prominent role in the 1973 horror classic *The Exorcist.*

Fortunately, nothing ominous awaits you at the top of the stairway on Prospect Street, which has some of Georgetown's oldest and most impressive houses. For an easier ascent to Prospect, go back east on M and turn left onto 34th Street. At the corner of 34th and Prospect stands the classic Georgian-style **Halcyon House** (1786). Built by Benjamin Stoddert, the first secretary of the Navy and an important Georgetown landowner, the house recently underwent a major restoration. A few buildings away is **Worthington House,** No. 3425, built in 1798 by prominent lawyer John Thomson Mason. Note the 24-paned windows lining both main floors. Just past 35th Street look for **Prospect House** (1788), No. 3508, another imposing Georgian, home of a 19th-century shipping merchant. Much of its structure and impressive gardens lie hidden behind a brick wall.

Prospect Street ends at 37th Street, the eastern edge of **Georgetown University** ❺, whose main entrance is at 37th and O. The Gothic-spired university is best known for its schools of medicine, law, and foreign service, and its basketball team.

From 37th, turn back east on N; across 34th on the north side runs a line of five stately brick town houses known as **Cox's Row** ❻, built in 1805 by Georgetown mayor John Cox. Down the block, in 1957–1961, Sen. John F. Kennedy and his wife, Jacqueline, lived at 3307 N Street, a three-story house with a fanlight and black shutters. On the corner of Potomac and O, Anglican services are still held at **St. John's Church** ❼, opened in 1804, and

Avenue and walk back up to M Street. This intersection is the area's busiest; the gold dome on the ornate old Farmers and Mechanics Branch of the Riggs National Bank serves as a landmark. Turn left heading west on M to the nearly block-long glitzy mall called **Georgetown Park** *(3222 M St.);* it has upmarket shops and restaurants on three levels, with skylit courtyards and chuckling fountains.

Continue west on M until you reach No. 3276, **Dean and Deluca,** a gourmet food shop where you can pick up lunch. Erected in 1865, the building sits on a site that also held markets in the 18th century.

A little farther down the street, just before Key Bridge, you'll come to the 1788 **Forrest-Marbury House** ❹ (now the Embassy of Ukraine). Here George Washington met with local landowners in 1791 to work out the agreement on the sale of their land to create designed by William Thornton, first architect of the Capitol.

East of Wisconsin Avenue lie several more blocks of elegant 19th-century houses. Bare brick alternates with stucco facades painted in muted shades of blue, gray, red, and yellow. Victorian bay windows and turrets are much in evidence. At the corner of Dumbarton and 31st Streets look for **Berry House,** built in 1810 when the street level was several feet higher. As a result, the front door stands unusually far above the street.

Walk one block south to N Street and turn left to see a noteworthy block. On your right is No. 3038, built in 1805, the longtime home of statesman Averell Harriman and his wife, Pamela. The large brick town house has a love-ly arched doorway and odd, shingled dormers.

In No. 3017 across the street, Jackie Kennedy lived for several months after the assassination of President Kennedy. Almost directly facing it stands the 40-room **Laird-Dunlop House,** No. 3014, built in 1799. Robert Todd Lincoln, the only son of Abraham Lincoln to survive into adulthood, lived here from 1918 to 1926. Especially notable is the raised fanlight doorway.

If you stroll on to 28th and Olive Streets, you'll come upon one of Georgetown's oldest and smallest houses. The tiny wooden cottage at 1222 28th St. was built sometime before the Revolution, though the date is uncertain. Very little has changed in its basic structure. ∎

Glitzy Washington Harbour, a splash both day and night.

Georgetown crawl

Before Adams Morgan and U Street became hip, anyone seeking nightlife went to Georgetown. Though club options have now spread to those and other locations in the city and suburbs, Georgetown still reigns supreme as party central. If you've a mind to join the fun, be aware that the revelry can be excessive at times, particularly on Halloween and the rare occasions the Redskins win the Superbowl. Traffic woes—Key Bridge, the main feeder from Virginia, is a solid jam on weekend evenings—and parking problems don't deter the crowds along M Street. Cabbing here makes the most sense; the fare for two from downtown costs about

as much as a single movie ticket.

There are many options to choose from. A sampler: The first thing you may notice when you enter **J. Paul's** (3128 M St., 202-333-3450) restaurant and tavern is the oyster shucking at the street-side raw bar. J. Paul's also features crab cakes and steaks and a 95-year-old mahogany bar. Down the street, **Clyde's of Georgetown** (3236 M St., 202-333-9180), with its interesting daily specials, old stone fire-place, vintage model planes, and gold record commemorating the 1976 hit song "Afternoon Delight"—inspired by Clyde's afternoon appe-tizers—offers a delicious dining experience. For simpler fare such as pizza, locals and stu-dents hit **The Tombs** (1226 36th St., 202-337-6668), a block from Georgetown University, beneath the upscale restaurant, **1789.**

If you're a sports fan, stop by **Champions** (1206 Wisconsin Ave., 202-965-4005) sports bar, where events are shown on multiple screens. Those who prefer music to sports will enjoy **Mr. Smith's** (3104 M St., 202-333-3104), which features a piano bar and an outdoor patio. Many people consider **Nathan's** (3150 M St., 202-338-2600) the place to go for week-end dancing.

If you want to find a table on the weekend at Georgetown's hot spots, arrive early. ∎

Dumbarton Oaks

Dumbarton Oaks

www.Doaks.org

🗺 Map p. 147

✉ Garden entrance, 31st & R Sts., N.W.; museum entrance, on 32nd bet. R & S Sts.

☎ 202-339-6401

🕐 Gardens & museum closed a.m.; museum also closed Mon.

💲 Gardens: $ April–Oct., free in winter; museum: donation

The Pebble Garden

AN ANTIQUE PROVENÇAL FOUNTAIN, A MINIATURE ROMAN amphitheater, and a 16th-century French-style arbor are among the many treasures awaiting you in Dumbarton Oaks's terraced gardens. Spring to fall, the gardens offer an ever changing display that includes early blooming dogwoods, magnolia blossoms, and cherries, peonies and roses, day lilies and chrysanthemums.

Presiding over the gardens is a federal-style house acquired in 1920 by Mildred and Robert Woods Bliss, stepsiblings and antiquities collectors who married and traveled widely in the Foreign Service. They hired the architectural firm McKim, Mead and White to renovate and enlarge the house for their extensive library and collection of Byzantine and pre-Columbian art. In 1940 they conveyed the property and museum to Harvard University, though they remained actively in-

volved in Dumbarton Oaks until their deaths (Robert in 1962, Mildred in 1969). In 1944 a series of informal conferences held here laid the foundation for the establishment of the United Nations.

Today the main part of the house functions as Harvard's center for Byzantine studies and is not open to the public. Visitors are allowed only into the gardens, music room, and museum. A garden library, built in 1963, is open by appointment only.

Orangery; a pre-Civil War fig tree climbs its walls. Through here you access the main gardens. Outside, to the right, a tremendous beech presides over the **Beech Terrace.** Next, steps take you down to the **Rose Garden,** planted with nearly 1,000 varieties of roses. Just below are gardens with fountains and a wisteria-draped arbor based on a 16th-century French design. At the property's edge, a winding walkway skirts the reflecting pool of Lovers' Lane and its small amphitheater. Farther north the garden becomes less formal, with flowering cherry trees, a hillside of golden forsythia, and views of Dumbarton Oaks Park, given by the Blisses to the National Park Service and now part of Rock Creek Park.

Head back uphill to the **Ellipse,** an oval formed by a double ring of hornbeams, pruned to a uniform 16 feet, enclosing a Provençal fountain. Up the steps lies another landscaping masterpiece: **The Pebble Garden** is composed of rounded stones embedded on edge to create a terrace of varying textures; espaliered magnolias and wisteria vines bedeck the walls. Walk on past the pool to the grassy sweep of the **North Vista,** behind the main part of the house.

Visit the **music room** and the **museum** through the 32nd Street entrance. The Renaissance-style Music Room is a must-see for its antique European decorations. El Greco's "The Visitation" hangs with other paintings and tapestries. Concerts are held throughout the year.

Filled with natural light, the museum galleries display Byzantine and pre-Columbian art objects. The Byzantine collection includes 6th-century ecclesiastical silver and 13th-century mosaic icons. The circular galleries holding exquisite pre-Columbian works were designed by Philip Johnson. ■

VISITING

The 10-acre formal gardens, designed by landscape architect Beatrix Farrand, spread across a gentle hill and down to a wooded valley. Ornate ironwork and stonework—in the form of gates and balconies, fountains and urns, pillars and stairways—adorn the grounds. Brick paths lined by boxwoods and perennial borders lead from one garden to the next, and little trellised bowers offer places to sit and admire the sound of birdsong, scent of flowers, and garden aesthetics.

A self-guided tour brochure, available at the entrance, highlights the gardens and plantings. Inside the gates to the right stands an old Katsura tree, its limbs almost touching the ground. Head up the path to the early 19th-century

Tudor Place Historic House and Garden

Tudor Place

www.tudorplace.org

⛰ Map p. 147

✉ Visitor entrance,
1644 31st St., N.W.

☎ 202-965-0400

🕐 House closed
Sun.–Mon., garden
closed Sun.

💲 $

🚇 Metro: Dupont Circle,
Foggy Bottom–GWU;
Bus: D6

SIX GENERATIONS OF THE PETER FAMILY, RELATIVES TO George Washington and Robert E. Lee, lived in this handsome neoclassic house. During those years (1805–1984), the country passed through many wars, two of them waged just outside the Peters' door.

Martha Custis, daughter of George Washington's stepdaughter, married Thomas Peter, son of Georgetown's first mayor. In 1805 the Peters purchased an 8.5-acre city block in Georgetown Heights; to design a home there, they hired William Thornton, architect of the Capitol—the building Martha would watch burn from a window of the house in 1814. The Peters' daughter Britannia inherited Tudor Place in 1854. A Southern sympathizer during the Civil War, she allowed Union officers to board at the house to prevent its becoming a hospital. In 1984 the house was transferred to the Tudor Place Foundation.

The one-hour guided tours of Tudor Place begin with a look at Thornton's design. On the south lawn, a domed "temple" portico projects from the two-story stuccoed main building, while one-

The south-facing temple portico presides over a serene sweep of lawn, set apart from the hubbub of Georgetown.

story hyphens connect the two wings, lending a pleasing symmetry. The curving portico creates a convex wall of windows, which can be lifted to allow a breeze to circulate. All the furniture, silver, porcelain, and decorative objects are original, some pieces acquired from an auction at Mount Vernon in the early 19th century. Not limited to one period, the furnishings reflect 180 years of family continuity. The restored Pierce-Arrow automobile out in the garage, for example, was maintained by Armistead Peter III from 1919 until his death in 1983.

The 5.5 acres of gardens include a sweeping south lawn, woodlands, and a formal federal-style garden on the house's north side. Among highlights are trees and roses planted in the early 19th century, and an old-fashioned "flower knot" pattern of English boxwoods and pathways. ■

Dumbarton House

Dumbarton House was built on a hill high above Rock Creek in the first years of the 19th century, when only a few large houses dotted the port of Georgetown. Originally called Cedar Hill, the federal-style brick house's second owner, Charles Carroll, changed its name in 1813 to Belle Vue; he sheltered Dolley Madison here the following year, after she fled the burning White House. In 1915, to make way for the extension of Q Street into Georgetown, the house had to be put on rollers and moved approximately 100 feet north, to its current location.

In 1928, the National Society of the Colonial Dames bought the house (which would become its headquarters), and renamed it Dumbarton House after the Rock of Dumbarton, the tract that originally encompassed much of present-day Georgetown. With great attention to detail, the Colonial Dames—one of the world's largest private historical preservation societies—restored the house to its early 1800s appearance.

The guided 45-minute tour here covers the parlor, dining room, library, music room, and three bedrooms, with furnishings primarily from the federal period, including furniture such as a mahogany sewing work table, silver, ceramics, textiles (including a carriage cloak belonging to Martha Washington's granddaughter), and paintings by artists such as Charles Willson Peale. Out back, the small formal courtyard and garden add a grace note to the estate. ∎

Dumbarton House
www.dumbartonhouse.org
- Map p. 147
- ✉ 2715 Q St., N.W.
- ☎ 202-337-2288
- ⏱ Closed. Sun.–Mon. & Aug. Tours at 10:15, 11:15, & 12:15
- 💲 $
- Ⓜ Metro: Dupont Circle, Foggy Bottom—GWU; Bus: D6

Oak Hill Cemetery

Occupying some of the city's finest real estate, this 1849 cemetery rambles over a hill above Rock Creek Park. William Wilson Corcoran, founder of the Corcoran Gallery and Riggs National Bank, bought 15 acres from George Corbin Washington, a great nephew of the first president. The following year he gave the parcel to the new congressionally established cemetery company, and James Renwick, architect of the Smithsonian Castle, designed the iron entrance gates and the English Gothic-style chapel.

At the attractive brick and sandstone gatehouse, you can buy a map showing the locations of 68 graves and mausoleums, including those of W. W. Corcoran, John Marbury, Edwin Stanton (Lincoln's secretary of war), Dean Acheson (Truman's secretary of state), and members of the Peter family from nearby Tudor Place. Also buried here is Philip Graham, publisher of the *Washington Post,* as is his widow Katharine, his successor at the *Post* until her death in 2001.

A murky overcast day makes a good time for wandering through this crowded village of the dead, with its elaborate Victorian monuments and obelisks. Winding paths circle knolls that offer views of adjoining Montrose Park, Rock Creek, and the parkway. Hiding behind trees and high walls, the property at the corner of 28th and R Streets is another Georgetown mansion with a long past: Evermay was built in the 1790s by Scotsman Samuel Davidson with funds acquired from selling some of his extensive property to the new federal city. Family members lie buried in Oak Hill. ∎

Oak Hill Cemetery
- Map p. 147
- ✉ 3001 R St., N.W.
- ☎ 202-337-2835
- ⏱ Closed Sat.–Sun., holidays, & during funerals
- Ⓜ Metro: Dupont Circle, Foggy Bottom—GWU; Bus: D6

Famous denizens of Georgetown

By day, the power of national government is exercised in the monumental edifices clustered around Washington's Mall and at both ends of Pennsylvania Avenue. At night, some of the action moves to Georgetown, residence down the decades of political leaders, media heavies, diplomats, legal minds, writers, and society doyennes—names in the news past and present. In elegant 19th-century houses, the House or Senate bill that seemed doomed by day may be quietly revived over cocktails or at a formal dinner party, where fine wines and informed conversation are equally savored.

Even Hollywood celebrities have found their way to Georgetown, though at times reluctantly. Elizabeth Taylor, married briefly to Virginia Sen. John Warner, has said she thought the couple would live on his hunt country estate, near Middleburg, where the talk centered on horses. Instead, she found herself in Warner's Georgetown house at 3240 S Street, where dinnertime chat explored the ins and outs of arms control and tax bills.

As a bachelor, Sen. John F. Kennedy lived in a Victorian town house at 1528 31st Street. In fact, John and Jackie first met at a Georgetown dinner party in 1951. He later claimed that he made up his mind at that party that she was "the one," though they dated only sporadically over the next year. He finally proposed, and a year later, he and his bride moved to 3271 P Street. President-elect Kennedy purchased the three-story brick town house at 3307 N Street in 1960, while Jackie was in the hospital giving birth to their first child, Caroline. Tastefully austere, the 1811 house occupies an especially handsome street of classic federal-style homes.

After her husband's death, Jackie Kennedy and her children moved temporarily to 3038 N Street at the invitation of statesman W. Averell Harriman. (His widow, Pamela, a celebrated hostess and Democratic party activist, later became President Clinton's Ambassador to France.) The former First Lady soon bought the house across the street at 3017 N Street,

but departed for New York after only a few months to escape the busloads of gawkers.

Just up the street at 3014 N Street stands another grand federal-style mansion with a presidential link. Built in 1799, it was the home of Robert Todd Lincoln, the 16th President's oldest son, a railroad lawyer who served as secretary of war and minister to England. He lived here until his death in 1926. The current owners, a prominent newspaper couple, consider themselves "caretakers" of the 40-room property.

The top ranks of government have always been well represented in Georgetown. Dean Acheson, President Truman's secretary of state, lived in the Georgian town house at 2805 P Street. Here Acheson hosted a farewell luncheon for the president on his last day in office. A four-story town house at 3018 Dumbarton Street is the one-time home of Supreme Court Justice Felix Frankfurter. Later Henry Kissinger, secretary of state under Presidents Nixon and Ford, briefly rented it.

Washington Post owner Katharine Graham, often called "the most powerful woman in America," lived in the mansion at 2920 R Street. Set well back from the street, it is approached by a semi-circular gravel drive—a real Georgetown luxury—that gives it the look of a French country estate.

Writers, too, have found Georgetown's vibrant society congenial. In 1922 Sinclair Lewis moved to Washington from his Minnesota hometown, calling it the perfect place to write, "with neither the country nor lake tempting one out to play, as in Minnesota, nor the noise and phone calls of New York." As soon as he made his fortune with *Main Street,* which later won him the Nobel Prize for Literature, he moved to a stately Georgetown house, at 3028 Q Street. In the early 1960s, Katherine Anne Porter reportedly completed her acclaimed novel *Ship of Fools* while a boarder at 3106 P Street; with the money it made her she bought her dream house complete with lawns and a rose garden—outside of Georgetown. ■

Washington Post owner Katharine Graham lived in the above house (R & 30th Sts., N.W.) from 1947 until her death in July 2001. Sen. John F. Kennedy bought a house (right and below) on N Street when he was elected president in 1960; from here he announced his Cabinet choices.

More places to visit in & around Georgetown

Tending bar at Martin's

BILLY MARTIN'S TAVERN

Opened by William G. Martin, a Georgetown University sports star who also played professional baseball in the early part of the 20th century, Billy Martin's Tavern has been operating at the southwest corner of N Street and Wisconsin Avenue since 1933. Four generations of Martins have managed the restaurant, and many of the staff have been here for years. Stop in for a draft or a meal and imbibe this Georgetown tradition.

Wood floors, dark paneling, and a friendly bar create the ambience of a European pub. Among menu offerings are crab cakes, bison steaks, linguine with clam sauce, and daily home specials such as meatloaf and corn beef with cabbage. The back of the menu lists some of the politicos and celebrities that have visited or been regulars, including former Secretary of State Madeleine Albright, actress Elizabeth Taylor, and the Kennedys. Martin's serves three meals a day, with a good brunch on weekends, at moderate prices.

✉ 1264 Wisconsin Ave., N.W. ☎ 202-333-7370 🚇 Metro: Foggy Bottom–GWU, Rosslyn; Bus: 32, 34, 35, 36

KREEGER MUSEUM

Designed by Philip Johnson and Richard Foster and completed in 1967, the modernist travertine house of late philanthropist David Lloyd Kreeger and his wife, Carmen, opened in 1994 as an art museum showcasing the Kreegers' collection of 19th- and 20th-century paintings and sculptures. A chairman of GEICO insurance company, Kreeger was famous for his contributions to the city's cultural life, at various times serving as president of the National Symphony, the Washington Opera, and the Corcoran Gallery of Art. The art collection, which the Kreegers began acquiring in 1959, includes more than 180 works by artists such as Monet, Cézanne, van Gogh, Rodin, Picasso, Miró, Munch, Kandinsky, and Chagall; among Washington artists represented are Gene Davis, Sam Gilliam, and Thomas Downing. Also on display are pieces of traditional African and Indian art. The building's spectacular **Great Hall,** with its 25-foot-high domed ceiling, was often the scene of concerts; an amateur violinist, Kreeger played his Stradivarius with such greats as Pablo Casals, Isaac Stern, and Pinchas Zukerman. www.kreegermuseum.org ✉ 2401 Foxhall Rd., N.W., 1.5 miles N of Georgetown ☎ 202-337-3050 🕐 Closed Sun.–Mon.; visit by guided 90-minute tour only. Reservations required 💲 Donation suggested

MOUNT ZION CEMETERY

When Mount Zion Methodist Episcopal Church realized in 1879 that it needed a place to bury its members, it leased a parcel of land on the edge of the Dumbarton Cemetery. On this site had already been buried several generations of slaves and freed blacks. The resulting Mount Zion Cemetery, now showing its age with toppled and crumbling gravestones, is Washington's oldest black burial ground. The last burial occurred here in the 1950s, and in 1975 it was designated a national historic landmark. At the back is a brick vault where slaves escaping to the North via the Underground Railroad are said to have hid. 🗺 Map p. 147 ✉ Q St., between 27th St. & the Buffalo Bridge ☎ 202-234-0148 🚇 Foggy Bottom–GWU, Dupont Circle; Bus: D6 ∎

A lively mix of cultures, cuisines, lifestyles, and music awaits in the neighborhoods beyond downtown, while stately mansions preserved as embassies and museums recall 20th-century glamour days.

Dupont Circle & Adams Morgan

A local artist at work in Dupont Circle

Dupont Circle
& Adams Morgan

AT THE INTERSECTION OF THREE MAJOR THOROUGHFARES, DUPONT CIRCLE anchors the city's buzzing residential neighborhoods, replete with row houses, cafés, bookstores, restaurants, and galleries.

Chess match at Dupont Circle

Dupont Circle sits at the crossroads of New Hampshire, Massachusetts, and Connecticut Avenues, marking a key interface between business and residential Washington. The circle itself, centered on a marble fountain, is in constant motion, with pedestrians passing through and traffic circling around. Yet it is also a place for casual picnics, jackets-off meetings, people-watching, and general loafing. Bicycle messengers form little impromptu gatherings, chess players study their next moves, joggers pound through. In 15 minutes the scene has changed, and a new series of small dramas has begun to unfold.

Starting in the 1870s, the area, then called Pacific Circle, began developing into the most elite neighborhood in Washington. New millionaires with fortunes from mining, steel, railroads, and shipping started putting up ornate beaux arts mansions and attending receptions and musicals in one another's houses, every hostess seemingly intent on outdoing her neighbor. A newspaper reporter in the 1880s wrote that going to lavish parties at Senator William M. Stewart's "Castle" (torn down in 1901) made him feel like Marco Polo at the court of Kublai Khan. This belle epoque

lasted only until the 1930s, when the stock market crash and Depression forced many of the wealthy to scale back.

Some mansions were razed, though many were sold to private clubs, organizations, and embassies; surrounding row houses became boarding establishments and apartments. In the 1960s, the area was a haven for hippies and other counterculturalists, and the circle became a focal point for marches and rallies. Development threatened many of the area's old "palaces" in the 1970s, but the efforts of preservation groups to save the neighborhood resulted in its designation as a historic district that stretches all the way to T Street.

Over the ensuing years Dupont Circle became the core of Washington's young gay community. Today the bars, restaurants, shops, and museums along the neighborhood streets attract a stimulating heterogeny of intellectuals, café-society devotees, and experimentalists of all stripes.

A residential zone of about ten blocks lies between the Dupont Circle neighborhood and the Latino enclave to the north—Adams Morgan, which centers on the intersection of Columbia Road and 18th Street, N.W. Adams Morgan has become a magnet for immigrants, artists, and young professionals, who now fill enormous apartment buildings or old brick houses and frequent the neighborhood's many restaurants and popular nightspots.

Running eastward from Adams Morgan into the Shaw neighborhood is the U Street corridor, where the black community was drawn beginning in the 1880s. This area possesses a rich legacy of music and culture—Pearl Bailey, Duke Ellington, and other greats once performed at its various theaters and clubs. Deteriorated after the 1968 riots, U Street has in recent years made a comeback, with restored theaters and new clubs, restaurants, and shops. ■

Washington, D.C.

NW   NE

Subject area

SW   SE

Virginia

Md.

Potomac

Anacostia

Md.

MOUNT PLEASANT

Mexican Cultural Institute

HARVARD ST.

ADAMS MILL RD.

ONTARIO PLACE

LANIER PLACE

COLUMBIA ROAD

MOZART PL.

FULLER

15TH STREET

16TH STREET

CALVERT ST.

EUCLID ST.

Duke Ellington Memorial Bridge

Rock Cr.

BILTMORE ST.

District of Columbia Arts Center

18th Street

ONTARIO ST.

17TH ST.

KALORAMA ROAD

CRESCENT PL.

Meridian Hill Park

MINTWOOD PLACE

20TH STREET

19TH STREET

CHAMPLAIN ST.

Meridian International Center

CONNECTICUT

BELMONT ROAD

BELMONT PL.

ASHMEAD PLACE

ADAMS MORGAN

W ST.

KALORAMA ROAD

WYOMING AVE.

FLORIDA AVENUE

SHAW →

KALORAMA

WYOMING AVENUE

CALIFORNIA ST.

COLUMBIA ROAD

CALIFORNIA ST.

VERNON ST.

V ST.

U STREET

To African American Civil War Memorial, Howard University, Lincoln Theatre, Mary Church Terrell House

23RD ST.

LEROY PL.

T STREET

WILLARD STREET

T STREET

BANCROFT PLACE

19TH STREET

18TH STREET

SWANN ST.

S STREET

S STREET

NEW HAMPSHIRE AVENUE

DECATUR PLACE

FLORIDA AVENUE

RIGGS PLACE

Scottish Rite Headquarters

15TH STREET

R STREET

R STREET

Sheridan Circle

Conner Contemporary Art and Gallery

CORCORAN STREET

Q STREET

16TH ST.

17TH ST.

Cosmos Club

MASSACHUSETTS AVENUE

The Phillips Collection

Anderson House

M Dupont Circle

CHURCH ST.

CHURCH ST.

Washington Club

P STREET

Rock Creek

Burton Marinkovich Fine Art

Wadsworth House

Dupont Circle

23RD STREET

22ND STREET

21ST ST.

P STREET

NEW HAMPSHIRE AVE.

Heurich House Museum

M Dupont Circle

MASSACHUSETTS AVENUE

CONN. AVE.

O STREET

Scott Circle

ISLAND AVE.

N ST.

RHODE ISLAND AVE.

MASS. AVE.

To Metropolitan Club

M STREET

Thomas Circle

| 0 | 200 yards |
| 0 | 200 meters |

The Phillips Collection

The Phillips Collection

www.phillipscollection.org

🅰 Map p. 163

✉ 1600 21st St., N.W.
(corner of 21st &
Q Sts.)

☎ 202-387-2151

🕐 Closed Mon.

💲 $$

🚇 Metro: Dupont
Circle; Bus: D1, D2,
D3, D6

WHEN ASKED WHAT THEIR FAVORITE LOCAL ART MUSEUM is, many Washingtonians name the Phillips. There are many reasons for this choice, and one of them is the location. Just two blocks from Dupont Circle, the Phillips Collection lies in the heart of an art-loving community. It's also far from the crowded Mall, close to a Metro station, and reasonably handy enough for many office workers to stop by during a long lunch break. Then there's the fact that the publicly supported, nongovernment museum is staffed with students, artists, and others who seem less like guards than friendly docents. Of course, the art itself is a big attraction.

Begun in the 1920s by founder Duncan Phillips (1886–1966), the Phillips Collection ranks as the first modern art museum in the United States. Its permanent holdings currently include more than 2,400 pieces of carefully chosen late 19th- and early 20th-century art.

Perhaps more than anything, the charm of the Phillips is its setting. You feel as though you have walked into a rich friend's comfortable old house and were free to wander, or were encouraged to plop down in a

A patron admires "The Luncheon of the Boating Party." This delightful painting by Renoir remains a highlight of the Phillips Collection.

museum holds one of the largest collections of works by this artist. Phillips also acquired art by such 18th-century masters as El Greco, Francisco Goya, and Jean-Baptiste-Siméon Chardin to show the influence of earlier painters on modern art. Currently, the permanent collection includes works by Paul Cézanne, Pierre-Auguste Renoir, Pablo Picasso, Thomas Eakins, Edgar Degas, Paul Gauguin, Vincent van Gogh, Claude Monet, Édouard Manet, Georges Braque, Winslow Homer, James Whistler, Georgia O'Keeffe, and Mark Rothko.

In 1930, Phillips and his family moved to a new home on Foxhall Road, opening up their entire former home, an 1896 brick-and-brownstone house, to the expanding collection. A new wing was added to the north side in 1960, and in the late 1980s it was renovated and renamed the Goh Annex— after Yasuhiro Goh, a donor of the Phillips. A skywalk connects the annex to the main building.

The growth of the museum in the 1980s was guided by Phillips's son, Laughlin, a founder of *Washingtonian* magazine. While no longer director, Laughlin Phillips is still the chairman of the board of trustees. Today the museum continues to live up to Phillips's original idea of a "joy-giving, life-enhancing influence, assisting people to see beautifully as true artists see."

VISITING

Begin your visit on the first floor of the **Goh Annex,** which displays several of the works in the rotating permanent collection. The second and third floors of the annex generally are reserved for special temporary exhibitions. Then take the skywalk to the **main building.**

Here you will discover more

plush chair and admire his taste in art. Indeed, that informal effect is what Duncan Phillips had in mind when, as a memorial to his recently deceased brother, James Laughlin Phillips, and their father, Maj. D. Clinch Phillips, he opened up two rooms of his home in 1921 so that other art lovers could enjoy the works that he and his brother had collected.

An heir to the Jones and Laughlin steel fortune, Duncan Phillips married artist Marjorie Acker, also in 1921. Soon after, the couple began assembling an outstanding group of Impressionist, Postimpressionist, and Cubist art. To Phillips, a key link between Impressionism and Expressionism was Pierre Bonnard, and today the

scene painted by Renoir. Phillips paid $125,000 for it in 1923, a record at that time for an Impressionist work. The painting depicts an easygoing mix of 20- and 30-somethings—Renoir and his friends—lounging around a table laden with wine and grapes, overlooking the Seine. One man straddles a chair backward; some people are down to their undershirts while others wear top hats.

Other famous pieces to look for include Pierre Bonnard's "The Open Window" (1921) and paintings from The Migration Series by Jacob Lawrence. But these are only a couple of the wonderful breadth of talent represented within these old walls.

On the first floor, take time to visit the **Music Room,** a perennial favorite, with its dark oak paneling, decorative ceiling, and elaborately carved stone and wood mantelpiece. Since 1941, Sunday afternoon concerts *(May–Sept. only, free with admission)* have showcased the talents of many musical artists, including Jessye Norman.

Besides concerts, the Phillips Collection also hosts traveling exhibitions and maintains a busy schedule of classes, lectures, workshops, and films. ■

Masters of color and light: Henri Matisse's "Interior with Egyptian Curtain" (1948, above) and Pierre Bonnard's "Woman with Dog" (1922, opposite)

exhibits from the museum's permanent collection. They are frequently rearranged, so there is no guarantee where you will find a particular piece. Be sure to look for the centerpiece of the Phillips's entire collection: "The Luncheon of the Boating Party" (1880–81), the delightfully warm and convivial

Collect your own

After a couple of hours at the Phillips, you may be in the mood to put an original Picasso in your own home. The Dupont Circle area is just the place to shop, with more than 25 galleries scattered about. One gallery recently offered a Toulouse-Lautrec lithograph for $70,000, a Picasso painting for a mere $16,000, and a piece by Miró for under $5,000. Stop in Burton Marinkovich Fine Art (1506 21st St.), for example, and you can purchase prints and

works on paper by the likes of Frankenthaler, Hockney, Motherwell, and Diebenkorn. Or check out Conner Contemporary Art (1730 Connecticut Ave.), which has had works by Annie Leibovitz, Claes Oldenburg, Roy Lichtenstein, Robert Indiana, and Andy Warhol. Other galleries specialize in African art, Inuit sculpture, and English and American crafts. To help you decide, pick up a free galleries guide, available in any of the galleries. ■

The Indonesian Embassy boasts 60 rooms and four stories behind its beaux arts facade.

A walk down Embassy Row

Walking west from Dupont Circle along Massachusetts Avenue takes you past the affluence and glamour of the early 1900s, when this was the fashionable neighborhood for Washington tycoons. After the Great Depression, many of the grand residences were sold to foreign delegations. Today the triangle formed by Massachusetts and Connecticut Avenues and Rock Creek holds more than 50 embassies, or about one-third of the city's total. It's about a mile from Dupont Circle to the Islamic Center, at the end of the walk, but you'll probably spend at least a good half day here if you stop for the museums. For a coffee or lunch break, you need to return to the circle; Connecticut Avenue on either side of Dupont has several good cafés and restaurants.

Start your walk a block east of Dupont Circle and take a look at the kind of structure wealthy people had in mind when they thought of the term "apartment building." On the northeast corner of 18th Street and Massachusetts Avenue stands the **National Trust for Historic Preservation ❶**, a beaux arts palace originally built in 1915 as the McCormick apartment building. The first floor contained two apartments, while five floors above each held an 11,000-square-foot apartment with six bedrooms and 14.5-foot ceilings. The most famous tenant, Andrew W. Mellon, founder of the National Gallery of Art and a U.S. secretary of the treasury, lived on the top floor from 1921 to 1937. In 1936 he paid 21 million dollars for paintings and sculptures owned by Sir Joseph Duveen, an art dealer leasing the apartment below; at the time, it was the largest art transaction on record. Robert Woods Bliss, owner of Dumbarton Oaks, also lived here in the 1920s.

Head west to the circle, where you can see more fine examples of turn-of-the-20th-century mansions that never became embassies. Now housing the Sulgrave Club *(private)*, a stalwart sorority of socially prominent Washington ladies, the circa 1900 **Wadsworth House** *(1801 Massachusetts Ave., N.W.)* was the winter residence of landowners Herbert and Martha Wadsworth of upstate New York. With a bow window facing the circle like the prow of a ship, the house is an early illustration of how a large building could be designed to fit the triangular lots around the circle.

Taking a different approach to the same problem, the Wadsworth's neighbor to the north, the ornate **Washington Club** *(private)*, fits into its wedge at 15 Dupont Circle with symmetrical wings and a concave front. Now a women's social club, the 1903 house was designed by Stanford White for Robert W. Patterson, publisher of the *Chicago Tribune*.

Standing in **Dupont Circle ❷**, you can see a striking example of how L'Enfant's city plan works, with grand avenues vectoring out from the central green. In the middle of the circle is a marble fountain designed in 1921 by Daniel Chester French, who is also known for the giant statue of Lincoln in the memorial. Spilling into a large pool, an upper basin is supported by a central column surrounded by three allegorical figures representing the sea, wind, and stars—elements that Civil War naval hero Samuel Francis du Pont would have known well. Benches around the circle and grassy plots under trees are constantly in use for lounging and informal lunching. Tables with built-in chessboards draw an egalitarian cross section of suits, uniforms, jeans, and cutoffs for serious games.

A block southwest, at 1307 New Hampshire Avenue, the **Heurich House Museum ❸** (see p. 176) preserves a piece of the 1890s and now houses the Historical Society of Washington, D.C.

Now head north 1.5 blocks to 2000

Massachusetts Avenue. This brick Victorian mansion was built in 1881 for Republican presidential candidate James Blaine, who lost in 1884 to Grover Cleveland. Shops occupy its first floor, with offices above.

On the same side of the street, the curving sweep of the **Indonesian Embassy ❹** *(2020 Massachusetts Ave.)* makes an impressive sight. Featuring marble columns, arched windows, and a red-tiled mansard roof, the mansion was built at the turn of the 20th century by Irishman Tom Walsh, who struck gold in a Colorado mine. He moved to Washington, built

---

🅼 See area map p. 163
▶ National Trust
⟷ 1 mile
🕒 3–4 hours
▶ Islamic Center

NOT TO BE MISSED
- Heurich House Museum
- The Phillips Collection
- Islamic Center

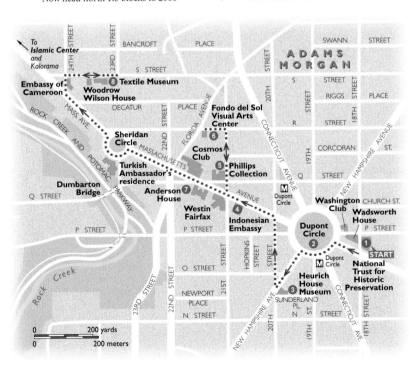

his dream house, and became part of the new moneyed class. His daughter, prominent hostess Evalyn Walsh McLean, was the last private owner of the Hope Diamond (now in the National Museum of Natural History; see p. 93); in 1951 she sold the mansion to the Republic of Indonesia.

At 2100 Massachusetts Avenue, the building housing the **Westin Fairfax,** dating from 1927, gives Embassy Row a European-style hotel flair. Al Gore lived here when his father was a U. S. senator. Across Massachusetts, a statue of Mahatma Gandhi stands in front of the Embassy of India. A block north on 21st Street, the **Phillips Collection** ❺ (see pp. 164–67) is one of Washington's most cherished museums.

If Latin American art interests you, continue north another block to **Fondo del Sol Visual Arts Center** ❻ *(2112 R St., 202-265-9235, closed Sun.–Mon., $),* which helps preserve and promote the cultural heritage of the Americas with exhibits, concerts, poetry readings, and lectures. A permanent collection of pre-Columbian and folk art is on display.

Back on Massachusetts, the double-winged mansion at 2118 Massachusetts Avenue is the **Anderson House** ❼ (see p. 176), headquarters of the Society of the Cincinnati. Across the avenue, at 2121 Massachusetts, stands the exclusive **Cosmos Club** *(private),* completed in 1902 as the home of Richard Townsend, president of the Erie & Pittsburgh Railroad. The fabulous limestone mansion was sold in 1950 to the club, whose members have earned recognition in the arts and sciences.

A number of embassies edge **Sheridan Circle,** named for Union general Philip H. Sheridan; the 1908 equestrian bronze in the center is by Gutzon Borglum, sculptor of Mount Rushmore. Among the impressive buildings nearby are the **Turkish Ambassador's residence** *(1606 23rd St.),* built in the 1910s for industrialist Edward Everett. A block south, the 1914 **Dumbarton Bridge**—often called the Buffalo Bridge for its bronze bison—carries Q Street over Rock Creek into Georgetown.

Back on Massachusetts, at the corner of Massachusetts and 24th, is the château-style **Embassy of Cameroon.** It was built in 1907 to house Norway's ambassador and legation, but it was never used as such because the ambassador died.

The Islamic Center's lofty minaret

Turn up 24th Street, then go east on S Street. Compared to many area houses, the **Woodrow Wilson House** *(2340 S St., 202-387-4062, closed Mon., $),* designed in 1915 by Waddy B. Wood, has a modest appearance. The president spent the last three years of his life in this Georgian Revival brick town house after leaving the White House in 1921; his wife stayed until her death in 1961.

Next door, the **Textile Museum** ❽ *(2320 S St., 202-667-0441, donation)* was founded in 1925 by President Wilson's neighbor, George Hewitt Myers, to house a collection of rugs and other textiles. The museum incorporates Myers's residence and the adjoining house he bought as his collection grew; John Russell Pope designed the latter house in 1913. The collection numbers over 17,000 carpets and textiles, dating from 3000 B.C. to the present.

About four blocks away is the **Islamic Center** *(2551 Massachusetts Ave., 202-332-8343),* a mosque richly embellished with tilework, arches, and pillars; in the carpeted sanctuary, shoes and shorts are not allowed, and women must cover their heads. The network of streets to the west is the prestigious Kalorama neighborhood, which holds several embassies and large houses. ■

Adams Morgan

THE CITY'S TRADITIONALLY HISPANIC NEIGHBORHOOD, Adams Morgan became in the 1980s and '90s the top apartment-and-nightlife nexus for artists and hip young professionals alike. With its international restaurants, funky shops, and rocking nightclubs, the little neighborhood sprang to life with a personality all its own, an enclave of bohemian flair in the center of staid Washington. Never mind that all this popularity meant there was no longer any place to park—especially on weekend evenings.

Adams Morgan

- Map p. 163
- Between Columbia Rd., 16th St., & Florida Ave., N.W.
- Metro: Dupont Circle (1.5 miles S) or Woodley Park–Zoo/Adams Morgan (0.75 mile NW)

The name itself alludes to the neighborhood's cultural mix: By combining the names of two schools—the mostly white Adams School and the predominantly black Morgan School—local citizens coined the term Adams Morgan in the 1950s for an area that had been part of four neighborhoods. In that same decade, the Spanish-speaking population swelled as an influx of students from Latin America and Mexican professionals added to the existing community of embassy workers. The early 1960s saw an increase in Cuban immigration, followed by large numbers from South and Central America through the next few decades. The ethnic influence still tends toward Latin—Spanish is heard on the streets as often as English; but in the smorgasbord of restaurants and shops, you'll find many other cultures, including Ethiopian, Chinese, Thai, Indian, and Vietnamese.

The heart of Adams Morgan is the intersection of **Columbia Road** and **18th Street.** On the northeast corner a kiosk provides lists of upcoming cultural events. At the intersection's southwest corner is a plaza where vendors set up shop on weekends and sell fresh produce and breads. Most of the area's action—eating, drinking, and dancing—takes place south of the intersection on 18th Street between Columbia Road and Florida Avenue, and along

a little branch west on Columbia Road to Belmont Road. That's pretty much it. Although the few attractions are worth seeing, they do not draw crowds.

VISITING

The three-story, brightly painted brick buildings lining the blocks of 18th Street south of the

Local Peruvians celebrate Our Lord of Miracles Day in Adams Morgan.

Shoppers examine local wares at a street fair on 18th Street—the heart of Adams Morgan.

Columbia Road–18th Street intersection hold most of the ethnic restaurants, bohemian bars, and boutiques. On sultry summer evenings, the sidewalks buzz with people strolling, walking dogs, or sipping cool drinks at sidewalk cafés and bars. Ethiopian seems to be the most sought-after cuisine here; among a number of places to give it a try is Meskerem *(2434 18th St., 202-462-4100)*, where diners scoop up communal stews with pieces of spongy sourdough bread.

If you're looking for some off-beat culture, try the **District of Columbia Arts Center** *(2438 18th St., 202-462-7833)*, which features the work of emerging artists and holds live performances in a 50-seat theater.

Columbia Road on either side of 18th also has several good restaurants—including Perry's, *the* place to be and be seen *(1811 Columbia Rd., 202-234-6218)*; its rooftop dining is one of the city's most pleasant experiences. Along Columbia you'll also find Latino grocery stores, outdoor jewelry stands, and vintage clothing and sundries shops.

Daytime Adams Morgan offers different sights to see. For grand interiors, walk down **16th Street.** Just below Columbia, the **Mexican Cultural Institute** *(2829 16th St., 202-728-1628, closed Sun.–Mon.)*, in a 1911 Italianate house, holds a huge tile-covered solarium, a lively stairwell mural, and ornately furnished salons; rotating exhibits are presented on two floors.

A few blocks farther, opposite Meridian Hill Park, **Meridian International Center** *(1624 & 1630 Crescent Pl., 202-667-6800, closed Mon.–Tues.)* promotes international understanding through cultural exchanges. The adjoining houses, with free art exhibits, were designed by John Russell Pope in 1911 and 1921; the 1630 address boasts antique French furnishings and a courtyard with 40 linden trees.

Pope also designed the glorious 1911 **Scottish Rite Headquarters** *(1733 16th St., 202-232-3579, closed weekends),* just beyond Adams Morgan at S Street; he modeled the building after the Mausoleum at Halicarnassus in Turkey.

The northwest portion of Adams Morgan, up 18th and onto Adams Mill Road and Calvert Street, is quieter, more residential, with tightly packed town houses. Just off Adams Mill, on the right, you can see one of the neighborhood's many colorful wall murals, this one dating from the 1970s and depicting life in Washington's barrio. If you follow Calvert, you'll come to the **Duke Ellington Memorial Bridge** over Rock Creek *(toward Woodley Park–Zoo/Adams Morgan Metro station).* ■

Chuck Brown

Since its birth some 25 years ago, go-go music appeared to be an indigenous creation that was not exportable beyond the Beltway. It's finally beginning to gain national attention. The "godfather" of go-go, Chuck Brown (1934–) cobbled the style by combining Latin and soul rhythms, jazz progressions, and gospel-style call-and-response lyrics. The result is a very funky sound that is more melodic and less aggressive than its rap and hip-hop cousins. Distinguishing features include long songs, heavy use of horns, cowbells, and congos, and undeniably danceable rhythms. For an introduction, try his *Greatest Hits* release, with "Bustin' Loose," "Back It On Up (Sho' Ya Right)," and "It Don't Mean a Thing (If It Don't Have the Go Go Swing)." Brown's latest album, *Your Game… Live at the 9:30 Club, Washington, D.C.,* was recorded in January 2001. ■

U Street

During the first half of the 20th century, the U Street corridor in the Shaw neighborhood—named for Robert Gould Shaw, the white colonel of the first African American regiment in the Civil War—was the center of black D.C. social and cultural life. It was often referred to as the "Black Broadway." People would dress in their finest outfits to frequent the restaurants, movie theaters, pool halls, and dance halls lining the street.

The baroque 1910 Howard Theatre *(624 T St.)* was the country's first legitimate theater built for black audiences and entertainers. Hosting vaudeville acts, musicals,

road shows, and concerts, the Howard commanded center stage: All the big names in entertainment played its boards. In 1922 the opulent Lincoln Theatre opened at 13th and U Streets. Both a movie palace and live-performance venue, it was designed to have the look and feel of a great opera house. Big bands played at the Colonnade, the dance hall in the basement.

At both theaters, the level of performance was so great that racial segregation was often ignored. Many white people also would come to see luminary performances by Duke Ellington, Cab Calloway, Ella Fitzgerald, Sarah Vaughan, and many more.

Ironically, desegregation in the 1950s led to the eventual decline of U Street's venues. The 1968 riots (which fanned out from 14th and U) led to further deterioration, and by the early '70s, both the Howard and the Lincoln had closed. In recent years, however, U Street has been revitalizing, though it is no longer the center of African American nightlife. Many nightclubs cater to crowds from all walks of life, and the eclectic mix of restaurants, cafés, and shops attracts a diverse group.

The Lincoln Theatre has been restored, and Bohemian Caverns *(11th & U Sts., 202-299-0800),* formerly known as Crystal Caverns, has returned; closed down in 1968, the Caverns was a haunt of Pearl Bailey, Miles Davis, John Coltrane, and others. You can catch live jazz every night except Tuesday. Other hot clubs include Republic Gardens, State of the Union, and the 9:30 Club.

Opposite: Edward Kennedy "Duke" Ellington (1899–1974) returned to his native Washington many times as a preeminent jazz bandleader and composer. Right: Another Washingtonian, singer and film star Pearl Bailey (1918–1990) strikes a seductive pose. Above: A chanteuse performs at Utopia on U Street.

At 1816 12th St., the Shaw Heritage Trust offers exhibits on the neighborhood in a 1912 building designed by W. Sidney Pittman, one of the country's first black architects. Another way to get to know this area's legacy is to take the U Street Heritage Trail, a self-guided, 90-minute walk past historical buildings relating to the once thriving black community. Pick up information from merchants along the trail.

For a taste of yesterday, stop by Ben's Chili Bowl *(1213 U St.)*. Opened in 1958, it still serves up half smokes and burgers beneath a pressed-tin ceiling and overhead fans. ■

More places to visit in Dupont Circle & beyond

ANDERSON HOUSE

This spectacular 1905 mansion serves as the headquarters and museum of the **Society of the Cincinnati,** a patriotic organization whose first president general was George Washington. The house was once the winter residence of diplomat Larz Anderson III, whose wife, Isabel Weld Perkins, inherited $17,000,000 from her grandfather's shipping fortune. After Anderson died in 1937, his widow turned the mansion over to the society, of which Anderson was a member.

A bulwark of fraternal tradition dating from 1783, the society's 3,500 members descend from officers in the Continental Army or Navy. Its name comes from the Roman senator Cincinnatus, who, like Washington, gave up farming to defend his country.

Among the first-floor treasures are walnut choir stalls from 16th-century Italy, decorative Japanese screens, and a ballroom with Verona marble columns. Off the ballroom, a sun-drenched winter garden room opens onto a Japanese garden. A billiard room holds society members' portraits by Gilbert Stuart and John Trumbull. On the second floor are English furniture, Belgian tapestries, Italian paintings, and Chinese jades and porcelains. A 42,000-title research library focuses on the military history of the American Revolution.

▲ Map p. 163 ✉ 2118 Massachusetts Ave., N.W. ☎ 202-785-2040 🕐 Closed Sun.–Mon. Ⓜ Metro: Dupont Circle; Bus: D1, D3, D6

HEURICH HOUSE MUSEUM

Built in 1895 for brewer Christian Heurich, this Romanesque castle now houses the **Historical Society of Washington, D.C.** As of press time, however, the house is being sold and its future uncertain. The historical society's main gallery, located in a back room on the first floor, is scheduled to move to the old Carnegie Library on Mount Vernon Square by 2003 (see p. 135).

Heurich, a poor German immigrant, came to the U.S. in 1872. Within seven years he had gotten married and purchased this property just off Dupont Circle. His first two wives died, but his third wife—the 33-year-old niece and namesake of his first wife, Amelia—

survived him by 11 years. After her death in 1956, their house was deeded to the Columbia Historical Society (as it was then called). A self-guided tour takes you through 11 rooms on three levels. Sumptuous decorations include a marble mosaic floor in the main hall and elaborately carved furniture in the dining room.

▲ Map p. 163 ✉ 1307 New Hampshire Ave., N.W. ☎ 202-785-2068 🕐 Closed Sun. Ⓢ $ Ⓜ Metro: Dupont Circle; Bus: L2

MARY CHURCH TERRELL HOUSE

The LeDroit Park neighborhood (*S of Howard University*) has been the home of many prominent African Americans since the 1890s. Civic leader Mary Church Terrell, wife of the city's first black municipal judge, lived a long, active life but is mostly remembered now for the work she did in her late 80s. In 1950, at age 86, she spearheaded a campaign to reinstate antidiscrimination laws that had been written in the 1870s. Her three-story brick house (*not open to the public*) is located at 326 T Street, N.W. Other blacks who have lived in this area include poet Paul Laurence Dunbar and Mayor Walter Washington. ■

Oliver O. Howard

Gen. Oliver Otis Howard (1830–1909) came to Washington after the Civil War and took charge of the new Bureau of Refugees, Freedmen, and Abandoned Lands (better known as the Freedmen's Bureau). Under Howard's leadership, the bureau bought the Barry Farm near what would become the Anacostia neighborhood, in southeast Washington, and sold off parcels to black families. The Freedmen's Bureau also helped fund and establish educational programs for freed people. In 1867 Howard University was founded (named for the general against his wishes) on land that was purchased by the bureau. The institution, located at Seventh and Bryant Streets, N.W., is now the country's leading black university, with an enrollment of more than 10,000. ■

With inducements ranging from the bucolic (Rock Creek Park) to the divine (Washington National Cathedral), this city-center enclave is a pleasing paradox: a tourist destination that provides a respite from touring.

Cleveland Park & beyond

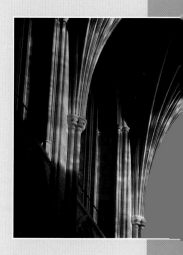

Soaring arches inside National Cathedral

Noodleheads spill onto the sidewalk of a Thai restaurant on Connecticut Avenue.

Cleveland Park & beyond

BY FOOT, METRO, OR BICYCLE, THE LEAFY NEIGHBORHOOD OF CLEVELAND
Park offers a pleasant afternoon of relaxed sight-seeing or lounging in cafés. Higher elevations and the nearness of Rock Creek Park provide relief from the heat of downtown.

Tourists who venture this far from the Mall generally come for the zoo. That's a great reason for a visit, made easy by the Metro's Red Line to Cleveland Park or Woodley Park–Zoo/Adams Morgan stations. And any of the outstanding sites nearby may land on your list of D.C. favorites.

The tony neighborhood of Cleveland Park is named for President Grover Cleveland, who spent the summers of his second administration (1893–97) at Woodley, a Georgian mansion built about 1800 at 3000 Cathedral Avenue. President Cleveland preferred the cool breezes that buffeted Woodley to the miasmas of the marshy lowlands around the White House about 2.5 miles away. Woodley is now part of the private Maret School.

When the city's trolley tracks were extended across Rock Creek valley at Calvert Street in the 1890s and thence up Connecticut Avenue, the area took on a fashionable cachet. Today Connecticut Avenue is still lined with big apartment buildings (the more ornate ones from the 1920s and '30s), behind which stand fine old houses with wide front porches

and trim gardens. Indeed, the city's largest hotel, the Marriott Wardman Park (*Woodley Rd. & Conn. Ave.*), got its start in 1928 as a luxury apartment building called the Wardman Tower. The tower's residents have included Herbert Hoover, Earl Warren, and Clare Booth Luce. Across Calvert Street, the 1930 Omni Shoreham has hosted inaugural balls since Franklin Delano Roosevelt took office in 1933.

Farther up Connecticut Avenue is one of the city's top attractions: the almost pastoral, 163-acre National Zoological Park. It abuts Rock Creek Park, a delightful preserve of trees, meadows, and cycling paths.

A mile west of the zoo, Washington National Cathedral towers gloriously on its high hill. Scores of stonemasons labored 83 years to complete this national architectural masterpiece. Unknown to many locals, the Hillwood estate to the north is a jewel box of Russian and French antiques. Afterward, reward yourself with a Frappuccino or some Thai food at one of the many establishments clustered near the Metro stops along Connecticut Avenue. ∎

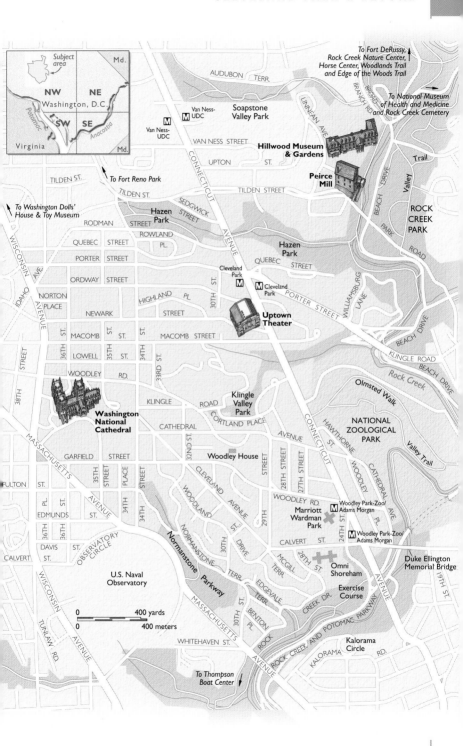

Subject area

NW   **NE**
Washington, D.C.

SW   **SE**

Md.
Virginia
Md.
Potomac
Anacostia

AUDUBON TERR.

To Fort DeRussy,
Rock Creek Nature Center,
Horse Center, Woodlands Trail
and Edge of the Woods Trail

To National Museum
of Health and Medicine
and Rock Creek Cemetery

Van Ness-UDC
Soapstone Valley Park

Van Ness-UDC

VAN NESS STREET

UPTON ST.

Hillwood Museum & Gardens

Peirce Mill

LINNEAN AVE.
BRANCH RD.
BROAD

Trail
BEACH DRIVE
PARK ROAD
Valley

ROCK CREEK PARK

To Fort Reno Park

TILDEN ST.
TILDEN ST.

TILDEN STREET

SEDGWICK STREET

To Washington Dolls'
House & Toy Museum

Hazen Park

RODMAN STREET
ROWLAND PL.

QUEBEC STREET

PORTER STREET

ORDWAY STREET

CONNECTICUT AVENUE

Hazen Park

QUEBEC STREET

Cleveland Park

Cleveland Park

PORTER STREET

WILLIAMSBURG LANE

WISCONSIN AVE.
IDAHO AVENUE

NORTON PLACE

NEWARK STREET

HIGHLAND PL.

STREET

30TH ST.

Uptown Theater

MACOMB ST.
LOWELL ST.

36TH ST.
35TH ST.
34TH ST.
33RD ST.

MACOMB STREET

WOODLEY RD.

KLINGLE ROAD
BEACH DRIVE

Rock Creek

KLINGLE

Washington National Cathedral

CATHEDRAL

Klingle Valley Park

CORTLAND PLACE

Olmsted Walk

Rock Creek

38TH STREET
MASSACHUSETTS

GARFIELD STREET

35TH STREET
34TH PLACE
34TH STREET
32ND ST.

CLEVELAND AVENUE

AVENUE

28TH STREET
27TH STREET

NATIONAL ZOOLOGICAL PARK

HAWTHORNE ST.
WOODLEY
CATHEDRAL AVE.

Valley Trail

FULTON ST.

PL. ST.
EDMUNDS ST.

36TH PL.
36TH ST.

DAVIS ST.

CALVERT ST.

AVENUE

34TH ST.
30TH ST.

WOODLAND DRIVE

NORMANSTONE TERR.

Woodley House

WOODLEY RD.

29TH ST.

Marriott Wardman Park

CALVERT ST.

Woodley Park-Zoo/
Adams Morgan

Woodley Park-Zoo/
Adams Morgan

24TH ST.

Duke Ellington Memorial Bridge

19TH ST.

OBSERVATORY CIRCLE

U.S. Naval Observatory

Normanstone Parkway

MASSACHUSETTS AVENUE

MCGILL TERR.

28TH ST.

EDGEVALE TERR.

BENTON ST.

ROCK CREEK DR.

Omni Shoreham

Exercise Course

AVENUE

WISCONSIN AVENUE

TUNLAW RD.

0   400 yards
0   400 meters

WHITEHAVEN ST.

30TH PL.

ROCK CREEK AND POTOMAC PARKWAY

KALORAMA RD.

Kalorama Circle

To Thompson
Boat Center

National Zoological Park

National Zoological Park

www.si.edu/natzoo

Map p. 179

3001 Connecticut Ave., N.W.

202-673-4717

Parking up to $11 per day

Metro: Cleveland Park, Woodley Park–Zoo/Adams Morgan; Bus: L1, L2, L4

THE NATIONAL ZOO WAS CONCEIVED AS "A HOME AND A city of refuge for the vanishing races of the continent." In 1887, Smithsonian taxidermist William T. Hornaday corralled some of North America's vanishing bison and a few other animals in a small zoo on the Mall. Two years later, Congress set aside acreage along a bend in Rock Creek to create the National Zoo "for the advancement of science and the instruction and recreation of the people."

Part of the Smithsonian Institution, the 163-acre biological park opened in 1891 and is now home to more than 3,600 animals representing 475 species. Nearly a third of the species—including Asian elephants,

Food **Gifts** **Restrooms** **Handicapped accessible** *Seasonal

Valley Trail, the steeper of the two zoo paths, includes major aquatic exhibits, birds, and Amazonia.

1 Tapirs
2 Bongos
3 Wetlands, Eagles
4 Bird House & Flight Exhibit
5 Australia Pavilion
6 Birds
7 Free-ranging Golden Lion Tamarins*
8 Beavers, Otters
9 Red Wolves
10 Seals, Sea Lions
11 Spectacled Bears
12 Amazonia, Amazonia Science Gallery

Olmsted Walk passes most indoor exhibits.

1 Visitor Center, Bookstore, Gifts, Wheelchairs, ATM
2 Cheetah Conservation Station, Zebras
3 American Prairie
4 Information*, Prairie Pavilion, Strollers, Wheelchairs
5 Giant Panda Exhibit
6 Elephants, Giraffes
7 Hippos, Rhinos
8 Camels
9 American Indian Heritage Garden
10 Small Mammal House
11 Great Ape House
12 Gibbon Ridge
13 Reptile Discovery Center
14 Invertebrate Exhibit
15 Think Tank
16 Servals, Caracals
17 Great Cats
18 Monkey Island
19 African American Heritage Garden
20 Bears
21 Police
22 Bat Cave
23 Mane Restaurant
24 Information*, Strollers, Wheelchairs

cheetahs, Sumatran tigers, giant pandas, western lowland gorillas, and Komodo dragons—are endangered. The animal enclosures aim to re-create natural habitats. Meanwhile, at the zoo's 3,150-acre Conservation and Research Center near Front Royal, Virginia, zookeepers have bred golden lion tamarins, red wolves, and black-footed ferrets for reintroduction to the wild.

VISITING

Given the zoo's 5 miles of hilly paths, it's hard to avoid at least some uphill walking. To minimize your efforts, pick up a map at one of the information stations at either end of the zoo's main east-west thoroughfare, the Olmsted Walk (landscape architect Frederick Law Olmsted designed the zoo's original layout). With more than 30 exhibit areas to choose from, you may want to hit a few highlights and save the rest for another day. Fall and winter are the least crowded seasons, but the buildings close early from mid-September through April.

If you begin at the visitor center inside the Connecticut Avenue entrance, the **Olmsted Walk** will lead you past the cheetahs, zebras, and other enclosures to the **Giant Panda Exhibit.** This indoor-outdoor area features Tian Tian and Mei Xiang, a pair of pandas on long-term loan from China. Within days of arriving in December 2000,

Pandas at play: Tian Tian ("more and more") and Mei Xiang ("beautiful fragrance"), born in Wolong, China, are star attractions at the zoo.

Rock Creek

15
16
17
22
24

Parking Lot E

To Harvard Street

Picnic Area

To Rock Creek and Potomac Parkway

Parking Lot D

the pandas had adapted so well that they were literally chewing up the scenery, devouring the decorative plantings of ornamental bamboo. The exhibit outlines efforts to save the panda, whose numbers have dwindled to about 1,000 in the wild and 140 in captivity.

Continue downhill and east past the Elephant House (stopping to see the calf born here in November 2001) to reach the **Small Mammal House,** where the challenge is to spot the golden lion tamarins, pygmy marmosets, two-toed sloths, and three-banded armadillos that occupy the glassed-in jungle. The **Great Ape House** next door is home to gorillas and orangutans. The latter can climb over an aerial pathway called the O Line to Think Tank, swinging on vinelike cables attached to a set of towers. A popular stop nearby, the **Reptile Discovery Center** features Komodo dragons, huge Aldabra tortoises, spiky matamata turtles, and hands-on exhibits.

Behind the center lies the fascinating **Invertebrate Exhibit.**

Here you'll find giant octopuses, anemones, and spiders; an adjoining greenhouse thrums with pollinators such as butterflies, hummingbirds, and honeybees. Continue on the Olmsted Walk to enter the **Think Tank,** where orangutans use tools and communicate with researchers via touch-screen computers. Beyond you'll find the Bat Cave, the Great Cats, and Monkey Island.

Head back to Connecticut Avenue on the **Valley Trail,** south of the Olmsted Walk. Your first stop will be the warm, humid **Amazonia** exhibit, which simulates a journey through a rain forest; here parrots and other tropical birds flit through kapok and mahogany trees beneath a domed 50-foot-high ceiling. Next on the Valley Trail is a delightful outdoor exhibit housing seals and sea lions, followed by enclosures for red wolves, beavers, otters, and free-ranging golden lion tamarins. Farther up the trail, the raucous **Bird House and Flight Exhibit** offers a walk-through aviary and a boardwalk spanning a wetland. ■

Feeding time for the sea lions is one of the zoo's most popular spectacles.

Rock Creek Park

WHEN YOU NEED TO GET AWAY FROM THE HURLY-BURLY OF urban living (or touring, for that matter), a peaceful Washington park awaits nearby. Rock Creek Park runs in a long strand of hilly woods and meadows from the National Zoo to the Maryland border 4 miles north, with tendrils of green branching off the main park into other parts of the city. At 1,739 acres—more than twice the size of New York's Central Park—Rock Creek is one of the nation's largest urban parks. Visitors and residents seek solace and rejuvenation in the park's 18-hole golf course, tennis courts, picnic areas, playing fields, nature center and planetarium, and more than 35 miles of trails for jogging, hiking, biking, and horseback riding.

Rock Creek Park
www.nps.gov/rocr
Map p. 179
Rock Creek Nature Center & Planetarium
5200 Glover Rd., S of Military Rd.
202-282-6828

For some 5,000 years, Algonquin Indians camped in the woods around Rock Creek above its run-in with the Potomac. There they gathered fruits and nuts and hunted deer, bear, and elk. They also quarried the Rock Creek valley, extracting quartz for tools and soapstone for bowls and other implements.

By the early 1700s, however, the Indians were gone, displaced by white settlers who cleared out more of the forest and built mills along Rock Creek. The only one remaining—restored 19th-century **Peirce Mill** (*Tilden St. & Beach Dr.*)—has

a museum where you can view the millworks and a historical film.

During the Civil War, Washington erected a ring of 68 forts to protect itself from Confederate attack. You can see some earthworks remaining from **Fort DeRussy,** half a mile north of the nature center. Other nearby fort sites—most of them long since reduced to fields for picnicking or playing ball—include **Fort Bayard Park** (*River Rd. & Western Ave.*); **Fort Reno Park** (*Chesapeake St. & Belt Rd.*), occupying the highest point of land in Washington; and partially recon-

Bridges, trails, and autumn glory are among the enticements of this sprawling urban sanctuary.

structed **Fort Stevens Park** (*13th St., N of Military Rd.*), the only Washington-area battlement that came under enemy fire.

Set aside in 1890, Rock Creek Park is today the city's playground, administered by the National Park Service. About 85 percent of the park is forested; the remainder is wildflower-dotted meadows and fields. Over the years, Theodore Roosevelt, Ronald Reagan, and other Presidents have availed themselves of the park's walking and bridle trails. Unlike them, the average citizen will need no bodyguards; the park is generally safe by day.

VISITING

Start your visit at the **Rock Creek Nature Center** (*closed Mon.–Tues.*). Here you can learn about the park's flora and fauna that fill this urban wildlife mecca, scope out its cycling and running paths, and pick up a trail map describing each route. The center's excellent displays include a bee colony, dioramas, and several hands-on exhibits; astronomy programs are staged in a planetarium.

Outside, two short nature loops—the **Woodlands Trail** and the wheelchair-accessible **Edge of the Woods Trail**— help you identify local trees and

plants. Towering oaks, hickories, and beeches are much in evidence; come spring the dogwoods, red-buds, and azaleas emerge in a gaudy show of blossoms.

From the nature center, you can also access the park's larger trail network. Some pathways are open to bikes and horses; others allow only foot traffic. One bike trail heads north from the nature center to the Maryland border and 14 miles beyond that to Lake Needwood. You can return the same way and pick up **Beach Drive;** normally a pulsing commuter artery, it closes on weekends, allowing cyclists a traffic-free ride from the Maryland border all the way to its intersection with Broad Branch Road. From there, a paved **bike trail** extends south beyond the park boundary, running alongside the Rock Creek and Potomac Parkway until it hits Memorial Bridge. About halfway along this trail, near Calvert Street and Connecticut Avenue, you'll come across a 1.5-mile **exercise course** with fitness-apparatus stations.

Hikers should seek out the moderate, blue-blazed, 5.6-mile **Valley Trail,** which winds along the east side of Rock Creek all the way from Boundary Bridge on the Maryland line down to Bluff Bridge at the park's southern end. Its analogue on the park's western edge is the strenuous, green-blazed, 4.6-mile **Western Ridge Trail.**

Just south of the nature center, sign up for a trail ride or lesson at the **Rock Creek Horse Center** (*202-362-0117*), an NPS concessioner amid a 13-mile web of bridle trails. Much farther south, where Rock Creek joins the Potomac, **Thompson Boat Center** (*202-333-4861*) rents canoes and kayaks for exploring the river and Theodore Roosevelt Island (see p. 209); it also rents bicycles. ■

Just spin 'em: Rock Creek Park's 10 miles of bike paths link to a Washington-wide web of other trails.

Frank O. Salisbury painted Marjorie Merriweather Post in 1934, when she was 47.

Hillwood Museum & Gardens

A HIDDEN GEM, THE HILLWOOD MUSEUM WAS THE FINAL home of cereal heiress Marjorie Merriweather Post (1887–1973). With her fabulous collection of Russian and 18th-century French decorative arts, she furnished the house with the idea that it would become a museum after her death. The site opened to the public in 1977, and Hillwood is now one of the top art collector's house museums in the country. Objects on display include Romanov family treasures, Fabergé eggs and other objets d'art, Russian religious icons, French tapestries, and Sèvres porcelain. The 25 acres of formal and natural gardens enhance the museum experience, while family photos and memorabilia remind visitors that Hillwood was once a home.

Hillwood Museum & Gardens

www.hillwoodmuseum.org

🅰 Map p. 179

✉ 4155 Linnean Ave., N.W.

☎ 202-686-5807

🕐 Closed Sun.–Mon. & all Feb.

💲 $$ (reservation deposit per person refunded by mail on request)

🚇 Metro: Van Ness–UDC; Bus: L1, L2, L4

As the only child of cereal magnate C. W. Post, Marjorie inherited a fortune at age 27 when her father died (just two years after her mother). She and her husband bought a mansion on Fifth Avenue in New York and began furnishing it with the help of flamboyant art dealer Sir Joseph Duveen, who became Post's mentor. She also educated herself by taking classes on tapestries, porcelain, and furniture at the Metropolitan Museum of Art.

In the course of a long and busy life, Post married and divorced four times and amassed a tremendous collection of European artwork. An astute businesswoman, she also donated millions of dollars to charities and other organizations, including $100,000 to help build the Kennedy Center (see pp. 124–25).

You can take a one-hour **guided tour** of the house at 11 a.m. or 1 p.m.; when a guided tour is not in progress, a self-guided **audio tour** is available. One-hour tours of the gardens take place from April through June and from September through November.

By contrast with the unremarkable exterior of the brick house, the inside customarily prompts a chorus of oohs and aahs. One highlight, the **Russian Porcelain Room,** contains Imperial Glassworks pieces from the 1730s.

More tsarist treasures are on display in the outstanding **Icon Room,** where you can feast your eyes on the diamond wedding crown worn in 1894 by Russia's last empress, Alexandra Fyodorovna; two Fabergé Easter eggs (one dates from 1914 and is studded with gold, diamonds, and pearls); and Russian Orthodox icons from the 16th century. Post discovered her love of Russian art while living in the Soviet Union from 1937 to 1938 with her third husband, American ambassador Joseph E. Davies.

The elegant **French Drawing Room** is furnished in the style of Louis XVI, with 18th-century tapestries designed by painter François Boucher and furniture by David Roentgen. Upstairs, Post's bedroom is likewise decorated in Louis XVI style; a display of her ball gowns, hats, and jewelry adds life and personality to the collection.

Almost as impressive as the house, the lovely **gardens** include 12 acres of lawns and formal plantings and 13 acres of native woodlands. A French parterre with a fountain, a circular rose garden, a crescent-shaped lawn, a Japanese-style garden, and an orchid-filled greenhouse round out the gardens. The trees and flowers bloom year round, making a stroll through Hillwood a delight in any season. ■

It was after her third divorce, in 1955, that Post purchased Hillwood—a 1926 Georgian house on the woodsy edge of Rock Creek Park. She spent two years renovating and enlarging the house, transforming it into a residence where she could entertain in legendary style. Hillwood parties routinely exceeded 200 guests, the politicians mixing with celebrities in the gardens. At formal dinners, guests ate off Post's antique porcelain and silver; informal dinners sometimes ended with square dancing in the Pavilion.

In the interstices between soirées, Post expanded her art collection, eventually turning Hillwood into a stunning showcase of decorative and fine arts. Today the museum is best known for its collection of 18th- and 19th-century Russian imperial art—the most comprehensive outside Russia—and for its distinctive array of French decorative art.

Post's treasures include the French Drawing Room (top) and Russian imperial Easter eggs created by Fabergé.

VISITING

Get oriented to the exhibits with a 15-minute film at the visitor center.

Washington National Cathedral

DOMINATING THE CITYSCAPE, WASHINGTON NATIONAL Cathedral is visible from points all over the district. Conversely, its lofty perch on Mount St. Alban gives cathedral visitors a commanding vista of the urban skyline. Officially known as the Cathedral Church of St. Peter and St. Paul, this towering Gothic church is one of Washington's most magnificent architectural achievements.

The idea of a national church occurred as early as Pierre Charles L'Enfant's design for the Federal City, which envisioned a "church… to serve as a moral lighthouse for the nation." But the constitutional separation of church and state scotched the idea until the 1890s, when it was revived by a group of Episcopalians and endorsed by President Benjamin Harrison.

In 1893, Congress chartered the Protestant Episcopal Cathedral Foundation. The church would be a house of prayer for all people, built and supported by private donations from people of many faiths. As contributions flowed in from every state, a 57-acre site was set aside atop Mount St. Alban.

After the cathedral's initial two designers died in 1917 with their plan still incomplete, up stepped Philip Hubert Frohman, an unknown whose dream it was to become the cathedral's architect. Frohman spent the next 50 years building the church. Obsessed with detail and scornful of expense, he once ordered all the molding on the central tower shifted by one-eighth inch because of its effect on the tower's shadow. He toiled away until 1972, when at age 85 he was hit by a truck on the cathedral close.

Others who dedicated their lives to the cathedral were the many masons, stonecarvers, and stained-glass artisans who conveyed 14th-century skills to the 20th. The 215 stained-glass windows, 3,000 stone sculptures, and other works of art were crafted to perfect the nation's "moral lighthouse." From the day Theodore Roosevelt laid the cornerstone in 1907 until the day President George H. W. Bush attended the dedication of the Tower of St. Paul in 1990, the cathedral took 83 years to construct. The building's 150,000 tons of Indiana limestone, says the U.S. Bureau of Standards, should stand without major restoration or reinforcement for 2,000 years.

VISITING

Guided tours *(donation)* are offered several times daily; you can also wander about on your own. There are daily services *(except Sat.)* from the Episcopal *Book of Common Prayer.* As an Episcopal institution, the church hosts many interfaith services; the building's main sanctuary and its other chapels are routinely used for weddings of cathedral-school alumni. Weekly **musical events** include organ demonstrations *(Wed.),* carillon recitals *(Sat.),* and ten-bell peals *(Sun. after a.m. service);* all take place around noon or 1 p.m.

Stroll outside to admire the flying buttresses, the arches, and some of the 112 **gargoyles** whose expressions range from silly to fiendish. In addition to warding off evil, the gargoyles repel rainwater; in storms they spout water well away from the building. The figures are

Washington National Cathedral
www.cathedral.org/cathedral
🅰 Map p. 179
✉ Massachusetts & Wisconsin Aves., N.W.
☎ 202-537-6200
🚍 Bus: N2, N3, N4, N6, & N7; or 30, 32, 34, 35, & 36

A stained-glass window shows Jesus urging followers to evangelize.

carved in various shapes: wild boars, mythical beasts, cats, dogs, even caricatures of people (such as master carver Roger Morigi) central to the construction or life of the cathedral. Binoculars are handy for inspecting the higher ones.

Outside is also the best place to drink in the immensity of the sixth largest cathedral in the world, and the second largest in the U.S. (only New York's St. John the Divine is bigger). The central Gloria in Excelsis Deo tower rises 300 feet, while the nave runs one-tenth of a mile.

The west-entrance central portal features Frederick Hart's spellbinding tympanum sculpture, "The Creation," in which half-formed men and women swirl about in a chaos of clouds and waves.

Walk inside and let the huge space swallow you up. Faithful to its Gothic style, the church was built in a cruciform shape. Stand at the crossing and look up; the massive piers rise 98 feet to the vaulting overhead. Instead of steel, the arches are held in place by a keystone and supported by buttresses.

The intricate pulpit, from which Dr. Martin Luther King, Jr., delivered his final sermon on March 31, 1968, was carved from stone donated by England's Canterbury Cathedral. The 10,500 pieces of glass in the spectacular **West Rose Window** cast a rich late-afternoon rainbow on the floor.

Running along the nave are memorial alcoves, or bays. The **Woodrow Wilson Bay** symbolizes the life of the 28th President, the only U.S. President whose final resting place is Washington, D.C. The floor of the **Lincoln Bay** is inset with 33 Lincoln-head pennies —one for each state in the Union at the time of the Great Emancipator's assassination. About halfway down on the right (south) side, the modernistic **Space Window** is captivatingly 3-D; a moon rock is embedded in the center lancet.

Scattered throughout, nine chapels vary from the tiny **Good Shepherd Chapel** to the church-size **Bethlehem Chapel** on the crypt level. Especially appealing is the intimate **Children's Chapel**, where every item has been scaled to the size of a six-year-old. Also on the crypt level is a store offering books, tapes, cards, and snacks.

For a closer look at the cathedral's towers and gargoyles (and a terrific view of the city), take an elevator to the **Pilgrim Observation Gallery** on the seventh floor of the St. Peter and St. Paul towers. ■

Bell appeal

National Cathedral's central tower holds ten peal bells and a 53-bell carillon. It is the world's only cathedral blessed with both kinds of bells in one tower.

Each peal bell is mounted on a wheel, from which a rope hangs down to the ringers' chamber. The pull must be smooth and even, so one ringer is assigned to each bell. Weighing 600 to nearly 3,600 pounds apiece, the bells cannot be rung fast enough to play a melody; instead, sequences of notes called "changes" are played.

Change ringing is difficult and dangerous: Lose your concentration and you not only sabotage the change but risk injury when the bell's momentum jerks you high off the floor. Peals *(Sun. after a.m. service)* can last from several minutes to the rare "full peal," a three-hour extravaganza of 5,000 changes. The joyous noise can be heard at the White House, 3 miles distant. ■

Opposite: The St. Peter and St. Paul towers on the west facade of Washington National Cathedral bask in the golden sunrays of late afternoon.

More places to visit in Cleveland Park & beyond

NATIONAL MUSEUM OF HEALTH & MEDICINE

Though it now stresses science over spectacle, this museum is not for the squeamish: Exhibits range from preserved human fetuses and a stomach-shaped hairball to a leg swollen by elephantiasis and a hands-on brain. The collection was begun during the Civil War as a research tool for military medicine and surgery. Included are photos of war wounds, fragments of Lincoln's skull, and microscopes from the crude to the complex. Permanent and chang-

Memorial (1890) by Augustus Saint-Gaudens was commissioned by historian Henry Adams to honor his wife, Clover. It depicts a seated figure wearing a heavy cloak, the face obscured by shadows. Mark Twain remarked that the sculpture embodied all of human grief, while Saint-Gaudens himself called his work "The Mystery of the Hereafter" and "The Peace of God that Passeth Understanding." Magnifying the work's mystery, it bears no inscription. ◩ Map p. 179 ✉ Rock Creek Church Rd. & Webster St., N.W. ☎ 202-726-2080

The last picture palace: The Uptown theater anchors upper Connecticut Avenue.

ing exhibits examine venereal diseases, women's health, heart disease, and other topics. ✉ Walter Reed Army Medical Center, 6900 Georgia Ave., N.W. ☎ 202-782-2200 $ Donation Ⓜ Metro: Takoma Park

ROCK CREEK CEMETERY

A mile and a half east of Rock Creek Park in the Petworth neighborhood, this 86-acre site exudes the feel of an old country parish. Set amid this pastoral glebe, St. Paul's (or "Rock Creek") Church is the city's sole surviving colonial church. The church was founded in 1712, long before Washington was a city; the current building dates from 1775, though only the walls are original.

Some of the city's finest cemetery memorials reside here. They honor crusading novelist Upton Sinclair, Cabinet members, Supreme Court justices, and National Geographic Society founder Gilbert H. Grosvenor. The cemetery also houses one of the finest works by one of America's greatest sculptors: The Adams

UPTOWN THEATER

Opened in 1936, the art deco Uptown is Washington's premier movie palace. Its 830 seats, including a balcony, make it the city's largest remaining cinema theater. A curved screen, 72 feet long and 32 feet high, wraps viewers in movie magic, while a Dolby digital sound system keeps the illusion up-to-date. Though the Uptown offers only one film at a time, almost anything looks great in a house this big. ◩ Map p. 179 ✉ 3426 Connecticut Ave., N.W. ☎ 202-966-5400 Ⓜ Metro: Cleveland Park

WASHINGTON DOLLS' HOUSE & TOY MUSEUM

Founded in 1975 by a doll house historian, this unusual museum presents a collection of antique dolls' houses, dolls, toys, and games, primarily from the Victorian period. The houses are drawn from all over the world. ✉ 5236 44th St., N.W. ☎ 202-244-0024 🕐 Closed Mon. $ $ Ⓜ Metro: Friendship Heights ∎

Alesser known niche away from the tourist center, the land east of the Capitol holds a few charms of its own, including a museum honoring African Americans, a dazzling basilica, and gardens galore.

East of the Capitol

**Stokes' aster at the
National Arboretum**

Rev. Willie Wilson plays washboard at Union Temple Baptist Church in Anacostia.

East of the Capitol

MORE THAN HALF THE CITY LIES EAST OF THE CAPITOL, AN AREA RICH IN AFRICAN American and military history, as well as gardens, marshes, and woods. Architecture lovers will find one of the city's most awe-inspiring buildings here, the nation's largest Catholic church.

The history of the eastern part of the city is tied to its river, the Anacostia, first seen by a European, explorer John Smith, nearly 400 years ago. Back then the Nacotchtank Indians (whose corrupted name, Anacostan, would be given to this East Branch of the Potomac) lived here, harvesting shad, catfish, and yellow perch. The arrival of white settlers meant the Indians' demise and the spread of tobacco plantations. In 1790 the lower Anacostia became part of the new capital. Soon developments arose on the northwest riverfront—the Washington Navy Yard (1799) and the U.S. Arsenal (1803).

Across the river from the Navy Yard, the city laid out its first planned, whites-only suburb, Uniontown, in 1854. During the Civil War, the military erected several forts east of the river. After the war, the Freedman's Bureau bought nearby, 375-acre Barry farm and sold

lots to 500 black families. Still the community, renamed Anacostia in 1886, remained mostly white until the 1950s. That changed with the migration of whites to the suburbs, and by 1970, Anacostia had become 86 percent black.

While the area along Martin Luther King Jr. Avenue (formerly Asylum Avenue) supports take-out restaurants, auto shops, and several other small businesses, the neighborhoods on U, V, and W Streets possess many early working-class row houses. The District government and private corporations have recently committed nearly a billion dollars to this area, hoping to improve neglected neighborhoods and enhance the waterfront. In the past decade, a rise in new housing and the arrival of the Metro have brought new residents, tourists, and life.

On the other side of the river, one of the last areas of the city to develop, the Northeast quadrant is anchored by the glorious grounds

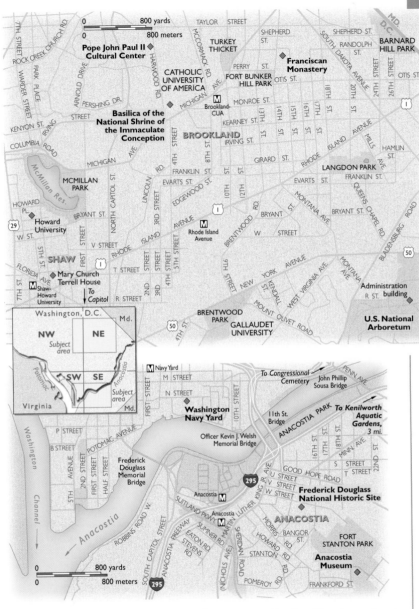

of the U.S. National Arboretum and by the Catholic University of America, home of the Shrine of the Immaculate Conception. Also in this area is Gallaudet University, the country's premier school for the deaf.

Sports fans know Northeast for the Langston Golf Course and RFK Stadium. The government built Langston in 1938 at the urging of black male and females golfers, who were barred from all but one of the District's courses. RFK Stadium, which opened in 1961, was once home to the Washington Redskins football team and the now defunct Washington Senators baseball team. Today the stadium draws crowds for its world-class women's and men's soccer teams and music concerts. ■

Frederick Douglass National Historic Site

Frederick Douglass NHS
www.nps.gov/frdo
🗺 Map p. 193
✉ 1411 W St., S.E.
☎ 202-426-5961 or 800-967-2283 (reservations)
🚌 Bus: B2

SITUATED AMONG THE ROW HOUSES OF ANACOSTIA, Cedar Hill—former home of abolitionist Frederick Douglass—harks back to a time when this area was a quiet country suburb. Built in the 1850s atop a grassy knoll, the 21-room white brick house offers a commanding view of the Washington skyline from its gracious front porch. A visit to this National Park Service site provides a fascinating glimpse into the life and work of the "sage of Anacostia," the most prominent African American orator of the 19th century.

The home of Frederick Douglass still offers a commanding view of the city.

Douglass was born a slave in Maryland's Talbot County in 1818, son of a black mother and a white father, possibly his owner. Sent to Baltimore as a servant, he taught himself to read; at 20 he escaped to New York, then Massachussetts, where he lectured for the Massachusetts Anti-Slavery Society. To elude slave hunters after publishing his autobiography, in 1845, he fled to Europe. The purchase of his freedom by friends allowed him to return two years later. He began the *North Star* newspaper and kept working for the rights of blacks and women.

After the Civil War, he moved to Washington, D.C. Appointed U.S. marshal of the District in 1877, he bought 9-acre Cedar Hill. He expanded it to 15 acres and enlarged the house by seven rooms. After his 1895 death, his widow, Helen, preserved Cedar Hill and organized the Frederick Douglass Memorial and Historical Association; the restored house opened to the public in 1972.

The guided one-hour tour begins in the **visitor center** with a 17-minute orientation film. Among items on display is a Lincoln cane given to Douglass by the President's widow. After the video, you climb the steps to the **Victorian house.** Inside, the tastefully appointed parlors, library, and dining room look much as they did in Douglass's time—some 90 percent of the furnishings are original. The kitchen, with its coal and wood-burning stove, and the adjoining washroom are reminders of the days before electricity and indoor plumbing. Upstairs, Douglass's bedroom has a 19th-century bootjack and pair of shoes tucked by the bed. To see the different styles of his two wives, peek into their separate bedrooms.

Outside, you'll find the **Growlery** (a reconstruction), the private study to which Douglass often escaped. Cedar Hill was originally a farm estate with chicken coops, barn, and carriage house; Hurricane Hazel destroyed all but two of the outbuildings in 1967. ∎

Kenilworth Aquatic Gardens

A cool feast of water lilies and lotuses floats on the waters of the Kenilworth Aquatic Gardens, on the east bank of the Anacostia. Started in 1880 by Civil War veteran Walter B. Shaw, this lovely 12-acre sanctuary is in full bloom in midsummer.

Popular with tourists in the 1920s, the pools were threatened when the U.S. Army Corps of Engineers began dredging marshes in the 1930s. Today the National Park Service manages the gardens.

A **visitor center** near the gardens' parking lot has exhibits on the area. From here, stroll onto the dikes around the 40 ponds to see willows and post oaks, geese and red-winged blackbirds. At the gardens' end, a 335-yard **boardwalk** extends into the marshes, where great blue herons and egrets stalk prey amid wild rice and duck potato. Other denizens include osprey, mallard, snapping turtles, and muskrat. The 0.7-mile (one way) **River Walk** offers a closer look at 77-acre Kenilworth Marsh, which borders the

Kenilworth Aquatic Gardens
www.nps.gov/nacel/keaq

🗺 Map p. 193
✉ 1550 Anacostia Ave., N.E.
☎ 202-426-6905
🚌 Bus: V7

An aquatic perennial indigenous to Asia, the sacred lotus flower opens in the early morning.

gardens. A city dump in the 1950s and '60s, the fill area is now rich in bird and plant life. Here American bittern, long billed marsh wrens, and spotted salamanders live in a cattail-fringed wetland.

The best time for seeing wildlife and catching night-blooming lilies is early morning. The gardens open at 7 a.m. ∎

Anacostia Museum

Located in Fort Stanton Park, where one of Washington's Civil War fortifications stood, this Smithsonian outlet opened in 1967 as a neighborhood museum devoted to the interpretation of the African American experience.

Exhibits have included retrospectives on black photographers, such as New Orleans's Jules Lion who began producing daguerreotypes in 1840, and inventors such as Benjamin Banneker, who helped to plan the capital city. Other exhibits have explored topics as diverse as African American quilts, black churches, the antebellum South, the

Civil Rights movement, Malcolm X, and race and ethnicity among black immigrants. Exhibitions of local artwork, including pieces by school children, and programs of music and dance are part of the museum's continuing mission to document and present the contemporary world of black Washington.

Reopened in February 2002 after an extensive renovation, the museum now has an expanded archives, library, and collections space. The premier exhibit, "Precious Memories: the Collector's Passion, Part I," promotes the preservation of historical materials. ∎

Anacostia Museum
www.si.edu/anacostia

🗺 Map p. 193
✉ 1901 Fort Pl., S.E.
☎ 202-357-2700
🚌 Bus: 92

U.S. National Arboretum

U.S. National Arboretum

www.usna.usda.gov

🏛 Map p. 193

✉ 24th & R Sts., N.E., or 3501 New York Ave.

☎ 202-245-2726

🚌 Bus: X6, B3

A BIT OFF THE BEATEN TOURIST TRACK, THIS WHOLLY delightful oasis of fields, ponds, fountains, gardens, and flowering trees is just the tonic for those in need of some outdoor beauty. Established by an act of Congress in 1927, the National Arboretum is run by the Department of Agriculture as a living museum and a research and education facility. The arboretum's 446 acres include 9.5 miles of gentle roadways that wind past a dozen garden areas.

A pleasure any time, the arboretum is especially beautiful in spring, with 15,000 multicolored azaleas and blossoming dogwoods, cherries, and crabapples blushing on the hillsides. The sweet fragrances of magnolias and roses blend with those of woodland wildflowers.

In summer, the delicate flowers of high grasses stipple meadows, while daylilies and crape myrtles take to the heat with ease, and water lilies bloom in the koi pool that surrounds one wing of the administration building. Fall enriches the color palette with the vivid yellows of hickory and tulip poplar and the wine reds of sweet gum and dogwood. The late flowers of witch hazel and spider lilies fan the flames.

In the cold quiet days of winter, the bright red berries of holly glisten like little beads, and dwarf conifers and other evergreens are often rimed with ice. Ornamental grasses and dry leaves chatter in the winds that sweep through the open fields.

VISITING

On the way to the administration building from the New York Avenue entrance, you'll notice beehive-shaped **brick kilns.** When the brickyard, dating from 1909, shut down in 1972, the acreage and buildings were sold to the arboretum.

At the administration building, you'll find maps and a list of gardens currently in bloom. Next to

Children create their own floral tableaus beneath a flowering "Tonto" crape myrtle at the arboretum.

this building, the recently redone **National Bonsai and Penjing Museum** has an outstanding collection of miniature trees from Japan, China, and America. Breezes lilt through feathery Japanese maples and gravel paths meander among bonsai pavilions.

Across the drive, the 2.5-acre **National Herb Garden** features some 800 varieties of herbs in ten themed gardens. Standing like ruins in a nearby field are 22 sandstone Corinthian columns, removed from the Capitol's east central portico in 1958 when the Senate side of the Capitol building was enlarged. To see other gardens, take the guided 40-minute open-air tram tour *(weekends mid-April–mid-Oct., $)* starting near the R Street entrance. Or drive or bike to most by looping the outer roads.

Heading southwest from the administration building, you come first to the **National Boxwood Collection**—more than a hundred species on 5 acres. Adjoining perennials include irises, peonies, and daylilies. Continue to the **azalea collections,** which peak in late April. To the east, on Crabtree Road, pull over for **Fern Valley** and its native plants of the eastern United States; a half-mile wooded path traipses past wildflowers, a meadow, prairie, and a stream. Plants are grouped by geographical origin—piedmont, southern mountains, coastal plain, and prairie. Along here is a specimen of Franklinia, a small tree with white flowers, discovered in 1765 in Georgia by naturalist William Bartram; by 1790 it was extinct in the wild, perhaps the victim of flooding or rampant collecting.

At the arboretum's far eastern end, the **Asian collections** are one of the city's highlights. Flora from Japan, Korea, and China have been planted on a hillside so that from strategically placed benches you have glimpses of a pagoda through the trees and views down to the Anacostia River. Ginkgos and bamboo bend in gentle breezes, and in spring Japanese wisteria and other flowers scent the air. To the north, the **Gotelli Collection of dwarf and slow-growing conifer** is considered to be among the world's best. The 1,500 specimens include juniper, cedar, spruce, fir, hemlock, and arborvitae. ∎

Anacostia River

Since the arrival of Europeans nearly 400 years ago, the Anacostia watershed has been used, overused, and abused. Runoffs from big farms in the 18th century silted the river, and urban growth has troubled the waters ever since. In the early 20th century, efforts to reshape the waterway and "reclaim" the adjoining swamps for development nearly killed the Anacostia.

Fortunately, the tide is turning. Government agencies as well as citizen groups, such as the Anacostia Watershed Society, are working to protect this valuable ecosystem, a vital part of the country's largest estuary—the Chesapeake Bay. Over the past decade, hundreds of tons of debris have been cleaned up, and some 12,000 trees have been planted. In the city, the river's watershed is essentially sidewalk and street drains, which means that unfiltered trash too often finds its way into the river. With an eye on the future, the Anacostia Watershed Society has enlisted the help of thousands of city youths to help clean up this river. ∎

Basilica of the National Shrine of the Immaculate Conception

THE BLUE DOME AND 329-FOOT-TALL CAMPANILE OF THE National Shrine preside over the skyline of Northeast Washington. Built along Byzantine and Romanesque lines, the National Shrine is the country's largest—and the world's eighth largest—Catholic church and one of the most beautiful and impressive pieces of architecture in a city renowned for its monuments.

Basilica of the National Shrine of the Immaculate Conception
www.nationalshrine.com
- Map p. 193
- Michigan Ave. & 4th St., N.E.
- 202-526-8300
- Metro: Brookland-CUA; Bus: 80

In 1913, while rector of the Catholic University of America, Bishop Thomas J. Shahan (1857–1932) presented Pope Pius X with plans for building a shrine to the Blessed Virgin Mary on the campus. With the Pope's support, work began in 1920; the building was dedicated four decades later, in 1959. In 1990, John Paul II designated the shrine a basilica because of its significance as a national center of worship.

You can join a free tour, or pick up a floor plan near the entrance and wander on your own. Sixty-five chapels and oratories, many funded by American ethnic groups, circle the perimeter of the crypt level and upper church. You should enter on the upstairs level, where the grandiose **Great Upper Church,** its vaulted ceilings soaring to a height of 100 feet, takes your breath away. Natural light floods the vast interior, stained glass casts color on walls and floors, and mosaics and candles sparkle in almost every niche and dome. Notice the swirling cosmos and the Garden of Eden depicted above the east transept and, in the west transept, the people rising toward a cloud-enthroned Jesus. The chancel dome holds a huge mosaic titled "Christ in Majesty," a hallmark of Byzantine art. A soothing contrast can be see in the green marble walls and trickling fountain of the **Mary Queen of Ireland chapel.**

Stairs lead downstairs to the **crypt level,** where inscribed black and white marble walls and pillars adorn **Memorial Hall,** as a remembrance to those who donated to the construction. Also noteworthy here is the **Crypt Church,** modeled on the Roman catacombs. It holds services six times a day during the week. In **Our Mother of Africa Chapel,** sculpture groups depict African American history from slavery to freedom. ∎

Pope John Paul II Cultural Center

Up the street from the Romanesque National Shrine is this modernistic limestone and granite multimedia museum (3900 Harewood Rd., N.E., 202-635-5411, closed Mon., $). Visitors watch a short orientation video about the center, then take a self-guided tour through galleries exploring such themes as church and papal history, community, and the Virgin Mary. Computer terminals offer background information and activities such as designing a stained-glass window. One room is filled with memorabilia of Pope John Paul II, while another—equipped with bell ropes and headsets—offers an opportunity for "virtual" change ringing. ∎

Opposite: The National Shrine's tiled dome and soaring bell tower punctuate the city's skyline.

More places to visit east of the Capitol

CONGRESSIONAL CEMETERY

Originally intended to contain the graves of congressmen and officials who died in office, the Congressional Cemetery, established in 1807, is the oldest national cemetery and the final resting place of many Washington notables. Beginning in 1839, sandstone monuments were created for every member of Congress, no matter when he died, though only 80 are actually occupied (the others are empty memorials to people buried elsewhere). Congress stopped the practice in 1877 after a furious debate, in which Senator George Hoar of Massachusetts argued that being buried under one of the massive monuments added "a new terror to death." Among its famous residents are Capitol architect William Thornton (1828), Civil War photographer Mathew Brady (1916), Marine Corps bandmaster John Philip Sousa (1932), and J. Edgar Hoover (1972), director of the FBI. Visitors are invited to stroll the grounds; a map is located at the entrance. ⚠ Map p. 193 ✉ 1801 E St., S.E. ☎ 202-543-0539 🚇 Metro: Stadium Armory; Bus: 96

FRANCISCAN MONASTERY

If you can't afford a trip to the Holy Land, this working monastery near the National Shrine of the Immaculate Conception offers a good

A monk leads a tour down into the catacombs of the Franciscan Monastery.

facsimile. Tours are offered hourly. Built in 1899 to educate missionaries, it contains full-scale reproductions of such sacred places as the Grotto of Lourdes, the Grotto of Gethsemane, the Tomb of the Virgin Mary, and the Holy Sepulcher of Christ. The Byzantine-style church is laid out in the shape of a five-fold Jerusalem or Crusader's Cross, with chapels at each end. Especially memorable are the Roman-style catacombs downstairs and the gruesome tales of Christian martyrs. In spring the gardens grace the monastery with flowering rosebushes, dogwoods, and cherry trees. You'll almost forget you're in the middle of a 21st-century city. ⚠ Map p. 193 ✉ 14th & Quincy Sts., N.E. ☎ 202-526-6800 🚇 Metro: Brookland–CUA; Bus: H2, H4

WASHINGTON NAVY YARD

Occupying a plot of land on the Anacostia set aside by George Washington, this lesser known gem of Washington tourism is considered the ceremonial "Quarterdeck of the Navy." Kids enjoy clambering through the passages and up and down the ladders of the decommissioned destroyer **U.S.S. Barry,** permanently moored here. The 424-foot-long ship took part in the 1962 Cuban missile crisis and in the Vietnam War. You can walk through the wardroom, bunk room, sick bay, galley and mess deck, and pilothouse. Just across the parking lot from the ship stands the **Navy Museum,** whose highlights include working periscopes with views to Virginia, a fighter plane, more than a hundred model ships, and hands-on antiaircraft guns. The **art gallery** and the **Marine Corps Historical Center,** in Building 58, are a bit more static, but you might want to look at **Willard Park,** a parade ground surrounded by 33 cannon captured as trophies from the 17th to 19th centuries, and the museum grounds. To the north are the Greek Revival arched gate and guardhouses designed in 1804 by Benjamin Henry Latrobe, one of the Capitol's architects. www.history.navy.mil ⚠ Map p. 193 ✉ 9th & M Sts., S.E. ☎ 202-433-4882 (Navy Museum), 202-433-3377 (U.S.S. *Barry*), 202-433-3534 (Marine museum) 🚇 Metro: Eastern Market ∎

Only on the Virginia side of the Potomac can you complete the story of the country's past, including colonial Alexandria and its early associations with the Revolutionary War, and Arlington, famous for its national cemetery.

Across the Potomac

Pineapple door knocker, symbolizing hospitality

Across the Potomac

GRACEFULLY ARCHING ACROSS THE POTOMAC RIVER, CONNECTING
Washington to Virginia, Arlington Memorial Bridge makes a powerful visual statement by
linking memorials dedicated to Union Commander in Chief Abraham Lincoln
and Confederate Gen. Robert E. Lee—a symbolic joining of North and South.
Overlooking Lincoln's templelike memorial on the Mall is Lee's Arlington House, high
on a hill in what is now Arlington National Cemetery, surrounded by the somber white
graves of Civil War veterans from both North and South, as well as servicepeople from
all succeeding wars.

Washingtonians seem reluctant to cross the
Potomac and enter Northern Virginia, a suburban mix of historic sites, residential neighborhoods, and shopping malls. But Arlington
and Alexandria, just on the other side, have
much to offer. Separated by the Crystal City
high-rises around Ronald Reagan Washington
National Airport, the two areas are connected
by the Metro system and highly scenic George
Washington Memorial Parkway.

Both suburbs originally belonged to
the District of Columbia, then a diamond-
shaped city straddling the river. But in 1846,
Virginia took back its part, the returned land
equaling about one-third of the entire city.
The fortunes of these two areas have been
tied to Washington ever since.

Already a tobacco port, Alexandria got its
official start in 1749 as a 60-acre townsite.
George Washington, who lived 9 miles south
at Mount Vernon, and Robert E. Lee, both
considered Alexandria their hometown.

Falling on hard times after the Civil War, the
town has prospered in recent years with the
sprucing up of its waterfront and the restoration of 18th-century town houses. Now a fashionable residential area, the town draws a
steady stream of tourists to its bars, boutiques,
restaurants, and riverside craft shops.
Historical sites give insight into the lives of
Washington, Lee, and other prominent locals.

One of the nation's smallest counties, and
containing no incorporated cities or towns
within its boundaries, Arlington did not exist
as its own separate entity until after 1846,
when the land was returned from Washington
to Virginia. Today it is home to Arlington
National Cemetery and the Pentagon. The
moving Marine Corps War Memorial,
Theodore Roosevelt Island and its tribute to
the 26th President, and the string of Potomac
River parks along the parkway are other good
reasons for venturing to the Virginia side of
the river. ∎

Theodore Roosevelt Memorial Bridge connects Washington with the burbs.

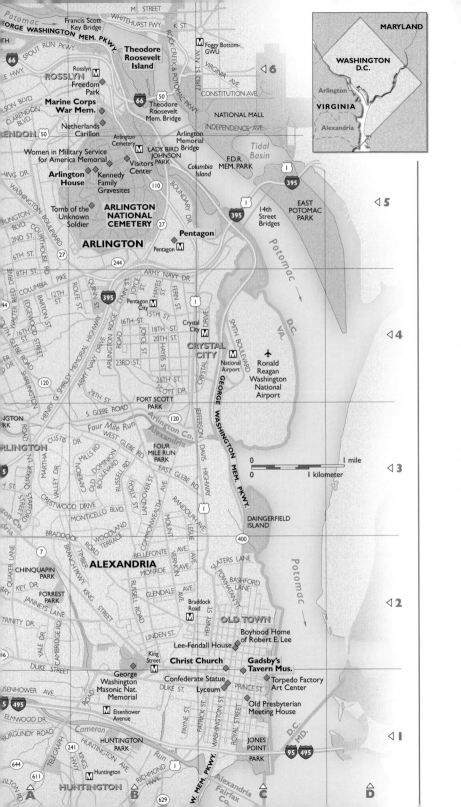

Potomac

Francis Scott Key Bridge
WHITEHURST FWY.

M STREET
K ST.

ORGE WASHINGTON MEM. PKWY.

Foggy Bottom-GWU M

66

SPROUT RUN PKWY.

Theodore Roosevelt Island

ROCK CREEK & POTOMAC PKWY.

N. 27TH ST.

VIRGINIA AVE.

◁ 6

ROSSLYN

Rosslyn M

Freedom Park

66

50

Theodore Roosevelt Mem. Bridge

CONSTITUTION AVE.

NATIONAL MALL

Marine Corps War Mem.

INDEPENDENCE AVE.

Netherlands Carillon

Women in Military Service for America Memorial

Arlington Cemetery

LADY BIRD JOHNSON PARK

Arlington Memorial Bridge

Tidal Basin

Visitors Center

M

Columbia Island

F.D.R. MEM. PARK

◁ 5

Arlington House

Kennedy Family Gravesites

110

1

395

EAST POTOMAC PARK

Tomb of the Unknown Soldier

ARLINGTON NATIONAL CEMETERY

27

BOUNDARY DR.

1

14th Street Bridges

ARLINGTON

27

244

Pentagon M

Pentagon

ARMY NAVY DR.

Potomac

VA.

D.C.

◁ 4

395

Pentagon City M

Crystal City M

CRYSTAL CITY

National Airport

SMITH BOULEVARD

Ronald Reagan Washington National Airport

FORT SCOTT PARK

120

GEORGE WASHINGTON MEM. PKWY.

JEFFERSON DAVIS HIGHWAY

Four Mile Run

FOUR MILE RUN PARK

0   1 mile
0   1 kilometer

◁ 3

ALEXANDRIA

1

DAINGERFIELD ISLAND

400

Potomac

7

CHINQUAPIN PARK

SLATERS LANE

BASHFORD LANE

◁ 2

FORREST PARK

Braddock Road M

OLD TOWN

Boyhood Home of Robert E. Lee

Lee-Fendall House

King Street M

Christ Church

Gadsby's Tavern Mus.

George Washington Masonic Nat. Memorial

Confederate Statue

Lyceum

Torpedo Factory Art Center

D.C.
MD.

Eisenhower Avenue M

Old Presbyterian Meeting House

5
495

JONES POINT PARK

95
495

◁ 1

241

HUNTINGTON PARK

Huntington M

1

611

HUNTINGTON

629

W. MEM. PKWY.

Alexandria Fairfax Co.

A   B   C   D

MARYLAND

WASHINGTON D.C.

Arlington

VIRGINIA

Alexandria

Arlington National Cemetery

Arlington National Cemetery

www.arlingtoncemetery.org

🅰 Map p. 203

✉ Virginia side of Arlington Memorial Bridge, off Va. 110

☎ 703-607-8052

🕐 Changing of the Guard, every hour Oct.–March, every half hour April–Sept.

💲 $ (parking fee)

🚇 Metro: Arlington Cemetery

Hundreds of thousands of servicemen and women lie buried beneath Arlington's green expanses.

ROWS OF WHITE HEADSTONES ON ROLLING HILLS, THE Changing of the Guard at the Tomb of the Unknowns, the eternal flame at John F. Kennedy's grave: These enduring images immediately bring to mind the nation's most famous national cemetery.

Another image, visible from the Washington side of the river, is the stately hilltop mansion called Arlington House (see p. 206). Once the beloved home of Robert E. Lee and his wife, Mary, it was on their surrounding plantation that the cemetery was established.

Shortly after Lee left to fight for the Confederacy in 1861, the federal government confiscated the property and put up fortifications. Union Quartermaster Gen. Montgomery Meigs recommended in 1864 that acreage on the Lee estate be set aside for a national cemetery. Later that year, Meigs's son was killed in the war; the high-relief tomb effigy of him lying slain in his uniform by the side of the road is one of Arlington's more unusual memorials.

Over Meigs's objection, Confederate soldiers were allowed burial in Arlington, though official decorations or observances were

not permitted. Meigs's bitterness largely kept Confederate widows outside the gates until the late 1800s. In a show of reconciliation, Congress in 1900 allowed a Confederate section of the cemetery to be set aside, and in 1914 the **Confederate Memorial** was dedicated by President Woodrow Wilson, with 3,000 veterans from both sides in attendance. As for the Lee family's fate, Lee's son, G. W. C. Lee, sued the government after the Civil War for confiscating their land. The Supreme Court ruled that he should be paid the market value, $150,000.

The 612-acre cemetery is now the final resting place for more than 260,000 servicepeople. With some 20 funerals conducted every weekday, the cemetery is expected to be filled by 2025, at which time it may be expanded onto other nearby government-owned land. To qualify for burial here, a serviceperson must have died on active duty, or be entitled to retirement pay, or have been awarded a high military decoration. Any veteran with an honorable discharge may have his or her cremated remains entombed in the Columbarium. For a funeral with full military honors, a flag-draped coffin is accompanied by an honor guard and a steady drum beat. After three rifle volleys, the coffin is lowered, while "Taps" is played. The guards then fold the flag and present it to the next of kin.

VISITING

As you approach the cemetery via the Ceremonial Entrance on Memorial Drive, you'll see the large, semicircular building of the **Women in Military Service for America Memorial.** Dedicated in 1997, it honors the nearly two million women who have served since 1776.

A guard will direct you to a left turn into the parking area for the cemetery's **visitor center.** Stop by for exhibits and a 12-minute film, as well as a good cemetery map. From here, quiet, tree-shaded streets and pathways meander to the main sites, making for a lovely stroll. Since the cemetery covers of lot of hilly ground, many people hop aboard the tourmobile *($)*, which stops at major points of interest.

Leaving the back of the visitor center, head up the pathway to reach the **gravesite of President John F. Kennedy.** At his funeral in 1963, his widow, Jacqueline, lit an eternal flame that continues to flicker even in the rain. She and their two infant children are also interred here. From this site, you have a grand view of the Lincoln Memorial, Washington Monument, and U.S. Capitol. Nearby, a white wooden cross marks the **grave of Senator Robert F. Kennedy.**

The best view of Washington from the cemetery, however, awaits farther up the hill at **Arlington House.** Appropriately, the grave of city designer Pierre Charles L'Enfant is situated here, in front of the mansion, facing Washington.

About a half-mile walk south from the house, adjacent to the amphitheater, the **Tomb of the Unknowns** holds the remains of unidentified servicemen, one each from the World Wars and Korea (the Vietnam veteran's remains were removed in 1998 when they

were identified). A 24-hour guard patrols this symbolic site, carrying an M-14 rifle with a ceremonial bayonet. The sentinel takes 21 steps on the plaza (symbolic of a 21-gun salute), then turns to face the tomb for 21 seconds. A dignified ritual, the Changing of the Guard always draws a crowd.

Others buried at Arlington include polar explorer Richard Byrd, boxer Joe Louis, 229 sailors from the U.S.S. *Maine* (sunk in Havana harbor in 1898), and Gen. John J. Pershing, the cemetery's highest ranking officer. Commander in chief of the American Expeditionary Forces in World War I, Pershing lies buried among the men with whom he served. ∎

A horse-drawn caisson and flag-draped coffin are standard at a full military funeral.

Arlington House

Arlington House
www.nps.gov/arho
- Map p. 203
- Arlington National Cemetery
- 703-235-1530
- Metro: Arlington Cemetery

BEFORE ARLINGTON CEMETERY, THERE WAS ARLINGTON House, the buff-hued Greek Revival mansion on a prominent hill above the Potomac. Built by Robert E. Lee's father-in-law in 1802–1817 and once anchoring a 1,100-acre plantation, it's now surrounded by the graves of servicepeople from many wars.

The Lees lived here off and on for 30 years while traveling between U.S. Army posts. Then, on April 18, 1861, when Virginia succeeded from the Union, Lincoln offered the 54-year-old Lee command of a Union Army that would invade the South. After a long and agonizing night Lee declined, deciding instead to accept command of Virginia's forces. His 32 years of distinguished service to the U.S. Army were over, and the country spiraled toward a long and bloody civil war.

"I can anticipate no greater calamity for the country than a dissolution of the Union," Lee later wrote. "I am willing to sacrifice everything but honor for its preservation." Loyal to his native state, home of his family for six generations, Lee left his home on April 22 to accept command of Virginia's forces, never to return. "I did only what my duty demanded," he said.

The Union Army soon moved in, using the house as a defense post headquarters. After the war, the cemetery superintendent lived and worked here for many years. In 1955 it officially was designated the Robert E. Lee Memorial.

Restored to its antebellum appearance, the gracious, high-ceilinged house looks much as it did during the Lee years. Though many heirlooms were looted, about one-third of the furnishings are original. A genuine touch is the original china, glassware, and silver in the Family Dining Room. After walking through the mansion's 15 rooms, you can take in some interesting exhibits on the Lee and Custis families in the slaves' quarters and museum out back. Vegetable gardens add to the authenticity of the site. From in front you can see the Lincoln Memorial, directly and symbolically connected by Memorial Bridge to Arlington House. ■

Overlooking Arlington National Cemetery, Arlington House honors Robert E. Lee and his family.

Marine Corps War Memorial

KNOWN AS THE IWO JIMA MEMORIAL, ONE OF THE NATION'S
most famous war monuments sits in a grassy park adjacent to Arlington
Cemetery. Its larger-than-life realism rests on the fact that the figures
are nearly six times life size, and the event they depict really happened.

There were, however, actually two
flag raisings. On Feb. 23, 1945, four
days into a vicious struggle for control of Iwo Jima, a detachment of
U.S. Marines made it to the top of
Mount Suribachi, the island's highest point, and raised a small
American flag. Later that afternoon,
after the slopes had been cleared of
enemy resistance, five Marines and
a Navy hospital corpsmen raised a
larger flag. It was this second flag
raising that news photographer
Joseph Rosenthal captured in the
famous image that won him a
Pulitzer Prize. The Marines' capture of the island three weeks

later was a crucial victory in the
Pacific campaign.

Sculptor Felix de Weldon, then
on duty with the U.S. Navy, was so
moved by the image that he cast it
in bronze. Dedicated in 1954, the 78-
foot-high sculpture depicts the soldiers standing atop a chunk of jagged
black granite that resembles the
island's volcanic rock, their cloth flag
flying 24 hours a day. On Tuesday
evenings in summer, the Marine
Corps presents a spirited parade here.

Nearby rises the **Netherlands
Carillon,** with 49 bells, presented
by the Dutch in 1960 in thanks for
American aid during the war. ∎

**Marine Corps
War Memorial**
www.nps.gov/gwmp/usmc
.htm

⬛ Map p. 203
✉ N. Meade St., just N
of Arlington
Cemetery
☎ 703-289-2500 or
703-289-2530
(concert & parade
information)
🚇 Metro: Arlington
Cemetery or
Rosslyn; Bus: 4A
or 4B

**Only three of the
six men depicted
in the memorial
survived the war.**

George Washington Memorial Parkway

George Washington Memorial Parkway

www.nps.gov/gwmp

Map p. 203

703-289-2530

The parkway in springtime splendor

OFFERING PEERLESS VIEWS OF THE CAPITAL CITY, THIS stunning roadway lends the perfect excuse for a leisurely drive. Ambling along the Potomac River between Mount Vernon and the American Legion Bridge, it links historic sites, riverside parks, and overlooks.

Beginning south of Alexandria at **Mount Vernon** (see pp. 220–222), the parkway winds north through maples, oaks, beeches, and tulip polars, chosen when the parkway was designed in the 1930s to give it the look of the Virginia countryside. Two miles beyond Mount Vernon sprawls **Fort Hunt Park,** preserving batteries that guarded the river approach to the city from 1898 to 1918. Look across the river to see its mate, **Fort Washington** (1824).

Ahead, a right turnoff leads to **River Farm** *(703-768-5700, closed weekends)*, once part of George Washington's estate. Beyond **Belle**

Haven Marina spreads a wide-sweeping upriver view—birders congregate along here to scan the water and sky for migrating geese and songbirds. For a closer look, take a stroll at **Dyke Marsh** *(Belle Haven Marina)*, a 240-acre bird haven.

Within **Old Town Alexandria** (see pp. 212–214), the parkway becomes Washington Street. Two blocks beyond King Street rises **Christ Church** (see p. 211), on the left. Beyond town you'll spot **Daingerfield Island,** site of a small marina and restaurant with a view.

Just north of Reagan Washington National Airport comes the most breathtaking stretch—the **Washington skyline** and its parade of monuments: the Capitol, Jefferson Memorial, Washington Monument, and Lincoln Memorial. The grassy riverbank here is ideal for picnicking. Beyond the 14th Street Bridges rises the **Navy and Marine Memorial.** Farther, you'll pass through the **LBJ Memorial Grove** and **Lady Bird Johnson Park,** abundant with flowers.

About a quarter mile beyond Roosevelt Bridge, you'll spy the turnout for **Theodore Roosevelt Island** (see opposite). The road passes beneath Key Bridge, with **Georgetown University's** spire looming across the river. The drive then climbs above the Potomac, offering overlooks of the increasingly wild and rocky river. About 1.5 miles beyond Turkey Run Park, the parkway ends at I-495 and the American Legion Bridge. ■

Theodore Roosevelt Island

Finding peace
and quiet near
the city's bustle

An arcadia of wooded paths and bird-filled marshes, this 91-acre island opposite the Kennedy Center is a favorite lunchtime retreat for office workers. Some 2.5 miles of trails are just right for walking, running, bird-watching, and general relaxing from city life stresses.

In 1967 the island was turned into a memorial to the charismatic, conservation-minded U.S. President. Many people heading over the footbridge for a walk are surprised to find, tucked in the middle of the woods, a rather grandiose **memorial** featuring a 17-foot-high bronze of Roosevelt, fountains, and

several enormous granite tablets inscribed with his words. About the outdoors, he remarked: "There are no words that can tell the hidden spirit of the wilderness, that can reveal its mystery, its melancholy, and its charm."

After a look at the memorial, you can choose between wooded or river-edged paths. One of the most delightful areas is the **boardwalk** through the swamp and marsh on the island's east side. Along here, herons stalk prey among cattails and pickerelweed, while bald cypresses and gnarled oaks suggest a pre-Washington landscape. ■

Theodore Roosevelt Island
www.nps.gov/gwmp/tri.htm
Map p. 203
Potomac River, 0.25 mile N of Theodore Roosevelt Bridge via George Washington Memorial Pkwy. north (no vehicle access southbound)
703-289-2530
Metro: Rosslyn

The Pentagon

It's certain that no one will look at this massive fortress quite the same way again following the tragic Sept. 11, 2001, crash of a hijacked jetliner into its south side. One of the world's largest office buildings, the 6.5-million-square-foot Pentagon was built in 16 months during World War II in order to combine the scattered offices of the War Department under one roof. The number five has no particular significance here—the building originally conformed to a five-sided site, and since President Franklin Roosevelt liked the unique shape it was kept.

Plans to reconstruct the damage are under way and could take as long as 1 to 3 years. It's undecided as of press time, however, whether tours will be offered again. If they are, you will be taken down a mile of hallways, where military art, model planes, and portraits of military leaders give insight into the nation's defense. Hidden away from public view are the War Room and other situation rooms in which top-secret meetings are held; in recent years Desert Storm and the Somalia operation were planned and controlled from here. ■

The Pentagon
Map p. 203
I-395 and Jefferson Davis Hwy. (Va. 110)
703-695-1776
Currently closed to the public
Metro: Pentagon; Bus: 9E, DASH 4

Alexandria

With its brick sidewalks, federal town houses, and quaint shops and restaurants, Alexandria's Old Town reminds many people of Georgetown. No coincidence here, since both arose as tobacco ports in the mid-1700s a mere 8 river miles from one another.

Scotsman John Alexander, for whom Alexandria is named, purchased much of present-day Alexandria in 1669 from an English ship captain for 6,000 pounds of tobacco. Incorporated in 1749, the town blossomed as a foreign port of entry. Strolling along Old plies—hundreds of thousands of soldiers tramped through on their way to postings and battles, and train after train rolled in with the wounded. Warehouses, churches, hotels, even large houses were requisitioned for use as military stations and hospitals.

King Street's panoply of shops and restaurants is housed in centuries'-old row houses.

Town's beautifully preserved wharf today, it's easy to visualize how Alexandria must have looked, when tall-masted brigs and schooners docked at the piers, mariners bustled between brick warehouses, and captains strutted cobbled lanes. Slaves and grain as well as tobacco added to the early prosperity of this genteel Southern town.

The Civil War, however, changed all that. As a buffer for Washington, only 100 miles north of the Confederate capital of Richmond, Alexandria was immediately occupied and soon overrun with Union forces. The fortified town became a crossroads for men and sup-

After the war, the small-town atmosphere was all but gone, and as Washington grew Alexandria sprawled and deteriorated. In 1946 the City Council stepped in to protect the splendid 18th- and 19th-century row houses, making Old Town the nation's third officially designated historic district.

Today, Old Town is a delightful place to spend a sunny afternoon, poking into shops, eating ice cream, watching boats glide by on the river. Especially on weekend evenings, crowds pack a spate of restaurants and pubs, enjoying the vibrant nightlife against its historical backdrop. ■

Christ Church

Historic Christ Church has sat behind its iron-gated fence on Washington Street since before Alexandria was established. Completed in 1773 in simple Georgian country style, it features a typical brick exterior and white-washed interior. The fine Palladian chancel window is unusual ornamentation for a church of its time.

George Washington was one of the first to buy a pew here, now marked by a silver plaque (No. 60). Tradition says that on the lawn he first declared to friends his intent to fight the war of American independence. Robert E. Lee was confirmed here on July 17, 1853 (a fact marked by another silver plaque, on the chancel), and he worshiped here with his family.

The tree-shaded **burying ground** was used for Alexandrians until 1808; the earliest tombstone is dated March 20, 1791. Look for one of the latest tombstones, for Anne Warren, a popular actress in her day. Her 1808 epitaph reads in part: "The unrivaled excellence of theatrical talents was surpassed by the mighty virtues…which adorned her private life. In her were contained the affectionate wife and mother and the sincere friend."

Docents lead **tours** daily; meet at the church's front door. ∎

Christ Church
www.historicchristchurch
.org
- Map p. 203
- 118 Washington St.
- 703-549-1450
- Metro: King St.; Bus: 10A

Gadsby's Tavern Museum

Consisting of a 1770s tavern, 1792 hotel, and three outbuildings, Gadsby's Tavern was colonial Alexandria's center of social, political, and business life. Festive balls, patriotic meetings, and presidential receptions once enlivened its rooms, earning it praise as the finest public house in America. Restored as a museum and operating restaurant, the tavern appears just as George Washington (a frequent visitor) might have seen it, complete with colonial decor and fare served on candlelit tables.

A 30-minute **guided tour** of the museum shows the taproom where patrons dined on whatever the tavern happened to be serving that night—perhaps ham and cheese "pye" or cream of County Surrey peanut soup. You learn that the drink of choice was rum, sometimes mixed with fruit juice and imported sugar to make a punch. You also see the dining room; ballroom; assembly room, where the Masonic Orders, the Alexandria Dragoons, and other local groups convened; and the third-floor communal bedchambers—the beds and floors were shared by as many travelers as could fit the space. ∎

Gadsby's Tavern Museum
- Map p. 203
- 134 N. Royal St.
- 703-838-4242
- $
- Closed Mon.
- Metro: King St. IF ROOM Bus: DASH 4, DASH 5

Setting up for lunch

Old Town by foot

Strolling is the best way to enjoy Old Town's colonial ambience, allowing you plenty of time to study the architectural details of historical row houses, admire postage-stamp gardens filled with peonies and begonias, visit the many historic buildings once frequented by Thomas Jefferson, George Washington, and Robert E. Lee, poke into specialty shops, and simply see what there is to see. The walk outlined here can be done in a couple of hours, but, depending on how many sites you stop by, you could easily spend a day.

Begin in the heart of the historic core at the two-story, yellow-frame **Ramsay House Visitors Center** ❶ *(221 King St., 703-838-4200)*, a reconstruction of the 1724 home of town founder William Ramsay. Across Fairfax

Street, **Market Square** holds a Saturday morning market that dates from 1749, making it one of the country's oldest.

From the visitor center, walk south on Fairfax Street. About half a block down on the right, the **Stabler-Leadbeater Apothecary Museum** ❷ *(105–107 S. Fairfax St., 703-836-3713, $, www.apothecary.org)* operated from 1792 to 1933. George Washington, James Monroe, and Robert E. Lee all knew these walls, stocked with all kinds of goods including medical supplies, house paint, and garden seeds. Preserved intact, the shop contains original potions, herbs, mortars, and journals.

Now go back to King Street and turn right. Situated along the river, the **Torpedo Factory Art Center** ❸ *(105 N. Union St., 703-838-4565, www.torpedofactory.org)* holds 80-odd studios where you can watch artisans sculpt, paint, weave, and make stained glass. A museum of local archaeological artifacts is on

The wharf (above) offers pleasant waterfront views. Dating from 1792, the Stabler–Leadbeater Apothecary Museum (left) was George Washington's pharmacy.

the third floor. Built in 1918, the factory turned out torpedo shell casings and other weaponry for both World Wars (look for the torpedo on view on the ground floor); the federal government used the spacious building for storage until the city of Alexandria bought it in 1969. The art center opened in 1974, and it was incorporated into a major waterfront development a decade later. Out back, you can

stroll along the boat docks, or park yourself on a bench and enjoy the fresh air.

Walk south on Union and make a right on Prince Street. Known as **Captain's Row,** this cobblestoned block is lined with sturdy federal town houses, many of which were owned by ship captains in the 18th century. Cross Lee Street, and on the right stands the 1851 pink stucco Greek Revival **Athenaeum** (*201 Prince St., 703-548-0035*), which once functioned as a bank; with the onset of the Civil War, the bank closed and documents were hidden until after the war, when customers were reimbursed. Now owned by the Northern Virginia Fine Arts Association, the Athenaeum features a contemporary art gallery. A little farther up the block, William Fairfax, an original trustee of Alexandria, lived at **207 Prince**

🅰 See area map p. 203
► Ramsay House visitor center
⟷ 2 miles
🕒 3 hours, without stops
► Carlyle House

NOT TO BE MISSED
* Torpedo Factory Art Center
* Christ Church
* Gadsby's Tavern Museum

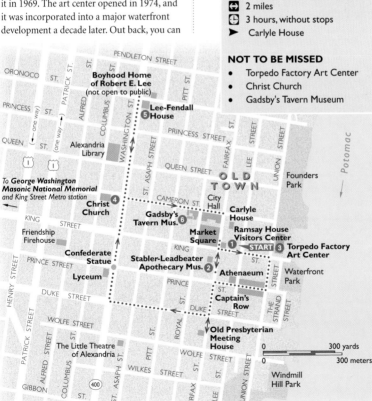

Green Christmas boughs adorn town houses on historic Queen Street.

Street, and next door at **209 Prince** lived Dr. James Craik, the surgeon-general who was with George Washington throughout the Revolutionary War, and who attended him at his death at nearby Mount Vernon.

At Fairfax Street, turn left and head south across Duke Street to the **Old Presbyterian Meeting House** (321 S. Fairfax St., 703-549-6670, sanctuary open Mon.–Fri.). Built in 1774, the church has a large unadorned interior with wood floors and clear windows; in the churchyard lies the Tomb of the Unknown Soldier of the American Revolution.

Proceed back up Duke Street to Washington Street, the main north-south thoroughfare, and head north. On the street's west side, the Greek Revival-style **Lyceum** (201 S. Washington St., 703-838-4994) was built in 1839 as a cultural center and library. It now maintains permanent and temporary exhibits on Alexandria's history.

At the intersection of Washington and Prince stands the bronze **Confederate Statue,** a memorial to the town's Confederate dead. Created by Casper Buberl and erected in 1889, the defeated-looking veteran faces south, head bowed, arms folded. A block north you're back at **King Street,** Old Town's main commercial avenue. Along here you can find a busy assortment of restaurants, bars, and boutiques. Antique shops pack the stretch to the west.

The monument rising on the hill a mile or so west is the grandiose **George Washington Masonic National Memorial** (King St. & Callahan Dr., 703-683-2007, www.gwmemorial.org), with sprawling views of Alexandria and Washington from the ninth-floor observation deck. The free one-hour tour lingers a bit much on Masonic history, but it is worthwhile for the good collection of Washington memorabilia, including his family Bible and leather field trunk. If you don't want to walk from Washington Street, it's an easy drive and there's plenty of parking.

Back at Washington and King Streets, the next block north holds historic **Christ Church** ❹ (see p. 211). Three blocks farther north on Washington, the **Lee-Fendall House** ❺ (614 Oronoco St., 703-548-1789, closed Mon., $) was built in 1785 by lawyer Philip Fendall, who married an aunt of Robert E. Lee. Family heirlooms are on display, including portraits, letters, and books. Across Oronoco Street, at No. 607, the **Boyhood Home of Robert E. Lee** was recently bought by private owners; although locals complained that the house would be closed to the public, no one came forth with the several million dollars needed for renovations and upkeep.

Head back down Washington and make a left on Cameron. To get a feel for how early Alexandrians dined out, stop by the **Gadsby's Tavern Museum** ❻ (see p. 211). Then walk east to the corner of Cameron and Fairfax Streets and end your stroll at the Georgian Palladian-style **Carlyle House** (121 N. Fairfax St., 703-549-2997, closed Mon., $), built in 1753 by Scottish merchant John Carlyle. British Gen. Edward Braddock convened a meeting here in 1755 with five colonial governors to discuss the financing of the French and Indian War. Interesting tours showcase the lifestyle of an 18th-century Virginia family and their servants and slaves. ■

Buzzing with life before Washington, D.C., was there, the land beyond the Beltway is laced with a wealth of historic sites that would be worth a peek even without the capital city nearby.

Excursions

Standing in formation at the U.S. Naval Academy, Annapolis

Excursions

WITH RIVERSIDE PARKLANDS AND COBBLE-LANED VILLAGES, COLONIAL plantations and busy harborfronts, Washington is blessed with an abundance of easy escapes within an hour's drive away.

Among the most accessible is the Chesapeake & Ohio National Historical Park, which preserves the ruins of a 19th-century canal and its towpath. Beginning in Georgetown and paralleling the Potomac River for more than 180 miles north, it's especially popular with walkers, bikers, and campers. Great Falls— its most distinctive feature and probably the most spectacular natural attraction anywhere between the Blue Ridge and the Chesapeake Bay—is only 5 miles beyond the Beltway (I-495). In this section of the park, you can hike, picnic, bird-watch, kayak, rock climb, and delve into local history that extends back to the early 1800s. Great Falls Park on the Virginia side of the river is also a popular place to view the falls; the remains of an earlier canal venture started by George Washington are here.

You'll find history that goes even further back on the Potomac River south of Washington. More than 250 years ago, Virginia colonists established vast plantations and manor houses, including Washington's Mount Vernon and Gunston Hall. Built by the slaves of early citizens, these historic houses, and the younger Woodlawn, stand today as tributes to the quality workmanship and to the tireless efforts of preservationists.

Annapolis, poised some 30 miles east of Washington at the point where the Severn River spills into the Chesapeake Bay, is equally well preserved. You couldn't ask for a more charming, history-saturated, seafood-proud water town. It's easy to fill a day—or two, if you're lucky—exploring the town's lively colonial historic center and admiring the sailboats.

To the north, Baltimore, with its vibrant Inner Harbor, sits on the Patapsco River off the Chesapeake Bay. Boasting a world-class aquarium, stellar museums, and the only Civil War-era vessel still afloat today, this popular, newly revitalized city makes for another good waterside excursion. ■

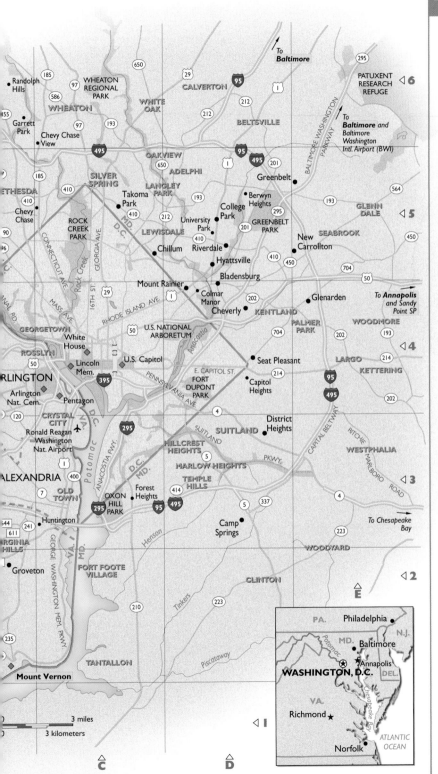

• Randolph Hills
185
97
WHEATON REGIONAL PARK
586
650
29
CALVERTON
95
To **Baltimore**
295
PATUXENT RESEARCH REFUGE
◁ 6

WHEATON
WHITE OAK
212
1

455
Garrett Park
97
193
BELTSVILLE
BALTIMORE WASHINGTON PARKWAY
To **Baltimore** and Baltimore Washington Intl. Airport (BWI)

Chevy Chase View
495
OAKVIEW
95
495
201

90
185
SILVER SPRING
650
ADELPHI
1
Greenbelt
564

BETHESDA
410
LANGLEY PARK
Takoma Park
• Berwyn Heights
295
193
GLENN DALE
◁ 5

Chevy Chase
410
212
College Park
University Park
201
GREENBELT PARK
New Carrollton
SEABROOK
450

96
ROCK CREEK PARK
LEWISDALE
410
Chillum • Riverdale
410
450
704
50

29
Mount Rainier
Colmar Manor
1
202
Glenarden
To **Annapolis** and Sandy Point SP

GEORGETOWN
White House
50
U.S. NATIONAL ARBORETUM
Cheverly
KENTLAND
704
PALMER PARK
202
193
WOODMORE
◁ 4

ROSSLYN
50
Lincoln Mem.
U.S. Capitol
Seat Pleasant
214
LARGO
214
KETTERING

ARLINGTON
395
E. CAPITOL ST.
FORT DUPONT PARK
214
Capitol Heights
95
495
202

Arlington Nat. Cem.
Pentagon
4
120
CRYSTAL CITY
Ronald Reagan Washington Nat. Airport
295
SUITLAND
District Heights
CAPITAL BELTWAY
RITCHIE MARLBORO ROAD
WESTPHALIA
◁ 3

1
400
HILLCREST HEIGHTS
5
MARLOW HEIGHTS

ALEXANDRIA
7
OLD TOWN
414
TEMPLE HILLS
5
337
4
To Chesapeake Bay

644
611
241
Huntington
295
OXON HILL PARK
95
495
Camp Springs
223
WOODYARD
◁ 2

VIRGINIA HILLS
Groveton
235
FORT FOOTE VILLAGE
210
223
CLINTON
△ E

TANTALLON
Piscataway

Mount Vernon

3 miles
3 kilometers

△ C
△ D
◁ 1

PA.
Philadelphia
N.J.
MD.
Baltimore
Annapolis
DEL.
WASHINGTON, D.C. ★
VA.
Richmond ★
Norfolk
ATLANTIC OCEAN

Chesapeake and Ohio Canal & Great Falls

C&O Canal NHP

www.nps.gov/choh

216 A5

Georgetown Visitor Center, 1057 Thomas Jefferson St., N.W.

202-653-5190

Great Falls Tavern Visitor Center, 11710 MacArthur Blvd., Potomac, MD

301-767-3714

$

SNAKING 184.5 MILES NORTHWEST FROM GEORGETOWN to Cumberland, Maryland, the Chesapeake and Ohio Canal National Historical Park has to be one of the longest, skinniest parks in the system. The most dramatic section is certainly the Great Falls area, just north of Washington, where the Potomac River hurls over steep, ragged rocks in a spectacular series of thundering falls before flowing through narrow Mather Gorge.

President John Quincy Adams broke ground for the C&O Canal on July 4, 1828. At that time, it was considered a Great National Project that would link Georgetown in Washington with Pittsburgh on the Ohio River, thus connecting the Atlantic Ocean with the Mississippi River. Plagued with problems from the start, however, including stiff competition by the new Baltimore & Ohio Railroad, the canal only made it as far as Cumberland.

Thousands of laborers—using hand tools, mule scoops, and black powder—toiled for 22 years to carve the trench, sometimes out of pure rock. A feat of engineering, its 74 lift locks raise it 605 feet in elevation from beginning to end.

The mule-drawn canal barges hauled coal, hay, fertilizer, and cement from the Appalachian Mountains to the city until 1924. In the early 1950s, Supreme Court Justice William O. Douglas led a movement to preserve the abandoned canal. The C&O was designated a national historical park in 1971.

VISITING

If you have the stamina, bike or hike the 14-mile towpath stretch from Georgetown to Great Falls, a

A kayaker hones his technique in the holes and waves below Great Falls.

lovely trek offering pretty river views; otherwise, you can drive, via MacArthur Boulevard, to the Great Falls Tavern section of the national historical park.

The big white stucco building overlooking the canal houses the **visitor center.** Built in 1831, the structure served as a lodge for travelers and boatmen for nearly a century. Exhibits tell about the area and the canal's history. Outside, hop aboard a narrated mule-powered canalboat for a ride through a working lock, a fun trip especially for kids *(April–Oct., $)*.

To see the falls, and perhaps bald eagles, head a short distance downstream on the towpath to the quarter-mile trail leading to **Great Falls Overlook.** A combination of boardwalk and bridges, the trail links the two sections of Olmsted Island, ending at a close-up look at frothing, roaring Great Falls as it narrows and tumbles 76 vertical feet over craggy boulders into swirling eddies.

Back on the towpath, continue downstream a little way. Before the stop-lock bridge, pick up the **Billy Goat Trail,** a wild, 2-mile romp over jagged rocks high on the river's edge and along Mather Gorge. In spring, trout lilies, jack-in-the-pulpits, and bluebells sprinkle the forest floor, and goose honks and songbird trills fill the air. On nice days kayakers play in the rapids below the falls and rock climbers scale the opposite gorge wall. The blue-blazed trail ends farther down on the towpath, allowing an easy 1.25-mile walk back to the visitor center.

Away from the water, the 4.2-mile **Gold Mine Loop** behind the visitor center winds through post oaks and river birches to the Maryland Mine. This little known outfit, now in ruins, operated from 1867 to 1939.

On the Virginia side of the falls,

a short distance as the crow flies but about 12 miles by car, lies 800-acre **Great Falls Park.** Learn about local flora and fauna, kayaking and rock climbing at the **visitor center.** Nearby overlooks provide splendid views of the wide river. The popular, blue-blazed **River Trail** ambles downstream from here for about a mile and a half, edging the bluff high above Mather Gorge.

Here, too, you'll find the ruins of the **Patowmack Canal,** started by George Washington in 1786 and closed in 1830 after work on the C&O had begun; five locks raised or lowered boats the height of the falls. A 2.2-mile trail runs alongside the canal's shallow ditch, taking you past the ruins of **Matildaville,** a town that served the needs of the canal industry. ∎

Great Falls Park
www.nps.gov/grfa
🗺 216 A5
✉ 9200 Old Dominion Dr., McLean, VA
☎ 703-285-2966
💲 $

Clambering along the Billy Goat Trail provides a chance to exercise and commune with nature.

Potomac River plantations

Mount Vernon

www.mountvernon.org

🗺 217 B2

✉ S end of George
   Washington Memorial
   Pkwy., Mt. Vernon, VA

☎ 703-780-2000

💲 $$

IN THE 18TH AND EARLY 19TH CENTURIES, LANDOWNERS built magnificent plantation houses along the Potomac south of present-day Washington, D.C. Three—Mount Vernon, Woodlawn, and Gunston Hall—lie within easy reach of the city. A visit to any one of these mansions, each carefully preserved in period detail, immerses you in the early slaveholding aristocratic life.

MOUNT VERNON

The stately Georgian-style home of George Washington sits on 500 acres of smartly kept grounds overlooking the Potomac, about a half hour from Washington by car. This estate richly deserves its ranking as the country's second most visited historic home; only the White House (see pp. 108–113) edges it out.

George Washington moved to Mount Vernon, home of his elder half-brother Lawrence, when he was in his teens; he acquired the estate from Lawrence's widow in 1754 at the age of 22. As commander in chief of the Continental forces, Washington rarely saw his home between 1775 and 1783. He then spent the next six years farming, expanding the plantation to

nearly 8,000 acres. After serving as the country's first President (1789–97), he had only a couple of years left to enjoy his beloved home before his death.

The Mount Vernon Ladies' Association purchased the estate from a Washington relative in 1858 and continues to own and operate it. Both the Confederate and Union Armies considered the estate neutral ground during the Civil War.

Visiting

Pick up a map at the entrance gate and check the schedule for various free tours around the estate. You can also rent audio tour cassettes here. Plan on at least two hours to see everything.

The 30-acre main area includes

Washington enlarged Mount Vernon—once a modest 1.5-story farmhouse—to its present appearance.

wasn't ever a permanent table, only chairs and sideboards; temporary tables were erected when the family entertained.

Washington's study and personal sanctuary sits at the other end of the house. The personal artifacts, including a telescope, globe, and an 884-volume library, reflect his varied interests. A small staircase connects the study to the **master bedroom** on the second floor. This simply decorated bedroom contains the four-poster bed in which Washington died in 1799. After his death, his wife, Martha, could not bear to stay in the room—she moved to a room on the third floor.

Back on the first floor, before you step onto the piazza, take note of the framed key hanging on a wall in the passageway; it's the key to the Bastille's west portal, which the Marquis de Lafayette sent as a gift to Washington in 1790. The piazza, looking east over a lawn that sweeps down toward a deer park, offers a grand view of the Potomac River.

Return to the house's west side to explore the formal grounds and various outbuildings. The walled-in upper and lower gardens flank the long, rolling bowling green. Tall trees edge the green—Washington planted the two 130-foot-tall tulip poplars, along with a dozen or so others.

The **outbuildings** sit along the perimeter of the formal grounds. The smokehouse, kitchen, washhouse, servant's hall, and other buildings offer a look at what it took to run a large, profitable 18th-century estate. A nearby building houses the **George Washington Museum.** You'll find silver, china, jewelry, swords, and other family heirlooms here, including the Houdon bust. French sculptor J.A. Houdon made this likeness in 1785 from a plaster mold of Washington's face. The **Archaeology &**

the mansion, numerous outbuildings, formal flower and kitchen gardens, and woodlands. Most people head straight for the house, a white mansion looking somewhat like a huge red-roofed barn with symmetrical wings; the wood exterior has the look of stone—sand thrown onto wet paint does the trick. All the details pertaining to the appearance of the house—down to the exact color of the interiors—are authentic.

The line to enter forms at the servants' hall on the left; come early in the morning to avoid crowds. Inside, the house is a treasure. Many of the furnishings are original to the house, others 18th-century duplicates. You may tour at your own pace; docents offer a steady patter of information about each of the 12 rooms.

Each room provides an interesting glimpse into life at Mount Vernon, but perhaps none more so than the large two-story green **dining room.** You'll think the table is missing, but the room appears exactly as it did in Washington's lifetime. Since he used the room for many different functions, there

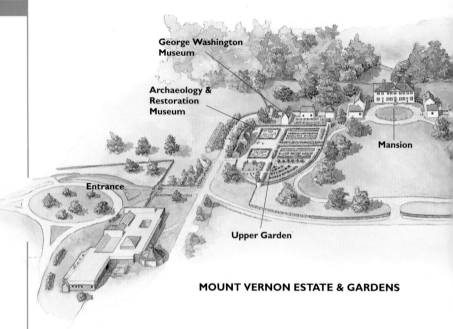

George Washington
Museum

Archaeology &
Restoration
Museum

Mansion

Entrance

Upper Garden

MOUNT VERNON ESTATE & GARDENS

Woodlawn

216 B2

9000 Richmond Hwy.
(US 1), 3 miles W of
Mount Vernon

703-780-4000

Closed Jan.–Feb.

$

Restoration Museum, in the
reconstructed greenhouse-slave
quarters complex next door,
displays unearthed artifacts that
reveal details of daily life. Other
exhibits explain the estate's building
techniques and craftsmanship.

Next, circle around the fruit gar-

Dogue Run gristmill

George Washington built
the Dogue Run gristmill
in 1771 to grind corn and wheat
into meal. He deeded it to his
step-granddaughter, Nelly
Custis, in 1799 as part of her
wedding gift. By 1850 the mill
had ceased functioning. First
reconstructed in the 1930s, it
was inoperable until a recent
renovation. A professional miller
explains how water power is
used to grind wheat into flour.
The mill lies just off Va. 235,
south of Woodlawn. ∎

den and nursery to the iron-gated
brick tomb that holds the remains of
George and Martha and other family
members. A nearby memorial marks
the estate's slave burial ground.

Downhill from here you'll find
the wharf. This restored version
dates from the 1800s, replacing an
earlier wharf that Washington used
to transport his goods to Alexandria. If you have time, stroll over to
the **George Washington:
Pioneer Farmer Site,** a 4-acre
demonstration area. Costumed
interpreters explain, in an appealing
and comprehensible fashion,
Washington's experimentation with
various crops and techniques.

WOODLAWN

George Washington gave Nelly
Custis, his step-granddaughter, and
Maj. Lawrence Lewis, his nephew,
2,000 acres of his estate in 1799 as
their wedding present and asked
William Thornton, first architect of
the U.S. Capitol, to design a house
for them. Thornton completed the

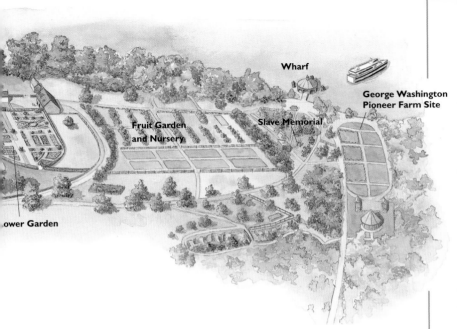

Wharf

George Washington Pioneer Farm Site

Fruit Garden and Nursery

Slave Memorial

...ower Garden

late Georgian/early federal-era two-story mansion in 1805. Typical of the period, the house is arranged symmetrically according to a five-part Palladian plan. There is no "front" or "back," rather two formal facades for approach by land or river.

The Lewis family and over 90 slaves lived on the estate for more than 40 years. The family sold the estate in 1846 to a Quaker community, which used the house as a nucleus for their growing abolitionist organization. The National Trust for Historic Preservation acquired the house and some of the land in 1951; the estate now comprises about 120 acres. The house is furnished much as it was during the Lewises' occupation, with some furnishings that the Lewises brought from Mount Vernon.

The refined **first-floor interior** includes a dining room, a family sitting room, and a parlor, where formal entertaining took place. The ceilings soar 13.5 feet high—the parlor excepted, which is a foot higher, in keeping with the grand proportions of the space. The second floor is divided into four graciously appointed chambers. In honor of its first patron, Woodlawn's **main hall** features a bust of George Washington commissioned by Nelly Custis Lewis; it stands on a pedestal at 6 feet 2 inches, the general's actual height.

Outside in the **formal garden** bloom lilacs, azaleas, and roses. From the riverside portico you can make out the Potomac, although silting over the past two centuries has pushed the river back. On the eastern horizon, tall trees block your view of Mount Vernon.

Before leaving Woodlawn, walk over to the 1940 **Pope-Leighey House** (*703-780-4000, $$*). This Frank Lloyd Wright-designed house was moved here in 1964 from Falls Church, Virginia, to save it from destruction. The small, low-ceilinged, flat-roofed dwelling is a classic example of Wright's Usonian style.

Gunston Hall

www.gunstonhall.org

🏛 216 B1

✉ Lorton, VA, on Va. 242, 4 miles E of US 1

☎ 703-550-9220

💲 $$

A rudimentary curtsying lesson at Gunston Hall

GUNSTON HALL

The farthest south of the three plantation houses, Gunston Hall anchors 550 magnificently lush acres, with tree-lined lanes, formal gardens, and farm animals. Its owner was Virginian George Mason (1725–1792), a lesser known but brilliant patriot and statesman.

Mason tried to quit public life after his wife's death in 1773, but the fledgling country would need him in the years ahead. Mason penned the 1776 Virginia Declaration of Rights, advocating religious tolerance and freedom of the press. Thomas Jefferson picked up, in some cases almost word for word, the same sentiments for the Declaration of Independence. Mason holds distinction as one of three delegates who refused to sign the Constitution in 1787. His passionate orations objecting that the Constitution gave the government too much power helped pave the way for the Bill of Rights.

Begin your tour at the **visitor center,** which holds several interesting exhibits, including family objects; a 12-minute film presents

Mason as a paradoxical man. Although an ardent supporter of human rights and intellectually opposed to slavery, Mason's 5,500 acres were tended by up to 90 slaves. He could not reconcile his desire to end slavery with a means to ensure the continued prosperity of his plantation.

Then head over to the two-story Georgian **brick house.** Designed in 1755 by indentured servant and soon-to-be-prominent architect William Buckland, each room has its own distinctive style. The Chinese-style formal parlor and the neoclassic, Palladian-style dining room, with arches and painstaking embellishments, are works of art. The rooms are furnished with family and period pieces.

In the **gardens,** a boxwood allée, likely dating from Mason's time, runs between formal plantings to the brow of a hill that provides a glimpse of the distant Potomac. You can take a 1-mile trail through coastal plain woods to the river, perhaps spotting deer, herons, and geese along the way. ■

Annapolis

YACHTS, MIDSHIPMEN IN CRISP UNIFORMS, STREETS LINED with colonial architecture, and restaurants serving world-famous crabcakes: The colorful port of Annapolis, less than an hour's drive east of Washington, offers big-time history in a small-town setting.

Puritans escaping persecution first settled at the strategic mouth of the Severn River, just off the Chesapeake Bay, in 1649. Named the Capital of the Proprietary of Maryland in 1694, the settlement grew to become one of the Colonies' most sophisticated towns by the eve of the American Revolution. As tobacco flowed out of its port, in flowed European luxuries to adorn beautiful Georgian homes and their elegant inhabitants.

Annapolis's political high point occurred between November 1783 and August 1784, when it served as the fledgling nation's working capital. After the capital was moved to Trenton, New Jersey, in 1784, however, the city dozed for two centuries.

The U.S. Naval Academy came in 1845, turning Annapolis into a sort of company town that catered to its guest institution. In the 1960s, interest in historic preservation brought about new life, as taverns, shops, restaurants, and museums moved into restored structures.

Today Annapolis showcases more than a dozen architectural styles spanning three centuries; some 1,300 buildings—all meticulously maintained—predate 1900. Much of the small city's charm owes to the fact that it preserves its 1695 radial street plan, which gives the highest elevations for the church (St. Anne's) and state (State House)—and offers many vistas of the picturesque waterfront. ■

Annapolis

⊿ 217 E4

Visitor information

www.visit-annapolis.org

✉ Annapolis & Anne Arundel County Conference & Visitors Bureau, 26 West St.

☎ 410-280-0445

Ego Alley in the heart of Annapolis is the place to show off your yacht.

The Maryland State House (1779) anchors Annapolis's 18th-century downtown.

Walking around Annapolis

The narrow streets and brick sidewalks in the historic center of Annapolis will enchant you. Plan to spend at least half a day strolling around and visiting its sights. With limited street parking available, your best bet is to park in one of the garages near the visitor center.

Start your stroll at the friendly, information-packed **visitor center** ❶ (*Annapolis & Anne Arundel County Conference & Visitors Bureau, 26 West St., 410-280-0445*). Just to the east, Church Circle features the Romanesque **St. Anne's Episcopal Church** ❷ (*410-267-9333*), built in 1858–59 as the third church on this site. The church still uses the communion silver set sent by King William III in 1696. Standing at the intersection of Church Circle and Main Street, the venerable 1772 **Maryland Inn** (*410-263-2641*) features wood balconies and a posh, award-winning restaurant, the Treaty of Paris. Proceed six blocks down Main Street, attractively lined with two-story brick and wood buildings harboring boutiques, restaurants, galleries, and bars.

At end of the street awaits Market Space and its busy waterfront, the **City Dock** ❸. No longer a thriving working dock, it's still the heart of the city, bustling with cafés, shops, and restaurants. The number of yachts moored here year-round attests to Annapolis's standing as one of the East Coast's great sailing centers; visiting boaters often cruise down the narrow, alleylike waterway fronting the dock to show off their boats (hence its local name, Ego Alley). Stop by the dockside 1858 **Market House** for a sandwich and join a life-size bronze of *Roots* author Alex Haley by the water's edge, where he sits telling a story to a group of children on the same spot where his ancestor, Kunta Kinte, arrived in 1767 on a slave ship. For fancier dining, head across Market Space to **Middleton Tavern** (*Randall & Pinkney Sts., 410-263-3323*), a cozy, dark-paneled establishment dating from 1750 that has welcomed the likes of George Washington, Thomas Jefferson, and Benjamin Franklin.

Just up Pinkney Street, step into the **Waterfront Warehouse** (ca 1815) and take a look at the scale model of the waterfront as it appeared in the 1700s. A few doors up, **Shiplap House** ❹ (18 Pinkney St.) dates from 1715; an exhibit inside details the worldwide trade network of slaves, china, linens, and cotton operated by Nathan Hammond, who ran a dry goods store here from 1759 to 1773.

Now go back down Pinkney and turn left on Randall; in two blocks turn right for the gates to the **U.S. Naval Academy** ❺ (410-263-6933) and follow signs to the visitor center. Established in 1845, the academy is now a 338-acre, four-year coed college attended by 4,000 midshipmen. Flanking the tree-dotted central green to the southeast is the enormous

⛰ See area map pp. 216–17
▶ Visitor center
↔ 1.8 miles
🕐 4 hours
▶ Maryland State House

NOT TO BE MISSED
- City Dock
- U.S. Naval Academy Chapel
- Hammond-Harwood House

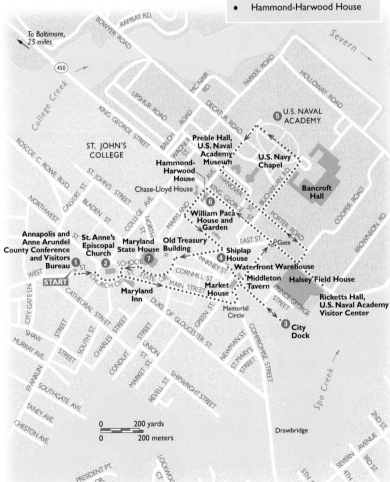

Sandy Point State Park

For a change of scenery, drive out to this Chesapeake Bay park (*9 miles E of Annapolis on US 50, 410-974-2149*). A sandy beach is great for swimming, as well as for views of the Bay Bridge and of freighters far out on the bay. Rowboats and motorboats are available for rent, and 5 miles of trails wind through woods and marshes. ∎

beaux arts **Bancroft Hall,** one of the world's largest dormitories. All of the midshipmen live and eat here. Step inside the palatial entrance hall to see paintings of historic sea battles. The nearby copper-domed **Navy Chapel** features a long, shiplike nave; don't miss the lavishly displayed marble tomb of Revolutionary War naval hero John Paul Jones in the chapel's crypt. Just to the northwest, Preble Hall houses the **Naval Academy Museum,** containing one of the world's finest collections of model warships. (Note: Visitors are allowed within the academy only on foot and must show a photo ID at the entrance gate.)

Back at the entrance gate turn northwest on King George Street, then southwest on Maryland Avenue. The 1774–75 **Hammond-Harwood House** ❻ (*19 Maryland Ave., 410-269-1714, $*) stands on the left, just beyond King George Street. This national historic landmark house was the last project of

The U.S. Naval Academy Band stays crisply in line and in tune.

architect William Buckland, once an indentured servant, who also designed Gunston Hall in Northern Virginia (see p. 224) and the interiors of the Chase-Lloyd House across the street. Many consider this house to be the finest example of Georgian architecture in colonial America. The furnishings date from the mid-18th and early 19th centuries.

Continue down Maryland Avenue to Prince George Street and turn left to the Georgian **William Paca House and Garden** (*186 Prince George St., 410-263-5553, $*), built in 1765. Paca was a signer of the Declaration of Independence and a three-term governor of Maryland. Inside and out, the house has been meticulously restored to its colonial appearance. Two acres of gardens have also been returned to their former glory, down to the terraced rose beds, brick canal, and Chinese Chippendale bridge.

Walking a block west on East Street brings you to State Circle, upon which sits the **Old Treasury Building** and the **Maryland State House** ❼ (*State Circle, 410-974-3400*). Completed in 1779, the state house is the nation's oldest continuously used capitol building. Two events of national importance took place in its old Senate Chamber during the nine months when Annapolis served as the new country's working capital: George Washington resigned his commission as commander in chief of the Continental Army on Dec. 23, 1783, and, three weeks later, Congress ratified the Treaty of Paris, officially ending the Revolutionary War. Return to your starting point via School Street and Church Circle. ∎

Baltimore

ONLY AN HOUR AWAY, BALTIMORE SEEMS LIKE AN ALTO-gether different place than Washington, its brick buildings, puffing factories, older ethnic neighborhoods, and active ship traffic giving it more of a "real city" feel. But it also has its share of world-class museums, including the Baltimore Museum of Art and the Walters Art Museum. And the Inner Harbor, a showcase of urban revitalization, ranks as one of the East Coast's top tourist destinations.

Strategically placed at the mouth of the Patapsco River at Chesapeake Bay, the Inner Harbor has long been a major port for coal and grain. Also considered an urban eyesore, it was targeted for demolition and renewal as far back as 1963. Buildings began coming down in the late 1960s, and the first sky-scrapers appeared in the early '70s. Restaurants, tourist attractions, and Oriole Park at Camden Yards followed thereafter, contributing to the harbor's vitality.

A wide promenade lined with shops and restaurants edges the waterfront and offers a delightful stroll past the harbor's various museums. Water taxis will ferry you from sight to sight if you'd rather ride than walk.

On the harbor's north side, at Pier 3, the seven-story **National Aquarium** (*410-576-3800, $$$$*) is Baltimore's biggest tourist draw. Inside, bottlenose dolphins perform feats in a 1.2-million-gallon ocea-narium; an Atlantic coral reef teems with colorful tropical fish; and sharks and manta rays glide effort-lessly through a pool that you cross on bridges.

The submarine U.S.S. *Torsk* and the lightship *Chesapeake* are moored alongside the aquarium. They, along with the Coast Guard cutter *Taney* and Seven Foot Knoll Lighthouse on Pier 5, form the **Baltimore Maritime Museum** (*410-396-3453, $$*). Exhibits aboard World War II veterans *Taney* and *Torsk* tell about U.S. naval history; the other two focus on local maritime history.

The last Civil War-era vessel still

Baltimore
🅜 217 D6
Visitor information
www.baltconvstr.com
✉ Baltimore Area Convention & Visitors Association, 100 Light St.
☎ 888-BALTIMORE

Led by the Inner Harbor, Baltimore has stepped into the limelight of urban revitalization.

The wonderful world of fish eyes at Baltimore's National Aquarium

Baltimore Museum of Art
www.artbma.org
✉ Corner of N. Charles & 31st Sts.
☎ 410-396-7100
🕐 Closed Mon.–Tues.
💲 $$

Walters Art Museum
www.thewalters.org
✉ 600 N. Charles St.
☎ 410-547-9000
🕐 Closed Mon.
💲 $$

Fort McHenry National Monument and Historic Shrine
www.nps.gov/fomc
✉ End of E. Fort Ave.
☎ 410-962-4290
💲 $

afloat, the **U.S.S. Constellation** is moored at Pier 1 (410-539-1797, $$). Climb aboard to learn about her many commissions. Launched in 1854, she has caught slave traders off the coast of Africa, blockaded ports during the Civil War, and served as a relief flagship of the U.S. Atlantic Fleet in World War II.

Walk past the cruise ship docks toward the harbor's south side and the **Maryland Science Center** (601 Light St., 410-685-5225, $$). You can easily spend half a day here exploring three floors of hands-on exhibits, seeing an IMAX film, and picking out constellations in the planetarium.

Located inland, on the harbor's north side, is the interactive **Port Discovery** (35 Market Pl., 410-727-8120, $$$). Exhibits let you decipher hieroglyphics, create musical instruments, and make chewing gum; the highlight is a three-story "urban treehouse," in which kids climb and crawl like monkeys. Outside, ride in the swaying gondola of a helium balloon, anchored by a steel cable, and take in breathtaking city and harbor views.

Within a short driving distance of the harbor are a number of other sights. Impressionist lovers will not want to miss the Cone Collection—works by Henri Matisse, Pablo Picasso, and others—on display at the **Baltimore Museum of Art.** The fascinating **Walters Art Museum** offers a broad look at over 55 centuries of world art, including Roman sarcophagi, Asian ceramics, Old Master paintings, and art deco jewelry.

Fort McHenry sits southeast of the harbor. During the War of 1812, as American forces valiantly defended the fort against the British, a young lawyer named Francis Scott Key felt inspired to pen some words as he saw its flag still waving in the early dawn light; later, these words became our national anthem. A tour of this restored monument to American freedom is illuminating.

At the end of the day, consider a jaunt to historic **Fells Point,** where the city took root in the early 1700s. Located east of the Inner Harbor, this salty waterfront district's brick row houses, congenial pubs, and snug restaurants have an enduring charm. ■

Travelwise

The soaring lines of Eero
Saarinen's Dulles
International Airport

TRAVELWISE INFORMATION.

PLANNING YOUR TRIP

WHEN TO GO/ CLIMATE

Until well into the 20th century, Washington was, because of its reputation for heat and humidity, classified as a hardship post for British diplomats. It is true that July and August in the capital are frequently hot and steamy, but Washington has relatively brief winters and often long and lovely springs and falls. Rain is fairly evenly divided throughout the year (an average of 3.21 inches per month), but afternoon thundershowers in July and August make rain slightly more likely during those months.

The busy season for tourism starts in April with school spring vacation, when busloads of schoolchildren visit the museums, monuments, and U.S. Capitol. Spring is also the time of the annual cherry blossoms display around the Tidal Basin, and when the blossoms are at their peak, the area around the monuments is packed with sightseers. Summer, despite the heat, is family vacation time.

The average high and low temperatures are as follows:

January—42°F/26°F
February—45°F/29°F
March—56°F/37°F
April—66°F/46°F
May—76°F/56°F
June—84°F/66°F
July—88°F/71°F
August—86°F/70°F
September—80°F/62°F
October—69°F/50°F
November—58°F/41°F
December—47°F/31°F

WHAT TO BRING

Heavy winter coats are usually essential only in December, January, and February, but a light coat or jacket can come in handy in the cooler spring or fall months. Government buildings and museums have miles of corridors with marble floors—comfortable shoes are a good idea.

TRAVELING TO WASHINGTON, D.C.

BY PLANE

Washington is served by three major airports: **Ronald Reagan Washington National Airport** (DCA), in Virginia about 4 miles from the city center; **Washington Dulles International Airport** (IAD), 26 miles west of Washington; and **Baltimore/Washington International Airport** (BWI), about 25 miles northeast of Washington.

Ronald Reagan Washington National Airport is the closest to the city and the most convenient to reach, because Washington's state-of-the-art Metro system has a station located there, adjacent to terminals B and C. (A shuttle bus connects terminal A to the Metro station.) Taxi fare to downtown Washington is about $12. Reagan National is also served by SuperShuttle, which picks up from and delivers passengers to their homes, hotels, and offices. Call 800/BLUEVAN or 202/296-6662 for reservations.

Dulles International Airport is served by its own Washington Flyer taxi fleet, which provides 24-hour service to and from the airport. For information, call 703/661-6655. Taxi fare to downtown Washington is approximately $45 to $50. Washington Flyer also operates a coach service (703/572-8400) connecting Dulles to the West Falls Church Metro station. An express bus, operated by the Washington Metropolitan Area Transit Authority, connects Dulles to L'Enfant Plaza downtown. For information call 202/637-7000. SuperShuttle, which operates on a shared ride-on-demand basis, also serves the airport (800/BLUEVAN).

BWI Airport is served by SuperShuttle (800/BLUEVAN), by taxi 410/859-1100 (about $55 to downtown Washington), or by train. Both MARC's Penn Line (800/325-RAIL) and Amtrak (800/872-7245) provide frequent service between Union Station in downtown Washington and BWI's own rail station; a free shuttlebus connects the station and the airport terminal. (MARC runs only during rush hours but is much cheaper than Amtrak.)

AIRPORT INFORMATION

For airport information (not information about specific flights), for Reagan National airport, call 703/417-8000; for Dulles airport, 703/572-2700; and for Baltimore/Washington airport, 410/859-7100.

AIRLINES

The Washington, D.C., metropolitan area is served by the following airlines. They fly into DCA, IAD, and BWI unless otherwise indicated.
Aeroflot 202/429-4922, www.aeroflot.com (IAD only)
Air Canada 888/247-2262, www.aircanada.com
Air France 800/321-4538, www.airfrance.com
Air Tran 800/247-8726, www.airtran.com (IAD & BWI only)
Alaska Airlines 800/252-7522, www.alaska airlines.com (DCA & IAD only)
America West Airlines 800/235-9292, www.americawest.com (DCA & BWI only)
American Airlines 800/433-7300, www.aa.com
American Trans Air 800/

435-9282, www.ata.com
(DCA only)

ANA 800/235-9262,
www.fly-ana.com (IAD only)

British Airways 800/247-9297,
www.britishairways.com
(IAD & BWI only)

Continental 800/525-0280,
www.continental.com

Delta Air Lines 800/221-
1212, www.delta.com

Frontier Airlines
800/452-1359, www.fly
frontier.com

Ghana Airways 800/404-4262,
www.ghana-airways.com
(BWI only)

Icelandair 800/223-5500,
www.icelandair.com
(BWI only)

JetBlue Airways 800/538-
2583, www.jetblue
airways.com (IAD only)

KLM 800/225-2525,
www.klm.com (IAD only)

Korean Air 800/438-5000,
www.koreanair.com
(IAD only)

Lufthansa 800/645-3880,
www.lufthansa.com (IAD only)

Midwest Express 800/452-
2022 (DCA & IAD)

Northwest Airlines
800/225-2525, www.nwa.com

Pan American Airways
800/359-7262,
www.flybangor.com(BWI only)

SAS 800/221-2350,
www.scandinavian.net
(IAD only)

Southwest Airlines 800/ 435-
9792, www.southwest.com
(BWI only)

Swissair 800/221-4750,
www.swissair.com (IAD only)

United Airlines 800/241-
6522, www.ual.com

US Airways 800/428-4322,
www.usairways.com

Virgin Atlantic 800/862-
8621, www.virgin atlantic.com
(IAD only)

Amtrak (800/872-7245) trains
arrive at Washington's spectacu-
larly refurbished Union Station
on Capitol Hill. The station, with
shops, restaurants, and a downstairs food court, is worth a visit

for its own sake. Although locals
use the train mostly as a fast,
convenient way to get to New
York on the Acela and Metroliner
trains, Washington is a major rail
hub, and it is connected by train
to most U.S. destinations with
rail service.

The Metro station at Union
Station provides easy access to
the rest of the city. The taxi
stand at the station sometimes
has long lines, and riders are
frequently expected to share
cabs with others going to nearby
destinations.

GETTING AROUND

BY PUBLIC TRANSPORTATION

METRO

The Washington Metropolitan
Area Transit Authority operates
the bus and subway systems in
the metropolitan area. The
impressively clean and efficient
system was designed primarily
to enable commuters to travel
easily to the downtown area.
Metrorail stations are marked
by large brown columns with
colored stripes that indicate
the lines served by the station.
Metro farecards are purchased
at vending machines in the
stations. The minimum fare is
$1.10, the maximum is $3.25,
based on the distance traveled
and time of day. Fare information is available near the ticket
machines. Metrorail opens at
5:30 a.m. on weekdays and
8 a.m. on weekends. It closes at
midnight Sunday through
Thursday. On Friday and Saturday nights, it runs until 2 a.m.

Route information: Call
202/637-7000 or log onto
http://rideguide.wmata.com.

BUS

Metrobus service covers the
city and the suburbs, with some
lines running 24 hours. The fare
for any destination within

METRO TIPS

Plan your trip before
arriving at the station by
visiting www.metroopen
doors.com.

The farecard machines bear
step-by-step illustrated
explanations of how to buy
a farecard. New Metro
patrons can even push a
button—designed primarily
for the vision impaired—to
hear the purchase
instructions.

Ask the station manager
(usually posted in the glass
kiosk near the farecard
machines) for help if you
continue to have difficulty
purchasing a card.

Carry plenty of one-dollar
bills for the farecard
machines. If not, you will
likely be saddled with a
Vegas-style payoff, since the
machines give change—up
to $6.25—in quarters only.

If making numerous trips
after 9:30 a.m., consider
buying a One Day Pass—at
$5 an excellent bargain.

On the escalators, stand
right, walk left. Otherwise
you risk being trampled by
others in a hurry.

If traveling in a group,
designate one person to buy
the farecards (one per rider)
for the entire group; that
way only one person needs
to learn how to operate the
station's farecard machine.

Washington is $1.10. Exact fare
is required. Drivers do not make
change. For route and fare
information, call 202/637-7000.

BY TAXICAB

Washington's taxi fleet may
not be the most modern in
the country, and the fares are

GETTING AROUND/PRACTICAL ADVICE

determined by a mysterious—to visitors and sometimes to locals as well—zone system, but cabs are plentiful and fairly inexpensive. It's usually possible to hail a cab on major streets.

The fare is $5 in the central zone, which covers the downtown from the Capitol on the east to 23rd Street on the west. There are frequent surcharges—$1.50 for each extra passenger, $1 for rush hour, $1.25 for an airport pickup. The driver may pick up extra passengers if it does not take the original passenger more than five blocks out of his or her way.

BY CAR

Visitors should consider the possibility that a car will be more an annoyance than a convenience. Parking is difficult, parking garages are expensive, and the most efficient branch of the city government is the one that gives parking tickets.

Should you find on-street parking, check the signs, since many streets become no parking zones during rush hour. If your car is not where you left it, call 202/645-5500 for information on its location.

Some streets are two-way most of the time, but during rush hour become one-way—including Rock Creek and Potomac Parkway and 17th Street, N.W.

CAR RENTALS

All three airports are served by the following national car rental companies:

Alamo	800/327-9633
Avis	800/831-2847
Budget	800/527-0700
Dollar	800/800-4000
Enterprise	800/325-8007
Hertz	800/654-3131
National	800/227-7368
Thrifty	800/847-4389

BY TOUR

Old Town Trolley Tours, 202/832-9800. This two-hour tour allows you to visit monuments and museums at your own pace, by simply getting off the bus to see what you want for as long as you want, and reboarding at will.

Tourmobile, 202/554-5100. Narrated shuttlebus tours of major monuments, museums, and attractions. You can get off the bus to visit any of these, and simply get on the next bus when it comes along.

DC Ducks: The Boats On Wheels, 202/832-9800. DC Ducks' amphibious vehicles allow you to tour the Mall by land, then splash into the Potomac River on the boats with wheels. Fully narrated 90-minute tours depart regularly 10 a.m.–4 p.m. from Union Station.

More tours: For specialty tours, please see pp. 261–62.

NEGOTIATING THE CITY

When seeking a site, first check the quadrant address, which indicates where it lies vis-a-vis the Capitol. Are you looking for N.W., N.E., S.W., or S.E.? The city is laid out in these four quadrants, with the Capitol building in the center. North Capitol, South Capitol, and East Capitol Streets radiate from this nucleus, separating the quadrants (the Mall runs west from the Capitol building).

Beware that many addresses can be found in more than one quadrant, and therefore are not the same place (for instance, there is a 400 M St. in N.E., S.E., S.W., and N.W.).

After locating the quadrant, note that there are three types of streets in Washington. First are the numbered streets—those

that run in a north–south direction from the Capitol. First Street, for instance, is located one block east or west of North or South Capitol Street, respectively.

The second street type is the lettered or named streets laid out in an east–west direction. Starting from East Capitol Street or the Mall, the streets run through the alphabet (with the exceptions of J, X, and Z). The ones nearest the Capitol are one-syllable words; when the alphabet has been run through, they become two syllables, then three. As such, you can tell how far a certain street is from the Capitol by the letter with which it begins and how many syllables it contains.

Finally, the avenues that are named after states run diagonally across the grid.

PRACTICAL ADVICE

COMMUNICATIONS

NEWSPAPERS
Washington, D.C., is a city of news. Most national and international news agencies have Washington bureaus. The Washington-based daily newspapers are the *Washington Post* and the *Washington Times*.

For upcoming local events, check the Weekend section of the *Washington Post,* published on Fridays, and the Washington Weekend section of the *Washington Times*. Both provide excellent suggestions for making plans. Also of local interest is the free weekly publication, the *Washington CityPaper,* published on Thursdays. It provides an up-to-date listing of what's happening in the clubs and theaters around town.

RADIO
WTOP (AM 1500) All news station (with the best traffic reports in town)

WXTR (AM 820) All news
WKDV (AM 1460) Asian
WDCT (AM 1310) Korean
WACA (AM 1540) Spanish
WAMU (FM 88.5) National
    Public Radio
WCSP (FM 90.1)
    CSPAN/Public Affairs
WETA (FM 90.9)
    National Public Radio
WMZQ (FM 98.7) Country
WIHT (FM 99.5) Top 40
WBIG (FM 100.3) Oldies
WGMS (FM 103.5) Classical
WJZW (FM 105.9) Jazz

TELEPHONE

Local and long-distance
    information, 411
Toll-free directory information,
    800/555-1212

Public telephones are located in all hotels, at tourist attractions and other public places, at most restaurants, and along some city streets. Local calls cost 50 cents. Long-distance calls are easier and cheaper if you use your home carrier's telephone calling card or purchase a prepaid calling card (available at post offices and larger drug-stores).

Area codes: The area code of Washington, D.C., is 202; for Maryland it's 301; and for Northern Virginia it's 703. For all Virginia calls, even local, you must always dial the area code with the number.

CRIME

Washington has a reputation as a dangerous city, but crimes of all sorts have been on the decrease in the last few years. Reduce your risk by following a few common-sense rules:

Don't wander onto deserted or ill-lighted streets or parks, particularly at night. If a neighborhood looks dangerous, it probably is. Stay with the crowds.
There's safety in numbers.

If someone tries to rob you, give the robber whatever he or she asks. Your life is more valuable

than your belongings.

Keep your wallet in a front trouser pocket—they're less vulnerable to pickpockets than rear pockets or breast pockets. Women should keep their purses close and not wear expensive jewelry. Don't carry large amounts of cash. Leave the credit cards you don't plan to use at home.

Don't leave valuables in your car. The trunk is more secure than the space under the seats.

MONEY MATTERS

ATM LOCATIONS
Cirrus, 800/424-7787
Plus, 800/843-7587

Banks and automatic tellers (ATMs) are located throughout the city, and most major attractions and shopping centers also have them. Check with your home bank to find out which system accepts your card. Credit cards, debit cards, and traveler's checks are accepted almost everywhere; make sure you have an official I.D. on you as some places require it before you can make a transaction.

NATIONAL HOLIDAYS

New Year's Day; Martin Luther King, Jr., Day (3rd Mon. in Jan.); President's Day (3rd Mon. in Feb.); Easter Sunday; Memorial Day (last Mon. in May); Fourth of July; Labor Day (1st Mon. in Sept.); Thanksgiving Day (4th Thurs. in Nov.); Christmas Day.

PLACES OF WORSHIP

The citizens and churches in Washington welcome people of all faiths and practices. With more than 2,000 established churches in the area, you will be able to find a service of your choice. Check with your hotel concierge or the local yellow pages for a listing of times and

locations. The *Washington Post* and *Washington Times* also publish listings of services in the religion sections in their Saturday editions.

SALES TAX

The price tags are misleading. Taxes will increase your hotel bill by 14.5 percent, restaurant bill by 10 percent, and rental car bill by 10 percent.

SECURITY

Security has become a major issue in many places worldwide, but you will note a special awareness in and around Washington's government buildings. A few things to note: Streets sometimes close with notice, sometimes without. Streets that you may have traveled on last year may be closed this year; just because the street is on a map does not mean it is not blocked by a concrete barrier.

Government buildings are generally open to the public, but they may close for security reasons with little or no notice. Be flexible, have alternate plans, and call ahead.

Metal detectors are now standard equipment in most public buildings. Be prepared for searches. If you have a pacemaker or some other medical device that might be affected, let the guards know. And, finally, do not bring anything that could be considered a weapon that you do not want to risk losing—e.g. Grandpa's pocketknife.

TIPPING

Leave at least 15 percent of the bill at restaurants (20 percent at upscale places). Taxi drivers should receive 10-15 percent, bartenders 10 percent, hairdressers 15 percent, porters at least a dollar a bag, valet parking attendees $2 or more, parking attendees $2 or more, and

236   TRAVELWISE

PRACTICAL ADVICE/EMERGENCIES & HEALTH CARE/ANNUAL EVENTS

doormen a couple of dollars every time they whistle you a cab. Tip the hotel concierge or restaurant maitre d' at your discretion, depending upon services performed.

TRAVELERS WITH DISABILITIES

Washington is a very accessible city for travelers with disabilities. The Washington, D.C. Convention & Tourism Corporation publishes a fact sheet detailing general accessibility of Washington hotels, restaurants, shopping malls, and attractions. For a free copy, call 202/789-7000, or write WCTC, 1212 New York Ave., N.W., Suite 600, Washington, D.C. 20005.

The Washington Metropolitan Area Transit Authority also publishes a free pamphlet on Metro's bus and rail system accessibility for the elderly and physically disabled. Call 202/962-6464 to order the guide, or visit the Metro's Web site at www.wmata.com.

Smithsonian museum buildings are accessible to wheelchair visitors. A comprehensive free publication called "Smithsonian Access" lists all services available to visitors with disabilities, including parking, building access, sign language interpreters, and more. To obtain a copy, call 202/357-2700.

VISITOR INFORMATION

The best source of visitor information is the **Washington, D.C. Visitor Information Center,** located in the Ronald Reagan International Trade Center at 1300 Pennsylvania Ave., N.W. (202/328-4748). Here you can obtain tickets, tour information, and maps. For up-to-the-minute events, pick up a copy of the *Washington CityPaper,* available for free at cafés, restaurants, and bookstores throughout the city.

EMERGENCIES & HEALTH CARE

USEFUL NUMBERS

- Emergencies (police/fire/ambulance) 911
- Washington, D.C., Police (non-emergency) 202/727-1010
- Metro Transit Police (emergency) 202/962-2121
- U.S. Park Police (emergency) 202/619-7300
- Travelers Aid 202/371-1937
- International Visitors Information Desk (offers multilingual information and assistance; located at Dulles) 703/572-2536

LOST CREDIT CARDS

American Express, 800/327-2177
Diners Club, 800/234-6377
Discover Card, 800/347-2683
MasterCard, 800/307-7309
Visa, 800/847-2911

ANNUAL EVENTS

JANUARY
Martin Luther King Jr.'s Birthday Mid-January. Lincoln Memorial, 202/619-7222. A military color guard salute at the site where King delivered his famous "I have a dream" speech.

Presidential Inauguration January 20, every fourth year. After the swearing-in on the Capitol steps, a parade follows down Pennsylvania Avenue to the White House.

FEBRUARY
Chinese New Year Parade Late January or early February, depending on the moon. Chinatown, H St., N.W., between 5th and 8th Sts. Colorful parade with firecrackers and dragons.

Abraham Lincoln's Birthday February 12. Lincoln Memorial, 202/619-7222. A reading of the Gettysburg Address and a wreath-laying ceremony at the memorial.

George Washington's Birthday February 22. Wreath-laying ceremonies at Mount Vernon (703/780-2000) and at the Washington Monument (202/619-7222).

MARCH
Smithsonian Kite Festival Late March or early April. 202/357-2700, http://kitefestival.org. Professional and amateur kitemakers and kite flyers compete for prizes at a contest on the Washington Monument grounds.

APRIL
National Cherry Blossom Festival Late March or early April. 202/547-1500. The annual display of blossoms around the Tidal Basin doesn't always coincide with the festival, but the city celebrates with two weeks of performances, exhibitions, and activities. The Cherry Blossom Parade is usually held on the first Saturday in April. For up-to-date information on when the blossoms will peak, consult the National Park Service at www.nps.gov/nacc/cherry.

Filmfest DC 202/724-5613, www.filmfestdc.org. Two weeks of international and American films, shown at local theaters and other auditoriums.

White House Easter Egg Roll Monday after Easter. 202/456-7041. This annual event dates back to 1878 during the Rutherford B. Hayes Administration. Children, ages three to six, have a chance to play on the South Lawn of the White House. The event includes storytelling, music, and costumed characters.

White House Spring Garden and House Tour April. 202/456-7041. A chance to tour the lovely spring gardens of the White House's South Lawn.

MAY
Georgetown Garden Day 2nd Sat. in May. 202/333-1950,

www.gtowngarden.org. A chance to visit the private gardens of some beautiful, historic homes.

Evening Parade Friday nights, May–Aug. U. S. Marine Barracks, 8th and I Sts., S.E., 202/433-6060. The evening begins with a concert by the United States Marine Band, followed by a demonstration of precision marching by Marine Drum and Bugle Corps, and the Marine Corps Silent Drill Platoon.

Memorial Day Celebrations Events on Memorial Day weekend include ceremonies at the Vietnam Veteran's Memorial (202/619-7222), the Tomb of the Unknowns at Arlington National Cemetery (703/607-8052), usually with an address by the President, and a concert by the National Symphony Orchestra on the West Lawn of the Capitol.

Washington National Cathedral Flower Mart Early May. Massachusetts and Wisconsin Aves., N.W., 202/537-6200. An annual flower and crafts show and sale on the cathedral grounds.

JUNE
Dupont-Kalorama Museum Walk Weekend 1st weekend in June. Dupont Circle neighborhood, 202/667-0441, www.dkmuseums.com. Visit museums and enjoy textile-weaving demonstrations, interactive tours, hands-on workshops, and concerts.

Capital Pride Festival Along Pennsylvania Ave. between 3rd and 9th Sts., N.W., 202/797-3510. A week-long celebration of the area's gay, lesbian, bisexual, and transgender residents, culminating in a parade through Washington and a festival on Pennsylvania Ave., N.W.

JULY
Smithsonian Folklife Festival Late June/early July. On the Mall, 202/357-2700. An annual two-week celebration of folk

cultures, American and foreign, with music, food, and handicraft demonstrations.

Fourth of July Celebrations The National Independence Day Parade takes place at 11:45 a.m. on Constitution Ave. between 7th and 17th Sts., N.W. The National Symphony Orchestra, with guest stars and soloists, performs at 8 p.m. on the West Lawn of the Capitol.

Fourth of July fireworks The show starts about 9:10 p.m. over the Washington Monument grounds (202/619-7222).

AUGUST
Virginia Wine Festival Mid-Aug. weekend. Great Meadows, The Plains, Va., 800/520-9670. A chance to sample the wares of Virginia's emerging wine industry with music, food, and entertainment.

SEPTEMBER
Labor Day Concert 202/619-7222. The National Symphony Orchestra closes its summer season with a concert on the West Lawn of the Capitol.

National Cathedral Open House Massachusetts and Wisconsin Aves., N.W., 202/537-6200. Washington National Cathedral holds its annual open house, with special tours, tower climbs, and entertainment.

OCTOBER
Taste of D.C. Festival 2nd weekend in Oct. Pennsylvania Ave., N.W., between 9th and 14th Sts. Two outdoor stages with live entertainment and food from many area restaurants are featured at this festival. Admission is free, but there's a charge for food tastings.

Marine Corps Marathon 800/786-8762, www.marinemarathon.com. Thousands of runners take part in this annual marathon. The race starts at the Iwo Jima memorial in Arlington at

8:30 a.m. and follows a course that crosses into Washington and passes all the major monuments on the Mall before ending back at the memorial.

NOVEMBER
Washington Craft Show Mid-Nov. Washington Convention Center, 203/254-0486. A juried show of American crafts, including basketry, ceramics, fiber decorative and wearables, furniture, glass, jewelry, leather, metal, mixed media, paper, and wood.

DECEMBER
Pageant of Peace/Lighting of the National Christmas Tree On the Ellipse south of the White House, 202/619-7222. The official kickoff of the Christmas season in Washington, with concerts and a Christmas tree from each of the states.

Washington National Cathedral Christmas Services Massachusetts and Wisconsin Aves., N.W., 202/537-6200. Christmas Eve services at 6 p.m. and 10 p.m. Passes are required.

FURTHER READING

The best book on Washington architecture is E. J. Applewhite's *Washington Itself.* Applewhite, a former CIA officer, has a keen eye for buildings and an ear for the details of history that make his opinions come alive.

For those interested in learning about where famous and not-so-famous events happened throughout the city, pick up a copy of *On the Spot: Pinpointing the Past in Washington, D.C.* (Douglas E. Evelyn and Paul Dickson, 1999).

Fiction lovers should check out one of Margaret Truman's many murder mysteries set in and around Washington, D.C.

HOTELS & RESTAURANTS

Where you sleep and eat can make all the difference between a good visit and bad. Washington offers a panoply of hotel and restaurant selections in all price categories and styles—something for every taste.

HOTELS

Washington hotels vary from the luxurious and expensive—the Four Seasons in Georgetown and the new Ritz-Carlton in the West End being good examples—to the basic and still fairly expensive—the large downtown hotels that cater mostly to the convention and meeting trade. Small and charming is harder to find, but the new boutique hotels being opened by the Kempton Group in Washington—Topaz is the first of them and more will follow—are a hopeful sign.

Because every major business in the country is affected by government legislation and regulations, Washington hotels cater to business travelers on expense accounts. That means high prices during the week, when businesses are paying the tab, but it also means weekend bargains for the leisure and family traveler. Similarly, prices are higher in the winter, when Congress is in session, and lower in the summer, when much of official Washington takes vacation time and flees the city for cooler climes.

Because hotels in the city are expensive, many visitors prefer to stay in less expensive places in suburban Virginia and travel into the city each day. It's always worth asking a hotel "Is this the best rate you can give me?"

Many hotels routinely offer rates cheaper than their posted rack rates, and many offer discounts through organizations such as AAA or AARP. All know that a room rented for a discounted price is income, but an unrented room is income lost forever.

RESTAURANTS

For many years, Washington was thought to hold little interest as a restaurant city. It's a city obsessed by power, the popular wisdom had it, and people cared more about whom they were eating with than what they were eating. Well, things have changed in the last decade. There's still plenty of meat-and-potatoes power dining—the late '90s and the first year of the new century saw an unprecedented number of steakhouses opening in the city and the suburbs. But a number of distinguished chefs running national-class restaurants now make Washington their home. Roberto Donna at Galileo, Michel Richard at Citronelle, and Gerard Pangaud at Gerard's Place are at the top of the class, but their students, many of whom have stayed in Washington and opened their own restaurants, continue to enrich Washington dining.

In addition to this wonderful but pricey dining, the Washington area has long been an attractive place for exiles from their own countries to locate, and they have brought their food with them. It is said that any upheaval in a foreign country enriches Washington dining. Refugees from Vietnam opened fine restaurants in the Virginia suburbs, particularly in the area surrounding the Clarendon Metro station. Washington has more Ethiopian restaurants than any other city in the country. Thailand, India, Pakistan, Laos, and Malaysia have all given the city fine restaurants.

Unless otherwise noted, all restaurants are air-conditioned and offer non-smoking seating. All restaurants are open daily unless indicated otherwise.

L=lunch
D=dinner

CREDIT CARDS

Many hotels and restaurants accept all major credit cards. Smaller ones may accept some or none, as shown in their entry. Abbreviations used are: AE American Express, D Discover, DC Diners Club, MC MasterCard, and V Visa.

ORGANIZATION

Hotels and restaurants are listed first by chapter area, then by price category, then alphabetically.

Hotel restaurants of note have been bolded in the hotel entries and indicated by a restaurant icon beneath the hotel icon (if they're unusually special, they are treated in a separate entry within the restaurant section).

CAPITOL HILL

HOTELS

🏨 THE HOTEL GEORGE
🍴 $$$$$
15 E ST., N.W.
TEL 202/347-4200 OR
800/576-8331
FAX 202/347-0359
A completely renovated
building originally built in
1928, the George is convenient to Capitol Hill offices
and attractions. The decor
is striking and modern. The
restaurant **Bistro Bis** (see
below) offers quality updated
French bistro fare. Around-
the-clock cigar-friendly
Billiard Room.
🛈 139 🅿 🎽 🅂 AE, D,
DC, MC, V 🚇 Union Station

🏨 HYATT REGENCY
WASHINGTON ON
CAPITOL HILL
$$$$–$$$$$
400 NEW JERSEY AVE., N.W.
TEL 202/737-1234
FAX 202/737-5773
This large convention hotel
occupies a full city block on
Capitol Hill. The Hyatt
Regency has two in-house
restaurants with a wide
range of American cuisine.
The rooftop Capitol View
Club overlooks the U.S.
Capitol and Senate Office
Buildings. The hotel is cen-
trally located to offer access
to museums, monuments,
and government buildings.
🛈 834 🅿 🌊 🎽 🅂 AE,
D, DC, MC, V 🚇 Union
Station

🏨 PHOENIX PARK
🍴 HOTEL
$$$–$$$$$
520 N. CAPITOL ST., N.W.
TEL 202/638-6900 OR
800/824-5419
FAX 202/638-4025
Named after the park in
Dublin, the Phoenix Park
calls itself "America's center
of Irish hospitality." The
adjoining **Dubliner Pub**
offers good pub cooking and
Irish entertainment.
🛈 150 🅿 🎽 🅂 AE, D,
DC, MC, V 🚇 Union Station

🏨 CAPITOL HILL SUITES
$$$
200 C ST., S.E.
TEL 202/543-6000
FAX 202/547-2608
Tucked behind the Library
of Congress on the House
side of the hill, Capitol Hill
Suites offers kitchenettes in
every suite. The hotel was
refurbished in 2000.
🛈 152 🅿 🅂 AE, D, DC,
MC, V 🚇 Union Station,
South Capitol

🏨 WASHINGTON COURT
🍴 HOTEL
$$–$$$$
525 NEW JERSEY AVE., N.W.
TEL 202/628-2100
FAX 202/ 879 7938
The Washington Court has
a dramatic four-story atrium
lobby with leather furniture
and luxuriant plant life.
The **Cafe and Grill
Restaurant** offers American
cuisine. Billiards and cigars
offered in the Club Room.
🛈 264 🅿 🎽 🅂 AE, D,
DC, MC, V 🚇 Union Station

🏨 HOLIDAY INN
WASHINGTON,
D.C. ON THE HILL
$$–$$$
415 NEW JERSEY AVE., N.W.
TEL 202/638-1616
OR 800/638-1116
FAX 202/638-0707
A newly remodeled hotel
with modern decor and
well-appointed guest rooms.
Senators Grill is a sports bar
in the hotel, with more than
40 TV sets, one of the
largest sports bars in
Washington.
🛈 343 🌊 🎽 🅂 AE, D,
DC, MC, V 🚇 Union Station

RESTAURANTS

🍴 B. SMITH'S
$$$
UNION STATION, 50
MASSACHUSETTS AVE., N.E.
TEL 202/289-6188
This gracious restaurant,
owned by former super-
model B. Smith, occupies
the former presidential
reception room at Union
Station, perhaps the grandest
dining room in Washington.
Chef James Oakley's menu
is a combination of traditional Southern, New
Orleans-style, and Mid-
atlantic seafood dishes.
🍽 268 🅿 In rear of station
🅂 AE, D, DC, MC, V
🚇 Union Station

🍴 BISTRO BIS
$$$
THE HOTEL GEORGE,
15 E ST., N.W.
TEL 202/661-2700
Owner Jeffrey Buben and
executive chef Cathal
Armstrong serve traditional
bistro fare and intelligently
updated versions of it in this
sleek, modern Capitol Hill
hangout. Start with a plate
of rabbit rillettes or a rare-
roasted Moroccan lamb
salad. For a main course, try
the classic *steak frites*,
accompanied by perfectly
crisp fries. Pastry chef Maura
Clark's desserts are a treat.
🍽 115 🅿 🅂 AE, D, DC,
MC, V 🚇 Union Station

🍴 LA COLLINE
$$$
400 N. CAPITOL ST., N.W.
TEL 202/737-0400
Traditional without being
stuffy, La Colline is the kind
of French restaurant that
makes you remember why
French cooking was the
cuisine responsible for the
current dining boom. The
coarse, country-style pâté is
a good place to start. There's
no better place in town to
have a plate of *tripes á la
mode de Caen*, but if that's a
bit too exotic, there's always
a terrific *steak frites*.
🍽 270 🕐 Closed Sun.
🅂 AE, DC, MC, V 🚇 Union
Station

DUBLINER
$$
520 N. CAPITOL, N.W.
TEL 202/737-3773
There are many things to eat at this lively Irish pub—fish and chips, shepherd's pie, even a burger—but the only thing to drink, particularly if you're Irish, is Guinness on tap, or maybe Irish whiskey. It all goes well with the Irish entertainment, every night after 9 p.m.
🔲 136 AE, DC, MC, V Union Station

THE MONOCLE
$$
107 D ST., N.E.
TEL 202/546-4488
Its position as the closest restaurant to the Senate side of the Capitol means that there's no better place in town for sighting politicos, either eating a meal or arriving for one of the frequent political fundraisers in the private rooms upstairs. Run by the Valonos family for 40 years, the Monocle serves an all-American menu of burgers, steaks, and seafood.
🔲 110 Closed Sat.–Sun. AE, DC, MC, V Union Station

TWO QUAIL
$$
320 MASSACHUSETTS AVE., N.E.
TEL 202/543-8030
A quirky place located in three town houses near Union Station, Two Quail draws its flea-market decor and its menu from eclectic sources. The cooking is basically Modern American—Caesar salad, portobello mushrooms to start, pasta and grilled meats for main courses.
🔲 80 Closed all Sat., & Sun. L AE, DC, MC, V Union Station

BANANA CAFÉ
$
500 8TH ST., S.E.
TEL 202/543-5906
This cheap and cheerful Mexican and Cuban restaurant has a bar and dining room on the main level and a piano bar above. You can order from a small selection of tapas to start, but the really interesting part of this menu is the Cuban specialties—ropa vieja (shredded flank steak cooked with tomato and spices), carnitas Cubanas (pork roasted with bitter oranges), and stuffed plantains. Don't miss the mango margaritas, a house specialty. Piano bar on Saturday evenings.
🔲 100 AE, D, DC, MC, V Eastern Market

SOMETHING SPECIAL

MARKET LUNCH
On Saturdays, the line for breakfast at the Market Lunch starts forming before the tiny restaurant opens, and it doesn't let up until noon. It's good Chesapeake Bay fare—pancakes and eggs for breakfast, maybe with a side of grits or scrapple, crab-cake sandwiches for lunch. The Market Lunch is one of those bits of an earlier Washington that locals hope will never change.
$
EASTERN MARKET
225 7TH ST., S.E.
TEL 202/547-8444
🔲 25 inside, 50 outside (in summer) Closed L, Sun. D, & all Mon. Cash only Eastern Market

THE MALL

HOTELS

LOEW'S L'ENFANT PLAZA
$$–$$$$$
480 L'ENFANT PLAZA, S.W.
TEL 202-484-1000
FAX 202/646-5060
The closest hotel to the Smithsonian museums, Loew's L'Enfant Plaza is attractive to both business and leisure travelers. The American Grill serves both Mediterranean and Pacific food.
🔢 370   AE, D, DC, MC, V L'Enfant Plaza

RESTAURANTS

LES HALLES
$$$$
1201 PENNSYLVANIA AVE., N.W.
TEL 202/347-6848
No restaurant in Washington feels more like Paris than this bustling French steakhouse. Service can be abrupt at busy times, but Washingtonians throng the place to eat the flavorful onglet, the hearty cassoulet, heaping platters of choucroute garnie, and the best French fries in town. The wine list is well-chosen and inexpensive.
🔲 186 Valet AE, D, DC, MC, V Metro Center, Federal Triangle

TENPENH
$$$
1001 PENNSYLVANIA AVE., N.W.
TEL 202/393-4500
Asian-American fusion cooking is everywhere these days, but few places do it more intelligently than this strikingly attractive downtown place. Chefs Jeff Tunks and Cliff Wharton have put together a menu that ranges from Vietnam to the Philippines, from Hong Kong to Thailand. Tunks's specialty, a Chinese-style smoked lobster, is a perfect marriage of East and West. Pastry chef David Guas's desserts are superb.
🔲 166 Valet Closed Sat. L, & all Sun. AE, D, DC, MC, V Metro Center

CAFÉ ATLANTICO
$$
405 8TH ST., N.W.
TEL 202/393-0812
With an attractive three-

level dining space tucked into an old power plant, Café Atlantico serves a fascinating menu of nuevo Latino dishes. Chef Christie Velie's menu changes frequently, but might include a soup of plantains with pork confit, followed by sea bass with spicy Salvadoran sausage. The bar makes great caipirinhas, and the wine list offers well-chosen South American wines at fair prices. 🏠 105 🅿 Valet 🐾 AE, DC, MC, V 🚇 Navy Memorial–Archives

🍴 SMITHSONIAN CASTLE, COMMONS RESTAURANT
$$
1000 JEFFERSON DR., S.W.
TEL 202/ 357-2957
The best food on the Mall is found in the impressive, high-ceilinged restaurant in the Smithsonian Castle. There's a lunchtime buffet, with good meat and fish dishes and a generous salad bar. The Commons is open to the public Saturday and for Sunday brunch. Reservations recommended.
🏠 120 🕐 Closed D 🐾 AE, D, MC, V 🚇 Smithsonian

🍴 NATIONAL GALLERY OF ART CAFES
$
6TH ST. & CONSTITUTION AVE.
TEL 202/737-4215
The **Garden Café** is the fanciest of the eateries in the National Gallery, offering a daily lunch buffet. The largest is the **Cascade Café** in the concourse between the two buildings, with a cafeteria menu of soups, salads, entrées, pizzas, and sandwiches. The newest is the **Sculpture Garden Pavilion Café**, serving pizzas, sandwiches, desserts, wine, and beer.
🚇 Archives

HOTELS

🏨 THE HAY-ADAMS HOTEL
$$$$$
ONE LAFAYETTE SQUARE, 16TH & H STS. N.W.
TEL 202/638-6600 OR 800/424-5054
FAX 202/638-2716
Built on the site where, alternately, President Lincoln's secretary John Hay and John Adams's grandson Henry Adams lived. The Hay-Adams Hotel is located just across Lafayette Park from the White House. The Lafayette Dining Room and guest rooms on the hotel's south side offer great views of the Executive Mansion.
🛈 145 🅿 🐾 AE, D, DC, MC, V 🚇 Farragut West, McPherson Square

🏨 PARK HYATT
$$$$–$$$$$
1201 24TH ST., N.W.
TEL 202/789-1234
FAX 202/457-8823
Located in Washington's West End, just three blocks from Georgetown, the Park Hyatt is comfortably but strikingly modern. The lobby is decorated with an impressive collection of modern art. Rooms are large and luxurious. The distinguished restaurant **Melrose** serves chef Brian McBride's accomplished Modern American cooking and a lavish Sunday brunch.
🛈 224 🅿 🐾 AE, D, DC, MC, V 🚇 Foggy Bottom

🏨 THE ST. REGIS
$$$$–$$$$$
923 16TH ST. AT K ST., N.W.
TEL 202/638-2626 OR 800/562-5661
FAX 202/638-4231
The St. Regis, well located near the White House and museums, is built in Italian Renaissance style with elabo-

rate plasterwork ceilings in the lobby. **Timothy Dean's** restaurant serves French and American fare. The Library Lounge is one of Washington's coziest bars.
🛈 194 🅿 🐾 AE, D, DC, MC, V 🚇 Farragut North

🏨 SWISSOTEL WASHINGTON, THE WATERGATE
$$$$–$$$$$
2650 VIRGINIA AVE., N.W.
TEL 202/965-2300
FAX 202/965-1173
Situated on the banks of the Potomac River, adjacent to the John F. Kennedy Center for the Performing Arts, the Watergate is part of the complex that gained notoriety after the 1972 break-in of the Democratic Party headquarters and subsequent cover-up. Rooms on the river side have spectacular views of the Potomac and of Virginia cities on the other side. The restaurant, **Jeffrey's at the Watergate,** added after the inauguration of George W. Bush, serves modern Texas cuisine.
🛈 250 🅿 🐾 AE, D, DC, MC, V 🚇 Foggy Bottom

🏨 WILLARD INTER-CONTINENTAL HOTEL
$$$$–$$$$$
1401 PENNSYLVANIA AVE., N.W.
TEL 202/628-9100 OR 800/327-0200
FAX 202/637-7326
A Willard Hotel has been located on this site since 1850. Abraham Lincoln stayed here before his inauguration; Julia Ward Howe wrote the "Battle Hymn of the Republic" while staying here. The hotel has been thoroughly remodeled and luxuriously decorated. The **Willard Room** is perhaps the grandest dining room in the city. The Round Robin Bar is one of the city's most popular gathering places.

H O T E L S   &   R E S T A U R A N T S

(i) 341 [P] 🍴 🚭 AE, D, DC, MC, V 🚇 Metro Center

🏨 JW MARRIOTT HOTEL
$$$$

1331 PENNSYLVANIA AVE., N.W.
TEL 202/393-2000
FAX 202/626-6991
Large, centrally located, and connected to the shops and boutiques of National Place, the JW Marriott is a convenient hub for explorations of the city. Two in-house restaurants.

(i) 774 [P] 🍴 🚭 AE, DC, MC, V 🚇 Metro Center

🏨 MONARCH HOTEL
🍴 **$$$–$$$$$**

2401 M ST., N.W.
TEL 202/429-2400 OR
877/222-2266
FAX 202/457-5010
Built around an attractive garden courtyard, the Monarch is in the West End near Georgetown. Rooms are luxurious, service is attentive. The fitness center, with pool, is one of the most complete in the city. **The Bistro** offers good Modern American cooking, while the Colonnade is open for Sunday brunch.

(i) 415 [P] 🍴 🚭 AE, D, DC, MC, V 🚇 Foggy Bottom

🏨 ONE WASHINGTON
🍴 **CIRCLE HOTEL**
$$$–$$$$$

ONE WASHINGTON CIRCLE, N.W.
TEL 202/872-1680 OR
800/424-9671
FAX 202/887-4989
Located near George Washington University, One Washington Circle has spacious rooms with private balconies, colorful furnishings, and a small-hotel atmosphere. **West End Café** has very good American food with Mediterranean influences.

(i) 151 [P] 🍴 🚭 AE, D, DC, MC, V 🚇 Foggy Bottom

🏨 THE WESTIN GRAND
🍴 **$$$–$$$$$**

2350 M ST., N.W.
TEL 202/429-0100
FAX 202/289-1728
This lovely hotel, located between Georgetown and the White House, is elegantly decorated and warmly welcoming. Rooms include executive-size desks and all-marble bathrooms with separate shower stalls. The **M Street Grille** features an elaborate morning buffet along with lunch and dinner. **Café on M** serves lunch, dinner, and cocktails in a clubby setting.

(i) 263 🚭 🍴 [P] Valet 🚭 AE, D, DC, MC, V 🚇 Foggy Bottom

🏨 HOTEL WASHINGTON
$$–$$$$$

15TH ST. & PENNSYLVANIA AVE., N.W.
TEL 202/638-5900
FAX 202/638-1594
Near the White House and the Treasury Department, the Hotel Washington is popular with locals and visitors for its seasonal rooftop bar offering great views (see p. 244). The in-house restaurant Two Continents offers American fare.

(i) 350 🍴 🚭 AE, D, DC, MC, V 🚇 Metro Center

🏨 WASHINGTON SUITES
GEORGETOWN
$$–$$$$

2500 PENNSYLVANIA AVE., N.W.
TEL 202/333-8060 OR
877/736-2500
FAX 202/338-3818
Located just over Rock Creek from Georgetown, this hotel is popular with performers at the nearby Kennedy Center. Each suite is more than 600 square feet in area and offers a living room with desk and sofabed, a separate bedroom with walk-in closet, two televisions, and a fully-equipped kitchen. The Italian restaurant **Donatello** is next door

---

PRICES

HOTELS
An indication of the cost of a double room in high season, excluding tax, is given by **$** signs.

$$$$$	$225+
$$$$	$175–$225
$$$	$125–$175
$$	$85–$125
$	Under $85

RESTAURANTS
An indication of the cost of a three-course dinner without drinks, tax, or tip is given by $ signs.

$$$$	Over $50
$$$	$35–$50
$$	$15–$35
$	Under $15

and provides room service for the hotel.

(i) 124 [P] 🍴 🚭 AE, D, DC, MC, V 🚇 Foggy Bottom

🏨 EMBASSY SUITES,
🍴 **WASHINGTON D.C.**
$$–$$$$

1250 22ND ST., N.W.
TEL 202/857-3388 OR
800/EMBASSY
FAX 202/293-3173
Built around an open, tropical atrium with waterfalls and plantlife, this popular hotel has an active lobby bar. The **Panevino Italian Ristorante** provides good basic Italian cooking.

(i) 318 🚭 🍴 🚭 AE, D, DC, MC, V 🚇 Foggy Bottom

🏨 GEORGE
WASHINGTON
UNIVERSITY INN
$$–$$$

824 NEW HAMPSHIRE AVE., N.W.
TEL 202/ 337-6620 OR
800/426-4455
FAX 202/298-7499
Situated on a quiet, tree-lined street in Foggy Bottom, two blocks from George Washington University and

---

the Kennedy Center, this well-located hotel has rooms with Williamsburg-inspired decor and 18th-century-style furnishings.

🛈 95 🅿 🚭 AE, DC, MC, V 🅰 Foggy Bottom

RESTAURANTS

🍴 EQUINOX
$$$$
818 CONNECTICUT AVE., N.W.
TEL 202/331-8118
Chef Todd Gray is fascinated by, but never limited by, the food of the Chesapeake Bay region. Many restaurants claim to use the freshest local ingredients, but few have taken the trouble, as Gray has, to research historical recipes and to update them for contemporary tastes while respecting their basic tastes. Gray's recent menus have included Virginia oysters on celery root purée as a starter and wild rockfish on country-style squash as a main course.
🪑 90 🕐 Closed Sat.–Sun. L 🚭 AE, DC, MC, V 🅰 Farragut West

🍴 GALILEO
$$$$
1110 21ST ST., N.W.
TEL 202/293-7191
The flagship restaurant of one of Washington's most popular and inventive chefs, Galileo offers a number of ways of dining. For a quick lunch or snack, the bar menu of sandwiches and salads is a great bargain. The main dining room has a large selection of dishes from chef Roberto Donna's native Piedmont, but for a real treat (and splurge), make reservations for Donna's Laboratorio, where the chef himself cooks a ten-course tasting menu based on what is available in the market.
🪑 175 🅿 Valet 🕐 Closed Sat.–Sun. L 🚭 AE, DC, MC, V 🅰 Foggy Bottom, Farragut North

🍴 KINKEAD'S
The popularity of this Foggy Bottom seafood restaurant makes reservations a must. Like most Modern American chefs, Robert Kinkead's repertoire includes dishes from a wide range of international cuisines and American regions: pepita-crusted salmon, roasted cod with crab imperial, rockfish with red curry and coconut-milk broth. His cooking is also impressive when he returns to his New England roots—Kinkead's has the best fried clams in town.
$$$$
2000 PENNSYLVANIA AVE., N.W.
TEL 202/296-7700
🪑 190 🅿 Valet 🚭 AE, D, MC, V 🅰 Foggy Bottom

🍴 MARCEL'S
$$$$
2401 PENNSYLVANIA AVE., N.W.
TEL 202/296-1166
Chef Robert Wiedmaier's Belgian-influenced French cooking is both sophisticated and robust. Start a meal with his wonderfully light *boudin blanc*; continue with a game dish, perhaps loin of venison in a subtle sauce of beets and blackberries. The wine list is particularly strong in red Burgundies and wines from the Côtes du Rhone.
🪑 120 🅿 Valet 🕐 Closed L 🚭 AE, DC, MC, V 🅰 Foggy Bottom

🍴 BOMBAY CLUB
$$$
815 CONNECTICUT AVE., N.W.
TEL 202/659-3727
The dark wooden chairs, ceiling fans, rugs, and leafy palms make this popular Indian restaurant near the White House seem like a trip back in time to the days of the British Raj. Lovers of spicy food might find the offerings here a bit tame, but

but the signature tandoori seafood dishes, and anything else from the tandoor clay oven, are wonderful.
🪑 96 🅿 Valet 🕐 Closed Sat. L 🚭 AE, DC, MC, V 🅰 Farragut West

🍴 OVAL ROOM AT LAFAYETTE SQUARE
$$$
800 CONNECTICUT AVE., N.W.
TEL 202/463-8700
Just across Lafayette Square from the White House, the Oval Room is a favorite lunch spot for senior executive branch staffers, drawn by the warm welcome and the innovative cooking of chef Frank Morales. Try the seared sea scallops with chorizo and squid, the loin of pork served with root vegetables, and finish with a selection of the perfectly kept cheeses.
🪑 125 🅿 Valet 🕐 Closed Sat. L & all Sun. 🚭 AE, DC, MC, V 🅰 Farragut West

🍴 TABERNA DEL ALABARDERO
$$$
1776 I ST., N.W.
TEL 202/429-2200
The small tapas bar at the entrance is a good first stop at this distinguished Spanish restaurant, perhaps for a glass of dry sherry and a plate of Serrano ham to whet the appetite. The main-course selections demonstrate that there is much more to Spanish cooking than paella—maybe lovely garlic soup or stuffed squid to start and a main course of a hearty rabbit stew.
🪑 162 🅿 Valet 🕐 Closed Sat. L & all Sun. 🚭 AE, D, DC, MC, V 🅰 Farragut West

🍴 OLD EBBITT GRILL
$$
675 15TH ST., N.W.
TEL 202/347-4801
Large, casual, and always crowded, the Old Ebbitt Grill feeds Washingtonians

and out-of-towners with a large menu that ranges from burgers to grilled fish and meat. There's no better place in town for oysters. The grill always has a large assortment of varieties from waters that are certified safe, and a crew of able shuckers to open them.

🍴 500 🅿 Valet
⬧ AE, D, DC, MC, V
🚇 Metro Center

🍴 SKY TERRACE, HOTEL WASHINGTON
$$

15TH ST. & PENNSYLVANIA AVE., N.W.
TEL 202/638-5900
The Hotel Washington's Sky Terrace, open from May through October, has spectacular views of Washington toward the south and the monuments and toward the west and the White House. It's a favorite summer place for drinks and also serves light American fare such as sandwiches, salads, and fish.

🍴 200 🕐 Closed Nov.–April ⬧ AE, D, DC, MC, V 🚇 Metro Center

🍴 BREAD LINE
$

1751 PENNSYLVANIA AVE., N.W.
TEL 202/822-8900
Owner Mark Furstenburg's popular lunch spot near the White House specializes in bread and bread-based dishes from around the world. Sandwiches are wonderful—if you're lucky enough to be in Washington in tomato season, try the BLT on brioche—but you can also find wonderful pizzas, empanadas, pirogis, and soups. It's a great place to buy a loaf of bread for a lunchtime picnic, but remember that it closes about 4 p.m.

🍴 100 🕐 Closed Sat.–Sun., & all D ⬧ AE, D, MC, V
🚇 Farragut West

🍴 MALAYSIA KOPITIAM
$

1827 M ST., N.W.
TEL 202/833-6232
Owners Penny and Leslie Phoon are hospitable guides to the food of Malaysia, which is less well known than it ought to be. The menu thoughtfully provides photos of the dishes, but the Phoons are glad to make recommendations—maybe appetizers of fish balls or a spicy lamb satay followed by Malaysian Chili Shrimp or a Chinese noodle dish.

🍴 110 🕐 ⬧ AE, D, DC, MC, V 🚇 Dupont Circle

DOWNTOWN

HOTELS

🏨 JEFFERSON HOTEL
$$$$$

1200 16TH ST., N.W.
TEL 202/347-2200
FAX 202/331-7982
Small boutique residential-type hotel, with every room unique. First an apartment house, in 1955 it was converted into a hotel. Oliver North resided here during the Iran Contra trials. During the '80s the Larry King radio program was broadcast live from within the Jefferson. Located four blocks from the White House.

🛏 100 🅿 ⬧ AE, D, DC, MC, V 🚇 Farragut North

🏨 THE MADISON
$$$$–$$$$$

15TH & M STS., N.W.
TEL 202/862-1600
FAX 202/785-1255
Opened in 1963, the Madison has antiques and works of art on display throughout. Federal-period decor is designed to be reminiscent of James and Dolly Madison's stately Virginia home, Montpelier.

🛏 353 🅿 🍴 ⬧ AE, D, DC, MC, V 🚇 McPherson Square

🏨 MORRISON CLARK 🍴 INN
$$$$

1015 L ST., N.W.
TEL 202/898-1200
OR 800/332-7898
FAX 202/289-8576
A Victorian mansion built as two separate town homes in 1864, with original turn-of-the-19th-century furnishings. The **Morrison Clark Restaurant,** located in the former drawing room, is known for its new American cuisine.

🛏 54 🅿 🍴 ⬧ AE, D, DC, MC, V 🚇 Mt. Vernon Sq.

🏨 GRAND HYATT WASHINGTON
$$$–$$$$$

1000 H ST., N.W.
TEL 202/582-1234
FAX 202/637-4781
Located near the Washington Convention Center and the MCI Center, this large hotel features a parklike atrium, lobby bar, sports bar, cigar bar, and a deli.

🛏 900 🅿 🍽 🍴 ⬧ AE, D, DC, MC, V 🚇 Metro Center

🏨 HENLEY PARK HOTEL
🍴 **$$$–$$$$**

926 MASSACHUSETTS AVE., N.W.
TEL 202/638-5200
FAX 202/638-6740
Quaint, Tudor-style hotel in the tradition of Europe's finest mall hotels—one of Washington's most charming. One hundred eighteen gargoyles and real lead windows decorate its exterior. The **Coeur de Lion** restaurant offers very good Modern American cooking. The Blue Bar has frequent live music and a menu of small plates.

🛏 96 🅿 🍴 ⬧ AE, D, DC, MC, V 🚇 Mount Vernon Square, Gallery Place/Chinatown

SOMETHING SPECIAL

RENAISSANCE MAYFLOWER HOTEL

Once the home to many members of Congress, the historic Mayflower has been the site of an inaugural ball for every President since its opening in 1925. J. Edgar Hoover had breakfast here every morning. The gracious lobby runs an entire city block from Connecticut Avenue to 17th Street. Café Promenade features Mediterranean cooking, and the Town and Country Lounge is a favorite gathering spot.

$$$–$$$$
1127 CONNECTICUT AVE., N.W.
TEL 202/347-3000 OR
800/228-7697
FAX 202/776-9182
🛏 660 🅿 🍸 🗝 AE, D, DC, MC, V 🚇 Farragut North

MARRIOTT AT METRO CENTER

$$–$$$$$
775 12TH ST., N.W.
TEL 202/737-2200
FAX 202/347-5886
Conveniently located at the flagship station of the city's Metro system, the Marriott at Metro Center is attentive to both business and vacation guests. The Metro Center Grille features New American cuisine.
🛏 456 🗦 🗝 AE, D, DC, MC, V 🚇 Metro Center

WASHINGTON RENAISSANCE HOTEL

$$–$$$$
999 9TH ST., N.W.
TEL 202/898-9000
The closest hotel to the Washington Convention Center and the MCI Center, the Washington Renaissance is a fully equipped business hotel well located for leisure travelers.
🛏 807 🗦 🍸 🗝 AE, D,

DC, MC, V 🚇 Gallery Place/Chinatown

HOTEL HARRINGTON

$–$$
436 11TH ST., N.W.
TEL 202/628-8140 OR
800/424-8532
FAX 202/393-2311
Low prices, a prime location, and very plain, clean rooms, make the Hotel Harrington popular with bus tours of schoolchildren who come to Washington for their spring breaks. The hotel restaurant serves breakfast, lunch, and dinner. **Ollie's Trolley** on the lobby level is good for burgers and shakes.
🛏 250 🗝 AE, D, DC, MC, V 🚇 Metro Center

RESTAURANTS

GERARD'S PLACE

$$$$
915 15TH ST., N.W.
TEL 202/737-4445
Chef Gerard Pangaud is the only Michelin two-star chef currently cooking in the U.S. In Pangaud's sparely elegant dining room, a mixture of food-loving locals and international officials enjoy classics and improvisations—a perfect roast chicken, his signature lobster in Sauternes, a simple roasted pear with vanilla ice cream.
🍴 55 🕐 Closed Sat. L & all Sun. 🗝 AE, DC, MC, V 🚇 McPherson Square

OCEANAIRE

$$$$
1201 F ST., N.W.
TEL 202/347-2277
This sophisticated seafood restaurant with its curving walls, cozy banquettes, and pink lighting that makes everyone look good, resembles the inside of an art deco ocean liner. The seafood is pristinely fresh and comes in enormous portions a lot like the gargantuan meals of ocean voyages—good oys-

ters on the half-shell, a Grand Shellfish Platter that is a meal for two, a heaping Fisherman's Platter of fried seafood, delicious Dover sole boned at tableside. The huge banana split should be attempted only by those with the heartiest appetites.
🍴 500 🅿 Valet 🕐 Closed Sat.–Sun. L 🗝 AE, D, DC, MC, V 🚇 Metro Center

TOSCA

$$$
1112 F ST., N.W.
TEL 202/367-1990
Chef Cesare Lanfrancone spent five years in the kitchen at Galileo before starting his own restaurant with a menu based on the food of his native region of Lake Como. The sophisticated modern setting is designed for private conversation—the widely spaced tables and well-designed acoustics give a measure of privacy, even when the room is full. The chef's signature dishes include a fascinating ravioli stuffed with amaretto cookies, roast meats and stews, and a wonderful tiramisu that makes you understand why this overserved dish was ever popular.
🍴 120 🅿 Valet 🕐 Closed Sat.–Sun. L 🗝 AE, DC, MC, V 🚇 Metro Center

JALEO

$$
480 7TH ST., N.W.
TEL 202/628-7949
There are main courses at Jaleo, but most diners choose to make a meal of the large selection of tapas—wonderful Spanish cheeses and coldcuts, eggplant flan, spicy octopus, sausages and beans. It's a great place for a light dinner before a performance at the nearby Shakespeare Theatre.
🍴 145 🅿 Valet parking 🗝 AE, D, DC, MC, V 🚇 Gallery Place/Chinatown

HOTELS & RESTAURANTS

GEORGETOWN

HOTELS

SOMETHING SPECIAL

🏨 FOUR SEASONS 🍴 HOTEL

Located on the very eastern edge of Georgetown, this luxurious hotel provides a nice link into the rest of the city. Seasons Restaurant, overlooking the C&O Canal, is the city's favorite power breakfast spot. The three-level fitness center with adjoining spa is one of the most opulent in town.

$$$$$+
2800 PENNSYLVANIA AVE., N.W.
TEL 202/342-0444
FAX 202/944-2076
ℹ️ 259 🅿️ 🏊 📺 🏧 AE, DC, MC, V 🚇 Foggy Bottom

🏨 WASHINGTON SUITES GEORGETOWN
$$$$$
2500 PENNSYLVANIA AVE., N.W.
TEL 202/333-8060 OR
877-736-2500
FAX 202/338-3818
Each suite at this moderately priced hotel has a 650-sq.-ft. living room/dining area, bedroom, and fully equipped kitchen. Located in the Georgetown/Foggy Bottom area, it's close to major landmarks and active Georgetown nightlife.
ℹ️ 124 suites 🅿️ 📺 🏧 AE, DC, MC, V 🚇 Foggy Bottom

🏨 HOTEL MONTICELLO
$$$$$
1075 THOMAS JEFFERSON ST., N.W.
TEL 202/337-0900 OR
800/388-2410
FAX 202/333-6526
Completely remodeled in 2000, this all-suite hotel is located in the center of Georgetown and is popular with international guests.

Rooms are bright, cheery, and spacious, and all have wet bars, microwaves, and refrigerators. It is close to the historic C&O Canal.
ℹ️ 47 🏧 AE, DC, MC, V 🚇 Foggy Bottom, then 32, 34, 36 bus

🏨 THE GEORGETOWN 🍴 INN
$$$$-$$$$$
1310 WISCONSIN AVE., N.W.
TEL 202/333-8900 OR
800/368-5922
FAX 202/295-2003
Opened in 1961, this pleasant redbrick hotel has colonial decor, large rooms, and marble bathrooms. It's conveniently located for Georgetown shopping and entertainment. The **American Grill** is reminiscent of the great American grills of the 1920s.
ℹ️ 96 🅿️ 🏧 AE, DC, MC, V 🚇 Foggy Bottom, then 30S bus

🏨 THE LATHAM HOTEL
🍴 **$$$$-$$$$$**
3000 M ST., N.W.
TEL 202/726-5000 OR
800/368-5922
FAX 202/337-4250
In the center of the Georgetown shopping area, the Latham Hotel has a variety of types of rooms and suites. The nearby C&O Canal towpath is convenient for jogging and bicycling. Michel Richard's **Citronelle** restaurant and cocktail lounge (see p. 247) offers exceptional food. **La Madeleine,** a French patisserie, is located in front of the hotel on M St.
ℹ️ 143 🏧 AE, DC, MC, V 🚇 Foggy Bottom, then 32, 34, 30 bus

🏨 HOLIDAY INN GEORGETOWN
$$$-$$$$
2101 WISCONSIN AVE., N.W.
TEL 202/338-4600
FAX 202/338-4458
Recently renovated, this moderately priced hotel in upper Georgetown is close

PRICES

HOTELS
An indication of the cost of a double room in high season, excluding tax, is given by **$** signs.

$$$$$	$225+
$$$$	$175–$225
$$$	$125–$175
$$	$85–$125
$	Under $85

RESTAURANTS
An indication of the cost of a three-course dinner without drinks, tax, or tip is given by $ signs.

$$$$	Over $50
$$$	$35–$50
$$	$15–$35
$	Under $15

to Dumbarton Oaks and Tudor Place.
ℹ️ 296 🏊 📺 🏧 AE, DC, MC, V 🚇 Foggy Bottom, then 30S bus

RESTAURANTS

🍴 CITRONELLE
$$$$
LATHAM HOTEL
3000 M ST., N.W.
TEL 202/625-2150
There's no more imaginative French cook at work in America than Michel Richard. The open kitchen at Citronelle, with banks of tables rising above it, is a fitting stage for his modern French cooking. The menu changes frequently, according to the availability of ingredients and the whim of the chef. For a sampling of Richard's talent, order one of his fixed-price menus, and don't forget dessert—Richard started life as a pastry chef.
🪑 100 🅿️ Valet 🕐 Closed Sat.–Sun. L 🏧 AE, D, DC, MC, V 🚇 Foggy Bottom, then walk 15 minutes

🍴 1789
$$$
1226 36TH ST., N.W.
TEL 202/965-1789
One of Washington's loveliest and most beloved restaurants, housed in a federal town house. There's no better way to spend a winter evening than at a table by the fireplace in the central dining room enjoying chef Ris Lacoste's rack of lamb, filet of beef, or pinenut-crusted chicken breast. Don't miss the pecan pie with bourbon ice cream for dessert. Downstairs you'll find the **Tombs,** where generations of Georgetown students have drunk countless pitchers of beer.
🛏 300 🅿 Valet 🕐 Closed L 🅰 AE, D, DC, MC, V 🚇 Foggy Bottom, Rosslyn; then Georgetown Metro Connect bus

🍴 HERITAGE INDIA
$$$
2400 WISCONSIN AVE., N.W.
TEL 202/333-3120
This elegant restaurant offers an unusually wide selection of cooking from the Indian subcontinent. Look for tandoori prawns, Kashmiri lamb curry simmered in a sauce of yogurt and saffron, baby eggplant in sesame sauce, and splendid vegetable curries.
🛏 100 🅿 Valet 🕐 Closed Sat. L 🅰 AE, D, MC, V 🚇 Tenleytown–AU, then 33, 34 bus

🍴 SEA CATCH
$$$
1054 31ST ST., N.W.
TEL 202/337-8855
The magnificent white Carrera marble oyster bar at the entrance to this dependable seafood restaurant gives you a suggestion about what to order first—a selection of oysters and clams on the half-shell. The seafood selection, always perfectly fresh, is based on market availability. Chef Jeff Shively, a Louisiana native, has a way with New Orleans-style seafood dishes, but his repertory is by no means limited to them. Try the steamed shellfish platter, seared sea scallops paired with lentils, or, in season yellow snapper from Florida.
🛏 200 🅿 🕐 Closed Sun. 🅰 AE, D, DC, MC, V 🚇 Foggy Bottom

🍴 BISTRO FRANCAIS
$$
3128 M ST., N.W.
TEL 202/338-3830
In a city where restaurants close early, this lively French bistro serves until 3 a.m. on weekdays and 4 a.m. on weekends. The classics of bistro cooking are dependably done: roast chicken with *pommes frites;* a hearty *cassoulet;* rabbit in mustard sauce.
🛏 150 🅰 AE, DC, MC, V 🚇 Foggy Bottom, then walk

🍴 CLYDE'S
$$
3236 M ST., N.W.
TEL 202/333-9180
The founder of the small Clyde's group of restaurants had the idea that he'd "rather eat in a bar than drink in a restaurant." This Georgetown original of the chain is built around a bar business, but offers an impressive menu of bar food, particularly in the summer when Clyde's makes a point of sending trucks to local farms for fresh produce. It's a good place for a restorative drink and light meal while shopping in Georgetown.
🛏 188 🅿 Georgetown Park Mall lot 🅰 AE, D, DC, MC, V 🚇 Foggy Bottom, Rosslyn; then Georgetown Metro Connect bus

🍴 SENSES
$$
3206 GRACE ST., N.W.
TEL 202/342-9083
Tucked away on Grace Street between the C&O Canal and the Potomac, Senses is the kind of small, out-of-the-way restaurant that travelers dream of finding. It's a good place for lunch, perhaps a salad and a quiche; for an afternoon pastry and coffee; or for an intimate dinner of a beautifully cooked rack of lamb, veal tenderloin, or salmon paired with mashed potatoes and a sauce of red wine and shallots.
🛏 42 🕐 Closed Mon. 🅰 AE, MC, V 🚇 Foggy Bottom, then Georgetown Metro Connect bus

🍴 SUSHI-KO
$$
2309 WISCONSIN AVE., N.W.
TEL 202/333-4187
Washington's original sushi bar, and there's still no better place locally for quality and variety of raw fish. Sushi-Ko has recently been remodeled into a hyper-cool, modern Japanese restaurant, with nontraditional sushi items. Owner Daisuke Utagawa thinks red Burgundy is the ideal accompaniment for sushi, and the restaurant has a wide selection.
🛏 100 🅿 Valet 🕐 Closed Sat.–Mon. L 🅰 AE, MC, V 🚇 Tenleytown–AU, then 32, 34, 35, 36 bus

🍴 WEST 24
$$
1250 24TH ST., N.W.
TEL 202/331-1100
Owned by Washington's political odd couple, Democrat James Carville and Republican Mary Matalin, West 24 offers a comfortable barn designed for political discussions and chef James Reppuhn's good Modern American cooking—for starters, tempura-battered softshell crab, jerk quail, or pan-seared foie gras; for a main course, barbecue-glazed pork tenderloin, buffalo strip loin, or honey-roasted chicken.
🛏 95 🅿 Valet 🕐 Closed

Sat. L & all Sun.
AE, D, DC, MC, V
Foggy Bottom

PATISSERIE POUPON
$
1645 WISCONSIN AVE., N.W.
TEL 202/342-3248
Primarily a bakery that makes wonderful fruit tarts, cakes, and Washington's best croissants, Patisserie Poupon has a small dining area and a small menu of sandwiches, soups, and salads.
26 Closed Mon. L & all D AE, MC, V
Tenleytown–AU, then 33, 34 bus

DUPONT CIRCLE & ADAMS MORGAN

HOTELS

THE CHURCHILL
$$$$$
1914 CONNECTICUT AVE., N.W.
TEL 202/797-2000
FAX 202/462-0944
Located just north of the vibrant Dupont Circle area in Kalorama, an area known for its stately residences and embassies, the Churchill offers a variety of suites and room with separate studies. The **Trocadero Café** offers French-inspired cuisine, and the Pullman Bar is a relaxing place for a drink.
144 AE, D, DC, MC, V Dupont Circle

JURYS WASHINGTON HOTEL
$$$$$
1500 NEW HAMPSHIRE AVE., N.W.
TEL 202/483-6000
FAX 202/328-3265
Owned and operated by Jurys Doyle Hotels, Ireland's largest hotel group, this recently remodeled hotel on Dupont Circle is one of the city's liveliest areas. Biddy Mulligan's Bar is a traditional Irish pub. **Claddagh Restaurant** has American

cuisine with an Irish twist.
309 AE, D, DC, MC, V Dupont Circle

RADISSON BARCELO HOTEL
$$$$$
2121 P ST., N.W.
TEL 202/293-3100
FAX 202/857-0134
Located between Georgetown and Dupont Circle, the Radisson Barcelo boasts some of Washington's largest guest rooms. The rooms have climate control, 3 phones, color cable TV, and radio. The restaurant **Gabriel** (see p. 249) serves Nuevo Latino cuisine and has one of the most popular Sunday brunches in the city.
301 AE, D, DC, MC, V Dupont Circle

TOPAZ HOTEL
$$$$$
1733 N ST., N.W.
TEL 202/393-3000 OR
800/424-2950
FAX 202/785-9581
This new boutique hotel, created from an older hotel on the site, is doing its best to spice up the hotel scene around Dupont Circle. It promises "cosmic energy and good karma." Decorated in a dazzling array of shapes and colors, all rooms are equipped with flat-screen Sony TVs, down comforters, and cordless speakerphones. A yoga exercise room provides instruction videos, and you can even get an energy drink on your way out in the morning. The **Topaz Bar** is open for meals and drinks.
99 AE, D, DC, MC, V Dupont Circle

WASHINGTON COURTYARD MARRIOTT
$$$$$
1900 CONNECTICUT AVE., N.W.
TEL 202/332-9300 OR
800/842-4211
FAX 202/328-7039

This pleasant Dupont Circle hotel is popular with conventioneers, and business- and vacation travelers. The lobby is welcoming with lush plantlife, the rooms gracious and modern. **Clarets** restaurant serves American cuisine.
147 AE, D, DC, MC, V Dupont Circle

WESTIN FAIRFAX
$$$$$
2100 MASSACHUSETTS AVE., N.W.
TEL 202/293-2100
FAX 202/293-0641
Opened in 1924 as the Fairfax Hotel, it was for many years the residential hotel favored by members of Congress. Former Vice President Al Gore grew up here. Guest rooms are luxurious, as one would expect from a hotel on Massachusetts Avenue's Embassy Row. **Cabo** restaurant, which has replaced the former Jockey Club, offers California cuisine.
206 AE, D, DC, MC, V Dupont Circle

CLARION HAMPSHIRE HOTEL
$$$
1310 NEW HAMPSHIRE AVE., N.W.
TEL 202/296-7600
FAX 202/293-2476
Located in a quiet neighborhood of office buildings, embassies, and other hotels, many of the Clarion Hampshire's comfortable, contemporary rooms have excellent views of the city, Georgetown, and Rock Creek.
82 AE, D, DC, MC, V Dupont Circle

TABARD INN
$$$
1739 N ST., N.W.
TEL 202/785-1277
FAX 202/785-6173
This small hotel is greatly loved by those who consider it quaint and love the Victorian clutter. Others hate it

for the same reason. Locals love the hotel's restaurant (see p. 250), which has a charming outdoor garden. The rooms vary widely in size, so it's wise to look before you commit.
🛏 40 🅿 🔲 AE, D, DC, MC, V 🚇 Dupont Circle

🏨 JURYS NORMANDY
$$$
2118 WYOMING AVE., N.W.
TEL 202/483-1350
FAX 202/387-8241
Remodeled in 1988, this pleasant mid-size hotel features a garden patio and glass conservatory with lush floral plantings.
🛏 75 🅿 🔲 AE, D, DC, MC, V 🚇 Dupont Circle

🏨 WINDSOR PARK HOTEL
$$
2116 KALORAMA RD., N.W.
TEL 202/483-7700 OR
800/247-3064
FAX 202/332-4547
A charming hotel with Victorian decor and Queen Anne and Chippendale-style furnishings. It overlooks Rock Creek Park and is near the National Zoo.
🛏 43 🔲 AE, D, DC, MC, V 🚇 Woodley Park

RESTAURANTS

🍽 THE PALM
$$$$
1225 19TH ST., N.W.
TEL 202/293-9091
The downtown branch of this steakhouse chain is the epicenter of Washington power dining. You'll see political figures, faces familiar from the news talk shows, and a flock of lesser Washington lights who like to be seen there. The main attractions are the Palm's steaks and five-pound lobsters, served by an efficient and irreverent crew of wisecracking waiters, but the Italian food is also very good.

🔲 185 🅿 Valet 🔲 Closed Sat.–Sun. L 🔲 AE, DC, MC, V 🚇 Dupont Circle

🍽 VIDALIA
$$$$
1990 M ST., N.W.
TEL 202/659-1990
Named after the sweet Georgia onion, Vidalia is one of the city's leading exponents of Southern cooking. In season, there's a large variety of Vidalia onion dishes. At other times of the year, onion offerings are likely to be limited to a dish of onion relish with your bread and the wonderful Five Onion Soup. Chef Jeffrey Buben's shrimp and grits is a signature dish, as is his roasted sweetbreads with lobster. For dessert, don't miss the lemon chess pie.
🔲 115 🅿 Valet 🔲 Closed Sat.–Sun. L 🔲 AE, D, DC, MC, V 🚇 Farragut West

🍽 CASHION'S EAT PLACE
$$$
1819 COLUMBIA RD., N.W.
TEL 202/797-1819
Chef Ann Cashion's Adams Morgan restaurant offers distinguished Modern American cooking in a setting that's casual enough for a weeknight dinner and attractive enough for a special occasion. The menus change frequently, but you'll usually find a perfectly roasted free range chicken, and if you're lucky, roast leg of pork with creamed collard greens, a fritto misto of crisply fried seafood, or a venison chop with aromatic vegetables. Desserts are a treat, particularly the chocolate cake and the frozen lemon tart.
🔲 100 🅿 Valet 🔲 Closed Mon. 🔲 MC, V 🚇 Woodley Park/Zoo–Adams Morgan, plus 15-minute walk

🍽 ETRUSCO
$$$
1606 20TH ST., N.W.
TEL 202/667-0047

Chef Francesco Ricchi is a native of Tuscany, and the cooking of his native region is reflected on the menu of this moderately priced Dupont Circle restaurant. Join neighborhood regulars for ribolita, a hearty Tuscan bread soup with Parmesan; rabbit sausage; a signature ragu of duck on pappardelle; and main courses such as roast rabbit or braised veal shank. Desserts include Grandfather's Cake, a chocolate treat, and a delicious pear cake.
🔲 130 🔲 Closed L 🔲 AE, MC, V 🚇 Dupont Circle

🍽 GABRIEL
$$$
RADISSON BARCELO HOTEL
2121 P ST., N.W.
TEL 202/956-6690
Gabriel has the best Sunday brunch in Washington, and one of the most popular. Chef Greggory Hill's groaning buffet tables feature a whole roast suckling pig surrounded by a selection of hot and cold vegetable dishes, and for the less adventurous, a traditional breakfast bar with bacon and eggs. Chef Hill's regular menu is an intelligent combination of Spanish cooking and the more robust flavors of Latin America. You can start your meal with a selection of tapas, then move on to more substantial dishes— perhaps bison tenderloin, a braised lamb shank, or a delicious rotisserie chicken with garlic mashed potatoes.
🔲 70 🅿 Valet 🔲 Closed L & all Sun.–Mon. 🔲 AE, D, DC, MC, V 🚇 Dupont Circle

🍽 NORA RESTAURANT
$$$
2132 FLORIDA AVE., N.W.
TEL 202/462-5143
Chef Nora Pouillon was a pioneer advocate of organic farming, and her restaurant is the first locally to be certi-

HOTELS & RESTAURANTS

fied organic by Oregon Tilth, an organization that promulgates standards for organic growers. This means that 95 percent of the ingredients at the restaurant comes from certified organic sources. But the handsome appearance and polished service at Nora Restaurant belie our '60s preconceptions of what an organic restaurant might be. The menu changes daily, but you will find wonderful first course salads, beautifully cooked organic chicken, fresh seafood, and spectacular pies for dessert. 🛏 80 🅿 Valet 🕐 Closed L, & all Sun. 💳 AE, MC, V 🚇 Dupont Circle

🍴 OBELISK
$$$
2029 P ST., N.W.
TEL 202/872-1180
At Obelisk, everything is small in scale except flavor. This tiny Italian restaurant holds fewer than 40 people, which makes it one of the hardest-to-get reservations in town. The $55 fixed-price menu, which changes too often to recommend specific dishes, offers two or three choices of antipasto, pasta, main course, and dessert. Chef Peter Pastan's cooking is simple but never precious and is likely to be a memorable culinary experience, based on fresh ingredients in the hands of a skilled chef. 🛏 36 🕐 Closed L, & all Sun.–Mon. 💳 DC, MC, V 🚇 Dupont Circle

🍴 TABARD INN
$$$
1739 N ST., N.W.
TEL 202/833-2668
The restaurant of this quaint hotel south of Dupont Circle serves New American cuisine in a well-worn dining room that's a popular lunch spot for the offices nearby. Sunday brunch is a favorite with the neighborhood, and the pleasant brick-walled

garden is a good place for a drink and dinner on a spring evening. 🛏 80 (30 summer patio) 🅿 Valet Fri. & Sat. 💳 AE, MC, V 🚇 Dupont Circle

🍴 BISTROT DU COIN
$$
1738 CONNECTICUT AVE., N.W.
TEL 202/234-6969
It's not a place for quiet conversation, particularly in the evenings when locals from the neighborhood crowd around the zinc-topped bar and fill the trestle tables, but Bistrot du Coin is a lot of fun. Owner Michael Verdun and chef Yannis Felix strike a good balance between good cheer and good cooking. Mussels are a good way to start a meal here, particularly the curried *mouclade de Charantes*. For a main course, it's hard to go wrong with *steak frites,* but the more adventurous can order *tripes à la Niçoise* or a delicious stew of rabbit and mushrooms. The house wines—a Beaujolais, a Rhone, and an Alsatian white—are good value. 🛏 100 💳 AE, D, DC, MC, V 🚇 Dupont Circle

SOMETHING SPECIAL

🍴 IRON GATE INN
There's no more charming spot in Washington for outdoor dining than the terrace at the Iron Gate Inn, with its overhead trellis and cooling fountain. The menu is Mediterranean-inspired and the kitchen does a good job on Middle Eastern dishes—stuffed grape leaves, braised lamb shank, shish kebobs with grilled vegetables.
$$
1734 N ST., N.W.
TEL 202/737-1370
🛏 120 🕐 Closed Sun., & Sat. L 🚇 Dupont Circle

PRICES

HOTELS
An indication of the cost of a double room in high season, excluding tax, is given by $ signs.

$$$$$	$225+
$$$$	$175–$225
$$$	$125–$175
$$	$85–$125
$	Under $85

RESTAURANTS
An indication of the cost of a three-course dinner without drinks, tax, or tip is given by $ signs.

$$$$	Over $50
$$$	$35–$50
$$	$15–$35
$	Under $15

🍴 JOHNNY'S HALF SHELL
$$
2002 P ST., N.W.
TEL 202/296-2021
Washington has a dearth of good seafood restaurants, particularly moderately prices ones. Johnny's Half Shell, with its menu of mid-Atlantic and New Orleans-style seafood, was a hit from the day it opened. Oysters are a treat here, either raw on the half-shell or crisply fried with an accompaniment of pickled vegetables. The gumbo, dark and filled with seafood, is delicious. Main dishes include a perfectly cooked filet of rockfish, or if you don't like seafood, a chicken with slippery dumplings. Two of Johnny's real treats are available only at lunchtime—a wonderful fried oyster po' boy sandwich (a half is enough for a normal appetite) and the best hot dog in town. Don't miss the chocolate angel-food cake for dessert. 🛏 54 🕐 Closed Sun. 💳 AE, MC, V 🚇 Dupont Circle

LAURIOL PLAZA
$$
1835 18TH ST., N.W.
TEL 202/387-0035
There's almost always a wait to get into this well-run Mexican restaurant, but there are good margaritas and baskets of chips and salsa to help you while away the time. The Mexican side of the menu is more interesting than the selection of international dishes—great fajitas, good enchiladas and burritos. The roof deck is a wonderful place to spend a summer evening over a pitcher of sangria or a few bottles of Dos Equis.
340 P AE, D, DC, MC, V Dupont Circle

MESKEREM
$$
2434 18TH ST., N.W.
TEL 202/462-4100
Washington has one of the largest concentrations of Ethiopian restaurants outside Addis Ababa, and Meskerem is a good place for an introduction to this appealing culture and cuisine. Alechas and wats, and spicy stews of meats, vegetables, and pulses form the center of this cooking. Eat with your hands, picking up small bites with pieces of injera, a large, floppy pancake. It's inexpensive and an unusual treat.
200 AE, DC, MC, V Dupont Circle

PERRY'S
$$
1811 COLUMBIA RD., N.W.
TEL 202/234-6218
It may sound like a meat-and-potatoes diner, but Perry's serves a combination of sushi and eclectic American fare. The Sunday drag brunch, with lip-synched entertainment by glamorous drag queens, is an Adams Morgan institution. The roof deck is the perfect spot for an evening dinner.
90 outdoors, 90 indoors P Valet Closed

Mon.–Sat. L AE, D, DC, MC, V Woodley Park/Zoo–Adams Morgan

SKEWERS
$$
1633 P ST., N.W.
TEL 202/387-7400
The food at this small Dupont Circle eatery, popular with the locals, is Middle Eastern with an overlay of pastas, salads, and sandwiches. Kebobs, both meat and vegetable, are very well done here and are available as an entrée or atop a salad, making for a light, healthy meal.
65 AE, MC, V Dupont Circle

COPPI'S
$-$$
1414 U ST., N.W.
TEL 202/319-7773
Popular with neighborhood residents and patrons of the clubs on U Street, this modest establishment turns out great pizzas from a wood-burning oven plus sandwiches and entrées. There's a good list of inexpensive Italian wines.
50 Closed Sun., & Mon.–Fri. L AE, D, MC, V U Street–Cardozo

BEN'S CHILI BOWL
$
1213 U ST, N.W.
TEL 202/667-0909
A fixture on the U Street corridor since 1958, Ben's has served chili dogs, chili burgers, and chili half-smokes to a generation of Washingtonians and visitors. Bill Cosby, a frequent visitor when he's in town, loves the chili half-smokes.
60 Cash only U Street–Cardozo

PIZZERIA PARADISO
$
2029 P ST., N.W.
TEL 202/223-1245
This small pizza parlor, which you will be able to recognize by the line reaching out the

front door and down the steps, makes simply the best pizza in Washington, maybe in the country. The crust, which tastes like good bread, is thin but supports the sparely applied toppings. This is not the place for a sweep-the-kitchen pizza. Order one of the set toppings—the spicy Atomica, the potato-and-pesto Genovese, or the delicious five-cheese combination. If you don't want pizza, there are also superb panini, Italian sandwiches, and salads.
40 DC, MC, V Dupont Circle

CLEVELAND PARK & BEYOND

HOTELS

MARRIOTT WARDMAN PARK HOTEL
$$$$$
2660 WOODLEY RD., N.W.
TEL 202/328-2000
FAX 202/234-0015
Still Washington's largest, the Wardman Park is set on six acres of flower-planted gardens within walking distance of the National Zoo. The Medici restaurant, serving Mediterranean food, is open for dinner; Perle's, an American café, serves breakfast and lunch.
1340 P AE, D, DC, MC, V Woodley Park/Zoo–Adams Morgan

OMNI SHOREHAM HOTEL
$$$-$$$$$
2500 CALVERT ST., N.W.
TEL 202/234-0700
FAX 202/265-7972
Opened in 1930 on 11 landscaped acres near Rock Creek, the Shoreham is a frequent convention site and location for large events. Its location gives it convenient access to the jogging trails and paths of Rock Creek

HOTELS & RESTAURANTS

Park. **Robert's Restaurant** provides elegant dining, or you can rub elbows with the international mix of guests at the Marquee Bar and Lounge. 🛈 835 🛌 🍴 🍷 AE, D, DC, MC, V 🚇 Woodley Park/Zoo–Adams Morgan

RESTAURANTS

🍴 PALENA
$$$$
3529 CONNECTICUT AVE., N.W.
TEL 202/537-9250
Chef Frank Ruta and pastry chef Ann Amernick met when both were working in the White House kitchen, and their collaboration can now be enjoyed even if you're not invited to a state dinner. Ruta's style is a combination of French, Italian, and Modern American, reflecting his background and experience. The menu changes frequently, so one of the best ways to become familiar with Ruta's style is by ordering his tasting menu—five courses for $48. You might find a terrine of foie gras with aspic, a gallette of fresh sardines, pigeon with lentils, cheese, and Ann Amernick's fine, homey desserts. 🪑 68 🕐 Closed Sun. & L 🗝 AE, D, DC, MC, V 🚇 Cleveland Park

🍴 YANYU
$$$–$$$$
3433 CONNECTICUT AVE., N.W.
TEL 202/686-6968
A beautifully designed, upscale pan-Asian restaurant, Yanyu cooks a much smaller number of dishes than most traditional Chinese restaurants, but what it does, it cooks well and presents beautifully. Start with little dragon buns, soup-filled Shanghai dumplings meant to be eaten whole and to release their rich stock in the mouth. The lily bulb dumplings, stuffed with shrimp, chicken, and lily buds, are equally delicious. Yanyu serves a wonderful Peking duck, one of the best in the area, and the server does the business of wrapping and rolling it for you. 🪑 150 🅿 Valet 🕐 Closed L & all Mon. 🗝 AE, DC, MC, V 🚇 Cleveland Park

🍴 NEW HEIGHTS
$$$
2317 CALVERT ST., N.W.
TEL 202/234-4110
A gracious second-floor dining room with large windows overlooking Rock Creek and a menu of creative New American cooking make this restaurant a perennial favorite. Sunday brunch, the only time the restaurant is open during the day, is particularly pleasant—almost, in the spring and summer, like eating in a tree house. 🪑 92 🅿 Valet 🕐 Closed Mon.–Sat. L 🗝 AE, D, DC, MC, V 🚇 Woodley Park/Zoo–Adams Morgan

🍴 ARDEO
$$
3311 CONNECTICUT AVE., N.W.
TEL 202/244-6750
This sophisticated neighborhood restaurant, with its warm woods, white tablecloths, and lively bar, has become a hangout for media types who live in Cleveland Park. It's the creation of restaurant entrepreneur Ashok Bajoj, who also owns the wine bar Bardeo next door. The kitchen starts with top-quality ingredients, and when it stumbles, it's because of bad combinations or faulty execution. So it's best to order simply—diver scallops, fresh fish, braised lamb shanks—and you'll eat well. 🪑 40 🅿 Valet 🕐 Closed Mon.–Sat. L, open Sun. brunch 🗝 AE, D, DC, MC, V 🚇 Cleveland Park

🍴 CACTUS CANTINA
$$
3300 WISCONSIN AVE., N.W.
TEL 202/686-7222
This many-chambered cantina, usually noisy and crowded, serves very good Tex-Mex food, both large combination platters and specialties from its mesquite grill. The tamales are a terrific way to begin, but for a main course, order from the grill: crispy quail, great grilled shrimp, or full-flavored spareribs. 🪑 130 inside, 30 outside 🅿 🗝 AE, D, DC, MC, V 🚇 Tenleytown–AU

🍴 LAVANDOU
$$
3321 CONNECTICUT AVE., N.W.
TEL 202/966-3002
A sunny, cheerful bistro with a loyal neighborhood following, Lavandou features the Provençal cooking of owner/chef Francis Devilliers. Soups are a good beginning here, the *soupe au pistou* with vegetables, basil, and garlic, or a country soup of leeks and beans. For a main course, try the daube of beef, cooked in wine to a melting tenderness, or the *carbounado* of lamb, a deeply flavorful stew of lamb, artichokes, and beans. 🪑 80 🕐 Closed Sat.–Sun. L 🗝 AE, DC, MC, V 🚇 Cleveland Park

SOMETHING SPECIAL

🍴 LEBANESE TAVERNA
There's no better place in Washington to experience the legendary hospitality of the Middle East—and its wonderful cooking—than at this busy Lebanese restaurant. It's possible to order a traditional three-course meal here, but you'll get to try a larger variety of dishes if your party makes a meal from mezze, the small appetizer plates that precede a Middle Eastern meal: spicy beef sausages,

stuffed vine leaves, tart hummous, babaganoush, Lebanese "pizzas"—count on about three dishes per person.
$$
2641 CONNECTICUT AVE., N.W.
TEL 202/265-8681
🔲 100 🅿 🕐 Closed Sun.
L 🚭 AE, DC, MC, V
🚇 Woodley Park/Zoo–Adams Morgan

EAST OF THE CAPITOL

RESTAURANT

🍴 COL. BROOKS' TAVERN
$
901 MONROE ST., N.E.
TEL 202/529-4002
A good place for a casual meal while visiting the nearby Shrine of the Immaculate Conception, Col. Brooks's Tavern has a Southern-inspired menu of steak and chicken dishes, burgers, and other sandwiches, all complemented by a large selection of beers. Live Dixieland Jazz on Tuesday nights.
🔲 100 🅿 🚭 AE, D, MC, V
🚇 Brookland–CUA

ACROSS THE POTOMAC

HOTELS

ARLINGTON, VA

🏨 RITZ-CARLTON 🍴 PENTAGON CITY
$$$$$
1250 S. HAYES ST., 22202
TEL 703/415-5000 OR
800/241-3333
FAX 703/415-5061
A part of the Fashion Centre mall, this hotel offers traditional Ritz-Carlton luxury with the added advantage of shopping. It is minutes from Reagan National airport. Dinner is offered in the club-like atmosphere of the **Grill**.

Afternoon tea is popular.
🛈 366 🅿 🚈 🍸
🚭 AE, D, DC, MC, V
🚇 Pentagon City

🏨 CRYSTAL CITY MARRIOTT
$$$–$$$$
1999 JEFFERSON DAVIS HWY., 22202
TEL 703/413-5500
FAX 703/413-0192
Located a mile from Reagan National airport, this hotel connects to the Crystal City Metro stop, so access to the memorials and Smithsonian museums is easy.
🛈 345 🚈 🍸 🚭 AE, DC, MC, V 🚇 Crystal City

🏨 KEY BRIDGE 🍴 MARRIOTT
$$$–$$$$
1401 LEE HWY., 22209
TEL 703/524-6400
FAX 703/524-8964
Another hotel just across the river from Georgetown, the Key Bridge Marriott offers easy access by Metro to downtown and its sites. **The View,** which overlooks Georgetown University and the National Cathedral in the distance, serves steak and Continental cuisine.
🛈 588 🚈 🍸 🚭 AE, DC, MC, V 🚇 Rosslyn

🏨 RESIDENCE INN BY MARRIOTT PENTAGON CITY
$$$–$$$$
550 ARMY NAVY DR., 22202
TEL 703/413-6630 OR
800/331-3131
FAX 703/418-1751
All rooms have fully equipped kitchens with cooking and eating utensils, microwave, and refrigerator with icemaker. Ronald Reagan Washington National Airport is a half-mile away.
🛈 299 🍸 🚭 AE, D, DC, MC, V 🚇 Pentagon City

🏨 DAYS INN CRYSTAL CITY
$$$
2020 JEFFERSON DAVIS HWY., 22202
TEL 703/920-8600
FAX 703/920-2840
A mile from downtown Washington, the Pentagon, and Reagan National airport, this Days Inn is in walking distance of the Crystal City Metro stop, two shopping malls, and many restaurants.
🛈 247 🍸 🚭 AE, D, DC, MC, V 🚇 Crystal City

🏨 HOLIDAY INN 🍴 ROSSLYN
$$$
1900 N. FORT MYER DR., 22209
TEL 703/807-2000 OR
800/368-3408
FAX 703/522-8864
An impressive orange-brick structure, this hotel is located in Rosslyn, just across the Key Bridge from Georgetown. For dinner, guests can go to one of the many restaurants in Rosslyn, cross the bridge to Georgetown, or stay in and enjoy dinner at the hotel's own **Vantage Point** restaurant.
🛈 306 🚈 🍸 🚭 AE, D, DC, MC, V 🚇 Rosslyn

🏨 BEST WESTERN PENTAGON
$$–$$$
2480 S. GLEBE RD., 22206
TEL 703/979-4400 OR
800/426-6886
FAX 703/685-0051
This Best Western provides a courtesy shuttle to Reagan National airport, Pentagon City Metro station, and the Fashion Centre Mall. The restaurant **Monuments** has traditional American cuisine.
🛈 206 🅿 🚈 🍸 🚭 AE, D, DC, MC, V 🚇 Pentagon City, then courtesy shuttle

🏨 QUALITY INN IWO JIMA
$$
1501 ARLINGTON BLVD. (US 50) AT FAIRFAX DR., 22209

TEL 703/524-5000
FAX 703/522-5484
It's easy to get to downtown D.C. and Old Town Alexandria from this modest hotel; and the Marine Corps War Memorial is just down the street. More than 100 restaurants within a 1-mile radius.
🏨 140 ⬛ ⬛ 📺 🕭 AE, D, DC, MC, V 🚇 Rosslyn

ALEXANDRIA, VA

🏨 EMBASSY SUITES
🍴 $$$$$
1900 DIAGONAL RD., 22314
TEL 703/684-5900
FAX 703/684-1403
Located at King Street's north end, this all-suite hotel is convenient to Old Town Alexandria. All suites have two rooms and a variety of amenities to allow for comfort and working space.
🏨 268 ⬛ 📺 🕭 AE, D, DC, MC, V 🚇 King Street

🏨 MORRISON HOUSE
🍴 $$$$–$$$$$
116 S. ALFRED ST., 22314
TEL 703/838-8000 OR 800/367-0800
FAX 703/684-6283
A modern hotel designed to evoke the atmosphere of Old Alexandria, the Morrison resembles an 18th-century manor house. Guest rooms are furnished in federal-period reproductions. Dinner offered at the hotel's very good **Elysium** restaurant.
🏨 45 🅿 🕭 AE, MC, V 🚇 King Street, then DASH bus to Old Town

RESTAURANTS

ARLINGTON, VA

🍴 MAESTRO
$$$$
RITZ-CARLTON HOTEL, 1700 TYSONS BLVD., TYSONS CORNER
TEL 703/917-5498
Maestro is one of the most

ambitious restaurants to open in Northern Virginia in the last few years, the successful collaboration of a team that includes chef Fabio Trabocchi and wine steward Vincent Feraud. Trabucchi divides his Italian menu in traditional and contemporary sections. The setting is sumptuous, the food is frequently dazzling, and the experience is worth the charge on the credit card. Where else might you be served sea urchin in its shell; lobster-and-black-truffle pasta; and three different preparations of lamb in the same meal?
🪑 86 🅿 Valet 🕘 Closed all Sun., Mon., & L 🕭 AE, D, DC, MC, V

🍴 QUEEN BEE
$$
3181 WILSON BLVD.
TEL 703/527-3444
Of the cluster of Vietnamese restaurants that surround the Clarendon Metro station, Queen Bee is the most dependable and popular. The spring rolls are the standard by which others should be judged. The shrimp and pork rolls are also delicious, as is the green papaya salad with beef jerky and spicy sausage. Good main course choices are the Hanoi-style grilled pork, the Saigon pancake, and the whole fried fish served with spicy sauce. Vietnamese iced coffee, sweetened with condensed milk, is the perfect dessert.
🪑 98 🕭 AE, DC, MC, V 🚇 Clarendon

ALEXANDRIA, VA

🍴 LA BERGERIE
$$$–$$$$
218 N. LEE ST.
TEL 703/683-1007
This dependable French restaurant has long been Old Town Alexandria's favorite place for special occasions. Chef David Craig has recently taken over the

kitchen, and the food and service remain consistently good. A recent meal started with a creamless chestnut soup garnished with duck confit. Main courses included a perfectly cooked veal loin and crisp sweetbreads with a slice of pan-seared foie gras. La Bergerie is one of the few restaurants that still go to the trouble of making dessert soufflés (order at the beginning of the meal). Hazelnut is the best.
🪑 70 🕘 Closed Sun. L 🕭 AE, D, DC, MC, V 🚇 King Street, then bus

🍴 BLUE POINT GRILL
$$$
600 FRANKLIN ST.
TEL 703/739-0404
The casually elegant dining room at Blue Point Grill is a wonderful place for a dozen oysters and a glass of wine, a shopping lunch on weekends, or a full-scale special occasion dinner. The prime draw is immaculately fresh fish and shellfish. You have to pass the impressive raw bar to get to your table, so let that be a clue to the best first courses. Main course selections depend on availability, but good picks have included sea bass margherita with black beans, tomato-corn relish, and cilantro; and seared halibut with creamy polenta.
🪑 66 🅿 🕭 AE, D, MC, V 🚇 King Street, then bus

🍴 MAJESTIC CAFÉ
$$$
911 KING ST.
TEL 703/837-9117
Chef Susan Lindeborg reopened this landmark Alexandria restaurant, which had been standing vacant for many years, and the result is impressive. The place has been modernized and many of its art deco elements preserved. Lindeborg's forte is home cooking—moist chicken breast served with cornbread dressing; a simple

gratin of oysters, Virginia ham, and cracker crumbs; richly satisfying spoonbread. And don't leave without a piece of the fabulous butter-milk pie.

🛏 72 🕐 Closed Mon.
🚭 AE, D, DC, MC, V
🚇 King Street, then DASH bus or Metro shuttle

🍽 EVENING STAR CAFÉ
$$
2000 MT. VERNON AVE.
TEL 703/549-5051
An ambitious American com-fort-food menu and an impressive wine program raise this appealing eatery out of the neighborhood restaurant category. A new bar offers wines by the glass and small plates for snacking. In fair weather, there's out-door seating.

🛏 70 🕐 Closed Mon. L
🚭 AE, D, DC, MC, V
🚇 Braddock Road

🍽 LE GAULOIS
$$
1106 KING ST.
TEL 703/739-9494
Loyal diners have followed this popular French restau-rant from its former home in Washington to its present one in Alexandria. What keeps them coming back is a menu of familiar classics of French bourgeois cooking, all done very well. You can get a comforting pot-au-feu in cool weather, a well-made omelet at lunch, and dinner specials such as chicken fricassée Normandy-style with a sauce made from apples, mush-rooms, calvados, and cream.

🛏 100 🕐 Closed Sun.
🚭 AE, D, DC, MC, V
🚇 King Street, then walk six blocks

🍽 ECCO CAFE
$
220 N. LEE ST.
TEL 703/684-0321
A large and popular Italian-American neighborhood pizza and pasta place.

🛏 150 🚭 AE, D, DC, MC, V 🚇 King Street; then bus

EXCURSIONS

RESTAURANTS

ANNAPOLIS, MD

🍽 TREATY OF PARIS
$$$
16 CHURCH CIRCLE
TEL 410/216-6340
The menu at this historic inn in the heart of Old Annapolis is not ground-breaking, but it's well pre-pared. Crab is king here. Crab Louis with a Cajun remoulade sauce is a good starter, as are the fried crab cakes. Seafood en papillote contains a mixture of fish, scallops, shrimp, and clams, and if you haven't had your fill of crab in the first course, the Crab Imperial is tradi-tional and good. There is also a good selection of meat dishes—beef Wellington, veal Oscar, rack of venison.

🛏 75 🅿 Valet 🚭 AE, D, DC, MC, V

🍽 CANTLER'S RIVERSIDE INN
$$
458 FORREST BEACH RD.
TEL 410/757-1311
A short drive from down-town Annapolis, Cantler's—owned by a family of water-men—is one of the city's most popular seafood restaurants. You eat at benches at communal tables, or at picnic tables on the deck, overlooking the docks and beautiful creek. Begin with a Styrofoam cup of she-crab soup. There are meat and chicken dishes, but the best main courses feature seafood from Maryland waters—crab cakes, softshell crabs, and rockfish.

🛏 318 🅿 🚭 AE, D, DC, MC, V

BALTIMORE, MD

🍽 CHARLESTON
$$$$
1000 LANCASTER ST.
TEL 410/332-7373
Chef Cindy Wolf's Charleston restaurant, located on the Inner Harbor, is Baltimore's most praised restaurant. As the name sug-gests, the specialty is low-country Southern cooking. Starters have included Charleston she-crab soup, cornmeal-crusted oysters, and fried green tomatoes with lobster and crab hash. Wolf frequently features traditional Carolina dishes such as seafood Perlau, or southern improvisations such as venison medallions with spoonbread or duck breasts with Madeira-poached pears and pecan rice. The wine selection is well chosen and well priced.

🛏 130 🅿 Valet 🕐 Closed Sun. & all L 🚭 AE, D, DC, MC, V

SOMETHING SPECIAL

🍽 OBRYCKI'S CRAB HOUSE
Don't leave Baltimore with-out eating at one of the city's traditional crab houses. Tables are covered with paper; steamed crabs coated with Old Bay Seasoning are dumped in the middle of the table; and if you don't know how to eat them, your friendly server gives you a quick lesson in the art of opening crabs with a knife and wooden mal-let. Obrycki's is closed for the winter and opens with crab season about the middle of March. You can also order crab cakes or softshell crabs, or just crabmeat sautéed in butter, all of which require less work than the hardshells to eat.
$$$
1727 EAST PRATT ST.
TEL 410/732-6399
🕐 Closed Dec.–Feb.

SHOPPING

Washington is the place to pick up that perfect political souvenir—from campaign buttons to White House Easter eggs to Presidential seal mousepads. But just as there is more to the city than what goes on atop Capitol Hill, there is more to Washington shopping than political paraphernalia. The museum stores, for starters, have wonderful inventories of unique books, arts and crafts, jewelry, and artifact reproductions. It's natural that in such a highly educated city you'll find countless excellent bookstores. And local markets feature interesting bric-a-brac.

For a real shopping experience, however, wander into the neighborhoods, which harbor neat little one-of-a-kind shops and boutiques. Georgetown's two main arteries—M Street and Wisconsin Avenue—has many fashionable boutiques, bookstores, art galleries, antique stores, and contemporary clothing stores. Dupont Circle is much funkier, with its eclectic boutiques, vintage clothing stores, antique furniture shops, plus stores catering to the neighborhood's gay population. Adams Morgan resembles Berkeley, California, more than anything found on the East Coast, with its down-to-earth selection of African goods and curious New Age paraphernalia. Across the river, Old Town Alexandria's historic core along King Street showcases a slew of antique shops, galleries, and carpet stores in 18th-century buildings.

This listing covers some of the more unique shopping experiences in the Washington, D.C., area.

ANTIQUES

Georgetown overflows with antique shops, especially on Wisconsin Avenue between P and S Streets, and along M and O Streets. Store after store features gorgeous furniture and such accessories as grandfather clocks, 19th-century paintings, and sterling tableware. **Adams Morgan** and **Dupont Circle** also offer a good selection of antiques. In **Kensington, Maryland,** Howard Avenue is

one of the foremost antique districts in the mid-Atlantic, with prices being better than those in Georgetown. Head to the lower, warehouse end of the street for serious antique shopping. The downtown Antique Row has cute, smaller shops full of collectibles. **Old Town Alexandria** has dozens of antique shops, purveying real Persian rugs, as well as French, English, and American period furniture.

ARTS & CRAFTS, GALLERIES

The best places to look for handmade works of art are Adams Morgan, Georgetown, Dupont Circle, and Old Town Alexandria. Seventh Street, N.W., between D Street and the MCI Center, has become a mecca of galleries.

Addison/Ripley Fine Art, 1670 Wisconsin Ave., N.W. (Georgetown), 202/338-5180. One of Washington's foremost galleries, established in 1981, featuring painting, sculpture, photography, and fine arts prints.

Appalachian Spring, 1415 Wisconsin Ave., N.W. (Georgetown), 202/337-5780; & Union Station (Capitol Hill), 202/682-0505. Traditional and contemporary crafts, including jewelry, gorgeous pottery, quilts, and woodcarvings.

Canal Square, 31st & M Sts. (Georgetown) Art galleries galore.

Torpedo Factory Art Center, 105 N. Union St., Alexandria (Across the Potomac), 703/838-4565. 84 working artists' studios (each one selling their works) and five galleries showcase sculpture, pottery, paintings in watercolor, acrylic, and oil, plus much more.

BOOKS

Chapters, 1512 K St., N.W. (White House & around), 202/347-5495. Metro: McPherson Square. Independent literary bookstore with current events, contemporary fiction, classics, and poetry.

Government Printing Office Bookstore, 710 N. Capitol St., N.W. (between G and H Sts.), (The Mall), 202/512-0132, closed weekends. Metro: Union Station. The largest general printing plant in the world, the GPO serves the printing needs of Congress. With nearly 16,000 titles (books and pamphlets) covering every conceivable area, from Cardiac Rehabilitation to the Dictionary of American Naval Fighting Ships, you should be able to find something that relates to any new hobby, interest, or activity. Also photography books, CD-ROMS and diskettes, prints, lithographs, and posters.

Kramerbooks & afterwords, 1517 Connecticut Ave., N.W., (Dupont Circle & Adams Morgan), 202/387-1400, open 24 hours on weekends. Metro: Dupont Circle. Small but good selection of books, including political, fiction, and religion. Late-night dining and entertainment at the café.

Olsson's Books & Records, 1307 19th St., N.W., 202/785-1133; 1200 F St., N.W., 202/347-3686; 418 7th St., N.W., 202/638-7610; www.olssons.com. Large and varied collection of books and a good selection of classical and folk records, tapes, and CDs.

**Politics and Prose
Bookstore & Coffeehouse,**
5015 Connecticut Ave., N.W.,
(Cleveland Park & beyond),
202/364-1919. Metro: Friendship
Heights. Topical novels and literary nonfiction, frequented often
by Washington's intelligentsia.
Frequent author readings. Café.

Second Story Books,
2000 P St., N.W. (Dupont Circle
& Adams Morgan), 202/659-
8884. Metro: Dupont Circle.
Used and rare books, including
first editions, fine bound volumes, and just plain used. Stays
open late.

DEPARTMENT
STORES & MALLS

**The Shops at Chevy Chase
Pavilion,** 5335 Wisconsin Ave.,
N.W., 202/686-5335. Metro:
Friendship Heights. Stores at
this popular mall include Pottery
Barn, Joan and David, and
Talbots. Food court.

Crystal City Shops, Crystal
Dr. between 15th & 23rd Sts.,
Arlington (Across the Potomac),
703/922-4636. Metro: Crystal
City. More than 125 stores with
clothing, gifts, and more. Dining.

**Fashion Centre at Pentagon
City,** 1100 S. Hayes St.,
Arlington (Across the Potomac),
703/415-2400. Metro: Pentagon
City. Four-story mall with 163
shops, including Macy's and
Nordstrom. Dining and cinema
as well.

Mazza Gallerie, 5330
Wisconsin Ave., N.W. Metro:
Friendship Heights. This complex
of exclusive shops, restaurants,
and theaters showcases Neiman
Marcus, Saks Fifth Avenue, and
Filene's Basement.

Old Post Office Pavilion,
1100 Pennsylvania Ave., N.W.
(Downtown), 202/289-4224.
Metro: Federal Triangle.
Clothing, souvenirs, gifts in a

historic 19th-century building.
Dining. Entertainment.

Potomac Mills Outlet Mall,
2700 Potomac Mills Circle,
Woodbridge, VA (Excursions),
703/490-5948. Off I-95 about 30
miles south of Washington.
Said to be Virginia's number one
tourist attraction, the 152-acre
shoppers' paradise has some
220 discount and outlet stores,
including Nordstrom Rack,
Ralph Lauren, Laura Ashley,
Coach, and L.L. Bean. IKEA, a
popular Swedish furniture store,
has recently expanded to twice
its original enormous space.

Shops at Georgetown Park,
3222 M St., N.W. (Georgetown),
202/298-5577. More than 100
upscale shops and boutiques,
including J. Crew, FAO Schwartz,
and Godiva Chocolatier, in a
restored tobacco warehouse.

Shops at National Place,
13th & F Sts., N.W.
(Downtown), 202/662-1212.
Metro: Metro Center. Three levels of shops, including men's and
women's clothing, jewelry, gifts,
shoes, and an enormous food
court.

Tyson's Corner Center,
1961 Chain Bridge Rd., McLean,
VA (Excursions), 703/827-7700.
Washington's largest mall, with
more than 230 shops and bou-
tiques, including Nordstrom,
Bloomingdale's, and Lord &
Taylor's. Dining.

Union Station,
50 Massachusetts Ave., N.E.
(Capitol Hill), 202/371-9441.
Metro: Union Station. 125-plus
stores on 3 levels, plus a food
court and cinema multi-plex, in
an active train station.

FARMER &
FLEA MARKETS

**Alexandria Farmer's
Market,** 301 King St.,
Alexandria (Across the
Potomac), Sat. a.m. only.

Traditional farmer's market with
the freshest fruit and vegetables,
preserves, pastries, and flowers.

Eastern Market, 225 7th St.,
S.E. (Capitol Hill), closed Mon.
Washington's last remaining
public market, where butchers
and greengrocers purvey
cheeses, meats, fish, baked
goods, flowers, and such local
delicacies as pigs' feet, baby back
ribs, and homemade jams in a
big redbrick building dating from
1870. Outside unfolds a farmers'
market (Sat.) and flea market
(Sun. March-Dec.). Popular
breakfast grill.

Georgetown Flea Market,
34th St. & Wisconsin Ave., N.W.
(Georgetown), Sun. only
March–Dec. A museum's worth
of antique musical instruments,
rugs, clothes, furniture, new jewelry and sunglasses, old cameras
and books, and much more. This
being Georgetown, don't expect
great bargains.

**Maine Avenue Seafood Mar-
ket,** Washington Channel, S.W.
A dozen canopied dockside
barges hold beautiful, gleaming
piles of the recently swimming
rockfish, bluefish, shad, catfish,
swordfish, pompano, crabs,
clams, and just about any other
catch you can name. A couple of
stands sell hot cooked crabs, for
those who can't wait.

GOURMET FOODS
& WINE

Dean & Deluca, 3222 M St.,
N.W. (Georgetown), 202/342-
2500. Gourmet foods in the historic Markethouse building, plus
kitchen accessories and gifts. Its
café is a wonderful place to pick
up a quick bite, including sandwiches on your choice of
baguette, focaccia, or onion roll;
sushi; and salads with such
clever touches as dried cranber-
ries in wild rice.

Marvelous Market, 5035
Connecticut Ave., N.W., 202/686-

4040; 1511 Connecticut Ave., N.W., 202/332-3690. Inventive sandwiches, small yet impressive selection of prepared foods, and wonderfully crusty bread.

Sutton Place Gourmet, 15 different locations in the Washington area, including 3201 New Mexico Ave., N.W., 202/363-5800. Modeled on European markets, featuring specialty foods and wines.

MUSEUM SHOPS

Bureau of Engraving & Printing, 14th and C Sts., S.W. (The Mall), 202/874-3019, closed weekends. Metro: Smithsonian. Engravings of Presidents, Washington landscapes, and government seals. Buy sheets of uncut $1 and $2 bills.

Decatur House museum shop, 1600 H Street, N.W. (White House & around), 202/842-1856. Reproductions of home accessories from the 18th and 19th centuries, including Presidential china. Books, jewelry, and children selections.

Hillwood Museum, 4155 Linnean Ave., N.W. (Cleveland Park & beyond), 202/686-8500 The former residence of Marjorie Merriweather Post, cereal heiress, includes a gift shop purveying French and Russian decorative arts and reproductions.

Hirshhorn Museum, 950 Independence Ave., S.W. (The Mall) 202/357-1300. Metro: Smithsonian.Contemporary jewelry that's fun and quirky.

John F. Kennedy Center for the Performing Arts, Rock Creek and Potomac Pkwy. & New Hampshire Ave., N.W. (White House & around), 202/467-4600, Metro: Foggy Bottom. Good selection of gifts with music, dance, theater, and opera themes.

Mount Vernon Inn Gift Shop, George Washington Memorial Pkwy., Alexandria (Across the Potomac), 703/780-0011. Reproductions of the Washingtons' belongings, including china and silver, as well as toys and souvenirs.

National Air and Space Museum, 7th St. & Constitution Ave., N.W. (The Mall), 202/357-1300. Freeze-dried ice cream (like what the astronauts eat), kites, books, and videos for aspiring pilots and astronauts.

National Archives Museum Store, 7th St. & Constitution Ave., N.W. (Downtown), 202/501-5000. Replicas of the Charters of Freedom, posters, and postcards.

National Building Museum, 401 F St., N.W. (Downtown), 202/272-2448. Architecture-related books, prints, posters, toys, and gifts.

National Gallery of Art, 600 Constitution Ave., N.W., (The Mall), 202/737-4215. Metro: Archives, Judiciary Square. Several shops in the museum feature quality prints and posters, art reproductions, gifts, and art books.

National Geographic Society, 1145 17th St., N.W. (White House & around), 800/638-6400. Metro: Farragut North, Farragut West. Wall maps, books, globes, and educational children's toys.

National Museum of African Art, 950 Independence Ave., S.W. (The Mall), 202/786-2147. Books for adults and children on African culture and history. Also African crafts, posters, dolls, jewelry, records, and tapes.

National Museum of Women in the Arts, 1250 New York Ave., N.W. (Downtown), 202/783-5000. Unique jewelry, decorative objects, books, and other gifts.

Phillips Collection, 1600 21st St., N.W. (Dupont Circle & Adams Morgan), 202/387-2151. Jewelry, ceramics, glassware, and other objects by contemporary artists, plus hand-painted scarves, reproductions, books, and more.

Renwick Gallery, Pennsylvania Ave. at 17th St., N.W. (White House & around).Features contemporary crafts of fiber, metal, ceramic, and wood, plus books, toys, posters, and more.

White House Gift Shop, National Press Bldg., 529 14th St., N.W. (Downtown), 202/662-7280.Gifts and collectibles, including glassware, jewelry, and clothing.

OTHER

ADC Map and Travel Center, 1636 I St., N.W. (White House & around), 202/628-2608, closed Sun. Metro: Farragut West. More than 5,000 maps from around the world, plus guidebooks, narratives, and globes.

Counter Spy Shop, 1027 Connecticut Ave., N.W. (White House & around), 202/887-1717, closed Sun. Metro: Farragut North. Gadgets for spies & aspiring 007s.

Washington National Cathedral, Wisconsin & Massachusetts Aves., N.W., 202/537-5766. Gothic- and Medieval-inspired ware, including window decorations, scarves, and stuffed gargoyles. Don't miss the Herb Cottage on the grounds.

ENTERTAINMENT

After traipsing around all day from site to site, be sure to save some energy for Washington after dark. Your choices are many: theater, a movie, dancing, or just hanging out at one of the local bars. Check the Friday Weekend section of the *Washington Post* for goings-on; as well as the weekly *Washington CityPaper*. *Washingtonian* magazine is another good source of information.

DANCE

Dance Place, 3225 8th St., N.E., 202/269-1600. Metro: Brookland. Dance Place presents programs of modern and ethnic dance most weekends.

Washington Ballet, 202/362-3606. The nationally recognized Washington Ballet presents a full season between September and May at the Kennedy Center and also presents the *Nutcracker* each Christmas at the Warner Theater and the Center for the Arts at George Mason University.

FILM

American Film Institute, Kennedy Center, New Hampshire Ave. and Rock Creek and Potomac Pkwy., 202/785-4600; www.afionline.org/net. Metro: Foggy Bottom. The AFI screens more than 700 movies each year at its theater in the Kennedy Center. Actors and directors often discuss their work at these showings.

Filmfest DC, 202/724-5613; www.filmfestdc.org. The DC International Film Festival, held in late April and early May, screens American and international films in a variety of local theaters and auditoriums.

National Gallery of Art East Building, 4th St. and Constitution Ave., N.W., 202/737-4215. The National Gallery shows free classic films and films relating to exhibitions in the galleries.

Reel Affirmations, 202/986-1119. D.C.'s gay and lesbian film festival, held for ten days in October each year, shows films of gay and lesbian interest at the Warner Theater (1215 U St., N.W.), the Jewish Community Center (16th and Q Sts., N.W.), and at the Goethe-Institut Inter Nationes (814 7th St., N.W.).

MUSIC

CHAMBER MUSIC
Corcoran Gallery of Art, 17th St. and New York Ave., N.W., 202/639-1700. Metro: Farragut West. Well known quartets appear in the Corcoran's musical evenings series from October to May.

Library of Congress, 1st St. and Independence Ave., S.E., 202/707-5502. Metro: Union Station, Capitol South. Both the Julliard String Quartet and the Beaux Arts Trio are in residence at the Library of Congress and present frequent free concerts.

Phillips Collection, 1600 21st St., N.W., 202/387-2151. Metro: Dupont Circle. Free Sunday-afternoon concerts in the Phillips mansion's wood-paneled music room.

CHORAL MUSIC
Choral Arts Society of Washington, 202/244-3669. Between September and May, this 180-voice ensemble, directed by Norman Scribner, presents frequent classical programs in the Kennedy Center Concert Hall.

OPERA
Washington Opera, Kennedy Center Opera House, 202/295-2400. Metro: Foggy Bottom. During the November to March season, the Washington Opera, directed by Placido Domingo, produces eight operas, sung in their original languages with English subtitles.

ORCHESTRA
National Symphony Orchestra, Kennedy Center Concert Hall, 202/416-8100. Metro: Foggy Bottom. From September to June, the NSO performs at the Kennedy Center. In the summer, there are concerts at Wolf Trap (703/225-1800) and at Carter Barron Amphitheatre.

NIGHTLIFE

The Birchmere, 3701 Mount Vernon Ave., Alexandria, 703/549-7500; www.birchmere.com. The Birchmere takes music very seriously—the club's no-talking policy is strictly enforced. But the performers and the sound are terrific; the food, from Alexandria's King Street Blues, is very good; and there's also a pool hall, a brewery, and a large bar.

Blues Alley, 1073 Wisconsin Ave., N.W., 202/337-4141; www.bluesalley.com. Metro: Foggy Bottom, then walk or bus. All the legends of blues have played at this small club—Dizzy Gillespie, Wynton Marsalis, Nancy Wilson, Charlie Byrd. Tickets are $16 to $60—and there's a $7 minimum. There are usually 8 and 10 p.m. shows, and sometimes on weekends a midnight set. Reservations are essential.

Bohemian Caverns, 2001 11th St., N.W., 202/299-0800. Metro: U Street–Cardozo. Bohemian Caverns was once a Washington institution, hosting Duke Ellington, Billie Holiday, Louis Armstrong, Jelly Roll

ENTERTAINMENT

Morton, Thelonious Monk, and others. The fake-cavern decor itself is worth seeing.

Chi-Cha Lounge, 1624 U St., N.W., 202/234-8400. Metro: U Street–Cardozo. Modern Andean cooking, Latin folkloric music, and a house drink called the Chi-Cha Morada, made of red corn, pineapple, cinnamon, cloves, and alcohol make this late-night lounge a favorite on U Street.

HR-57 Center for the Preservation of Jazz and Blues, 1610 14th St., N.W., 202/667-3700; www.hr57.org. Named for the House of Representatives resolution that honored jazz as a national treasure, this non-profit music cultural center holds jazz jam sessions on Wednesday, Friday, and Saturday nights. On Thursdays, a big band performs.

IOTA Club & Cafe, 2832 Wilson Blvd., Arlington, 703/522-8340. Metro: Clarendon. Iota consistently books some of the best folk, alternative country, and rock music in the area, and the food's good, too.

Kramerbooks & afterwords café, 1517 Connecticut Ave., N.W., 202/387-1462; www.kramers.com. Metro: Dupont Circle. "Serving latte to the literati," this bookstore with attached café is the informal community center for the Dupont Circle neighborhood. It's open all night Friday and Saturday nights, and has live music Wednesday through Saturday.

Madam's Organ, 2461 18th St., N.W., 202/667-5370; www.madamsorgan.com. The popular Madam's Organ has a full schedule of bluegrass, R&B, and blues. Try to arrive before 10 Thursday through Saturday—after 11, you'll probably wait in line.

Modern, 3287 M St., N.W., 202/338-7027. Metro: Foggy Bottom, then walk or bus. You may not be sure if it's a bar or a retro furniture store, but this handsome, friendly bar with couches, coffee tables, a hardwood dance floor, and a dress code is a delightful exception to the rule that Georgetown bars are only for students.

9:30 Club, 815 V St., N.W., 202/265-0930; www.930.com. Metro: U Street–Cardozo. The 9:30 Club is where Bob Dylan plays when he comes to Washington. It has a great sound system and is always crowded—and that's the way its fans want it.

Strike Bethesda, 353 Westbard Ave., Bethesda, MD, 301/652-0955. Bowling is hip again. Sister establishment to New York's wildly popular Bowlmor Lanes, Strike Bethesda features 34 lanes, a VIP room, state-of-the-art sound and video systems, and a restaurant serving New American cuisine. It's open until 1 a.m. weeknights, and 2 a.m. weekends.

Visions, 1927 Florida Ave., N.W., 202/667-0090; www.visionsdc.com. Metro: Dupont Circle. An art movie house theater cum coffeehouse, it has a full bar with a funky coffeehouse atmosphere—plus a bistro that serves Mediterranean, Middle Eastern, and Indian tapas-style food; a bar; and a coffee selection worthy of the Pacific Northwest. Two narrow theaters show the latest independent and foreign films.

THEATER

Arena Stage, 6th St. and Maine Ave., S.W., 202/488-3300; www.arenastage.com. This respected resident theater company presents a busy season on its three stages.

Ford's Theatre See p. 172.

Howard Theatre See p. 174.

Lincoln Theater See p. 174.

National Theatre See p. 173.

Shakespeare Theatre, 450 7th St., N.W., 202/393-2700. Metro: Gallery Place/Chinatown Widely acknowledged as one of the best Shakespeare companies in America, the Shakespeare Theatre stages four plays a year in a custom-built, state-of-the-art theater. See p. 134.

Signature Theatre, 3806 S. Four Mile Run Dr., Arlington, 703/218-6500; http://www.sig-online.org. Especially known for its productions of modern musical theater.

Source Theatre, 1835 14th St., N.W., 202/462-1073. Metro: U Street–Cardozo. The Source Theatre company specializes in new plays, contemporary works, and bold reinterpretations of the classics.

Studio Theatre, 1333 P St., N.W., 202/332-3300. Metro: Dupont Circle. The third largest producing theater in Washington, Studio Theatre presents the best of contemporary theater. It is the home of Studio Theatre Acting Conservatory, which runs a widely-respected school for the theater.

Warner Theatre See p. 144.

Woolly Mammoth, 917 M St., N.W., 202/393-3939; www.woollymammoth.net. Metro: Gallery Place/Chinatown. *Variety* comments on Woolly Mammoth's "fierce dedication to the offbeat," a dedication that is pursued with genuine devotion and solid production values.

ACTIVITIES

From boating to golfing to ice skating, Washington offers an amazingly diverse selection of options for outdoor enthusiasts. If you're in the mood to watch others do the work instead, you have a number of big-name sports teams from which to choose, including Michael Jordan's Wizards. For something a little different, join one of the many specialty tours—a chance to see the city from a different point of view, by walking, boating, or even by bike.

OUTDOOR ACTIVITIES

BOATING
Jack's Boats, 3500 K St., N.W., 202/337-9642.
Open April–Oct.
Located under Key Bridge in Georgetown, Jack's rents canoes, kayaks, and row boats.

Thompson Boat Center, 2900 Virginia Ave., N.W., 202/333-9543. Open April–Oct. Canoes, rowing shells, and kayaks for rent. Lessons available. Also, all-terrain and cruiser bike rentals.

GOLF
East Potomac Park Golf Course, 972 Ohio Dr., S.W., 202/554-7660. This public course near the Mall consists of one 18-hole, par-72 course and two 9-hole courses. Open daily from dawn until dusk. Daily cart fees.

Langston Golf Course, 268 Benning Rd., N.E., 202/245-2726. The Langston Golf Course is an 18-hole, par-72 public course that also offers a golf school, golf shop, driving range, putting green, and snack bar.

Rock Creek Park Golf Course, 16th and Rittenhouse Sts., N.W., 202/882-7332. This 4,798-yard, par-65 public course has a hilly and challenging terrain. Amenities include a golf school, golf shop, a putting green, and a snack bar. The course is open every day from dawn to dusk.

ICE SKATING
National Gallery of Art Sculpture Garden Ice Skating Rink, 7th St. and Constitution Ave., N.W., 202/737-4215. Beautifully designed, this rink on the Mall affords skaters views of the wonderful works of modern sculpture in the museum garden. The state-of-the-art sound system provides uniform sound to the skaters without distracting other visitors to the garden.

TENNIS
East Potomac Tennis Center, 1090 Ohio Dr., S.W., 202/554-5962. Indoor and outdoor courts, seasonal membership or walk-in court rental, tennis lessons, and racquet stringing.

Rock Creek Park Tennis Center, 16th and Kennedy St., N.W., 202/722-5949. The facility has a total of 25 outdoor tennis courts: 10 hard courts and 15 clay courts. Five indoor courts are heated and available in winter.

SPECTATOR SPORTS

Baltimore Orioles, tickets through TicketMaster, 888-848-2473. Baseball at Oriole Park at Camden Yards, Baltimore.

Baltimore Ravens, 410/261-7283. NFL football in Baltimore.

DC United, 703/478-6600. Professional soccer at RFK Stadium.

Washington Capitals, 202/266-2277. Professional hockey at the MCI Center.

Washington Mystics, 202/432-7328. Professional women's basketball at the MCI Center.

Washington Power, 866/769-3752. Lacrosse.

Washington Redskins, 301-276-6050. NFL football at FedEx Field.

Washington Wizards, 202/661-5050; www.nba.com/wizards. Professional basketball at the MCI Center, starring Michael Jordan.

SPECIALTY TOURS

WALKING TOURS
Anecdotal History Walks, 301/294-9514. Author Anthony Pitch leads tours around Georgetown; around the White House; the Capitol to the White House; Adams Morgan; and sites relating to the Lincoln assassination. Most Sundays. Private tours any day by appointment.

U Street Walking Tours, 202/232-2915. Long before the Harlem Renaissance, the U Street area was known as Black Broadway, the city's African American social, cultural, and intellectual center. Among the 14 stops included on this 90-minute guided walk through that neighborhood are the block where Duke Ellington lived, the city's first black YMCA, and the African American Civil War Memorial. Tours begin at 10 a.m. at the Duke Ellington Mural, U Street–Cardozo Metro Station.

Washington walks, 202/484-1565. Among the walks offered are Capital Hauntings, which seeks out the ghosts that frequent the area around Lafayette Square and the White House; Embassy Row, Washington's grandest boulevard; and Goodnight, Mr.

Lincoln, in which families clad in pajamas learn about the 16th President at the base of the Lincoln Memorial.

BOAT TOURS & CRUISES
Dandy Restaurant Cruise Ship, Zero Prince St., Alexandria, VA, 703/683-6076. The *Dandy* cruises from Old Town Alexandria to Georgetown, under the Potomac River bridges and past the monuments and memorials. Dinner is served aboard, and there's a marble dance floor.

Gangplank Marina Odyssey Cruises, 600 Water St. S.W., 202/488-6000. The *Odyssey* cruise features a four-course meal, award-winning wine list, and live professional entertainment while taking in the sites of the nation's capital. Three-hour lunch cruise and four-hour dinner cruises available.

OTHER
BeyondGuide, 301/816-0303. Beyond Guide offers self-guided tours over your cell phone, allowing you to see what you want at your own pace.

Bike Sites, 202/966-8662. Lisa and Gary Olner arrange bicycle tours—bikes included—of Mount Vernon, Civil War statues, bridges, early Washington, D.C., and a general tour visiting 55 historic landmarks.

Scandal Tours, 202/783-7212. This irreverent tour of Washington's infamous scandal sites is hosted by the critically acclaimed comedy group, Gross National Product, who give you an impudent commentary on Washington's embarrassing moments. Reservations required.Offered from April Fool's Day through Labor Day weekend on Saturdays at 1 p.m., pick-up at the Post Office Pavilion.

SpyDrive, 866/SPY-DRIVE. Former intelligence officers (U.S. and foreign) host this two-plus-hour bus tour of sites where spies operated.

Washington Photo Safari, 202/537-0937. Professional photographer David Luria offers half-and full-day workshops in landmark photography. Tours are given in English, French, and Spanish.

You and Me Travel, 202/841-8106. Shopping trips to Potomac Mills and Leesburg discount malls.

HEALTH CLUBS

Bally Total Fitness
Call 800/695-8111 for information on all locations, or visit www.ballyfitness.com. No daily guest rate; must be a Bally Total Fitness member. The 12 clubs in the Washington area include:
> Downtown: 2000 L St., N.W. #1B, 202/331-7788
> 1 Tysons Corner Center, McLean, VA, 703/356-0106

Fitness Company
There are 17 clubs in the Washington area including the following. Visit www.thefitnesscompany.com for other locations.
> International Square: 18751 St., N.W., 202/833-2629. Guest fee: $15
> Washington Center: 1001 G St., N.W., 202/637-4747. Guest fee: $15

Gold's Gym
There are nine Gold's Gyms in the Washington area, including the following. Visit www.goldsgym.com for other locations.
> Van Ness area: 4310 Connecticut Ave., N.W., 202/364-4653
> Capitol Hill: 408 4th St., S.W., 202/554-4653

Sport and Health Club
Call 800/88-CLUBS for information on all locations; www.sportandhealth.com. There are 22 Sport and Health Clubs in the Washington area, including:
> Watergate area: 2620 Virginia Ave., N.W., 202/298 4460. Guest fee: $12 daily
> Tenleytown area: 4000 Wisconsin Ave., N.W., 202/362-8000. Guest fee: $14.00 if you are a member of the International Health, Racquet and Sportclub Association (IHRSA) or $25 walk-in.

Washington Sports Club
Visit www.washingtonsport.com for information on all locations. The five clubs in the Washington area include:
> Downtown: 1990 M St., N.W., 202/785-4900. Guest fee: $15.00 if a member of the International Health, Racquet and Sportclub Association (IHRSA) or $25 walk-in.
> Kalorama: 1835 Connecticut Ave., N.W., 202/332-0100. Guest fee: $15.00 if a member. of the International Health, Racquet and Sportclub Association (IHRSA) or $25 walk-in.

ILLUSTRATIONS CREDITS

One of the world's largest nonprofit scientific and educational organizations, the National Geographic Society was founded in 1888 "for the increase and diffusion of geographic knowledge." Fulfilling this mission, the Society educates and inspires millions every day through its magazines, books, television programs, videos, maps and atlases, research grants, the National Geographic Bee, teacher workshops, and innovative classroom materials. The Society is supported through membership dues, charitable gifts, and income from the sale of its educational products. This support is vital to National Geographic's mission to increase global understanding and promote conservation of our planet through exploration, research, and education.

For more information, please call 1-800-NGS LINE (647-5463) or write to the following address:

National Geographic Society
1145 17th Street N.W.
Washington, D.C. 20036-4688
U.S.A.

Visit the Society's Web site at www.nationalgeographic.com.

Published by the National Geographic Society

John M. Fahey, Jr., *President and Chief Executive Officer*
Gilbert M. Grosvenor, *Chairman of the Board*
Nina D. Hoffman, *Executive Vice President,*
    President, Books and School Publishing
Kevin Mulroy, *Vice President and Editor-in-Chief*
Elizabeth L. Newhouse, *Director of Travel Publishing*
Charles Kogod, *Director of Photography*
Marianne Koszorus, *Design Director*
Cinda Rose, *Art Director*
Carl Mehler, *Director of Maps*

Staff for this book:

Barbara A. Noe, *Senior Editor and Project Manager*
Melissa G. Ryan, *Illustrations Editor*
Kay Hankins, *Designer*
Allan Fallow, *Senior Editor*
Jane Sunderland, Carolina E. Averitt, Jarelle Stein, *Text Editors*
Caroline Hickey, *Senior Researcher*
Victoria Garrett Jones, *Editorial Researcher*
Matt Chwastyk, Joseph F. Ochlak, Nicholas P. Rosenbach, Gregory
    Ugiansky, XNR Productions, *Map Edit, Research, and Production*
R. Gary Colbert, *Production Director*
Richard S. Wain, *Production Project Manager*
Janet Dustin, *Illustrations Assistant*
Connie D. Binder, *Indexer*
Lise Sajewski, *Editorial Consultant*
Lawrence Porges, *Editorial Coordinator*
Elizabeth Erskine, Marianne G. Koszorus, *Contributors*

Map art drawn by Chris Orr & Associates, Southampton, England
Artwork by Maltings Partnership, Derby, England

ISSN 1538-5515

Printed and bound by R.R. Donnelley & Sons, Willard, Ohio
Color separations by Quad Graphics, Alexandria, Virginia
Cover printed by Miken Inc., Cheektowaga, New York

Visit the society's Web site at http://www.nationalgeographic.com

The information in this book has been carefully checked and to the best of our knowledge is accurate. However, details are subject to change, and the National Geographic Society cannot be responsible for such changes, or for errors or omissions. Assessments of sites, hotels, and restaurants are based on the author's subjective opinions, which do not necessarily reflect the publisher's opinion. The publisher cannot be responsible for any consequences arising from the use of this book.

NATIONAL GEOGRAPHIC
TRAVELER

A Century of Travel Expertise in Every Guide

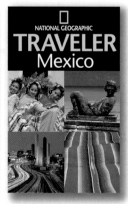
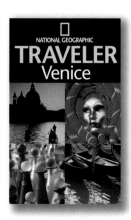

- **Amsterdam** ISBN: 0-7922-7900-X
- **Arizona** ISBN: 0-7922-7899-2
- **Australia** ISBN: 0-7922-7431-8
- **Barcelona** ISBN: 0-7922-7902-6
- **Boston & Environs** ISBN: 0-7922-7926-3
- **California** ISBN: 0-7922-7564-0
- **Canada** ISBN: 0-7922-7427-X
- **The Caribbean** ISBN: 0-7922-7434-2
- **China** ISBN: 0-7922-7921-2
- **Costa Rica** ISBN: 0-7922-7946-8
- **Egypt** ISBN: 0-7922-7896-8
- **Florence & Tuscany** ISBN: 0-7922-7924-7
- **Florida** ISBN: 0-7922-7432-6
- **France** ISBN: 0-7922-7426-1
- **Great Britain** ISBN: 0-7922-7425-3
- **Greece** ISBN: 0-7922-7923-9
- **Hawaii** ISBN: 0-7922-7944-1
- **Hong Kong** ISBN: 0-7922-7901-8
- **India** ISBN: 0-7922-7898-4
- **Italy** ISBN: 0-7922-7562-4
- **Japan** ISBN: 0-7922-7563-2
- **London** ISBN: 0-7922-7428-8
- **Los Angeles** ISBN: 0-7922-7947-6
- **Mexico** ISBN: 0-7922-7897-6
- **Miami and the Keys** ISBN: 0-7922-7433-4
- **New Orleans** ISBN: 0-7922-7948-4
- **New York** ISBN: 0-7922-7430-X
- **Paris** ISBN: 0-7922-7429-6
- **Rome** ISBN: 0-7922-7566-7
- **San Francisco** ISBN: 0-7922-7565-9
- **Spain** ISBN: 0-7922-7922-0
- **Sydney** ISBN: 0-7922-7435-0
- **Thailand** ISBN: 0-7922-7943-3
- **Venice** ISBN: 0-7922-7917-4
- **Washington, D.C.** ISBN: 0-7922-7903-4

AVAILABLE WHEREVER BOOKS ARE SOLD